Big Data and Analytics

Vincenzo Morabito

Big Data and Analytics

Strategic and Organizational Impacts

 Springer

Vincenzo Morabito
Department of Management and Technology
Bocconi University
Milan
Italy

ISBN 978-3-319-10664-9   ISBN 978-3-319-10665-6   (eBook)
DOI 10.1007/978-3-319-10665-6

Library of Congress Control Number: 2014958989

Springer Cham Heidelberg New York Dordrecht London
© Springer International Publishing Switzerland 2015
This work is subject to copyright. All rights are reserved by the Publisher, whether the whole or part of the material is concerned, specifically the rights of translation, reprinting, reuse of illustrations, recitation, broadcasting, reproduction on microfilms or in any other physical way, and transmission or information storage and retrieval, electronic adaptation, computer software, or by similar or dissimilar methodology now known or hereafter developed.
The use of general descriptive names, registered names, trademarks, service marks, etc. in this publication does not imply, even in the absence of a specific statement, that such names are exempt from the relevant protective laws and regulations and therefore free for general use.
The publisher, the authors and the editors are safe to assume that the advice and information in this book are believed to be true and accurate at the date of publication. Neither the publisher nor the authors or the editors give a warranty, express or implied, with respect to the material contained herein or for any errors or omissions that may have been made.

Printed on acid-free paper

Springer International Publishing AG Switzerland is part of Springer Science+Business Media (www.springer.com)

Foreword

Few organizations understand how to extract insights and value from the recent explosion of "Big Data." With a billion plus users on the online social graph doing what they like to do and leaving a digital trail, and with trillions of sensors now being connected in the so-called Internet of Things, organizations need clarity and insights into what lies ahead in deploying these capabilities. While academic scholars are just beginning to appreciate the power of big data analytics and new media to open up a fascinating array of questions from a host of disciplines, the practical applicability of this is still lacking. Big data and analytics touches multiple disciplines ranging from sociology, psychology, and ethics to marketing, statistics, and economics, as well as law and public policy. If harnessed correctly it has the potential to solve a variety of business and societal problems.

This book aims to develop the strategic and organizational impacts of Big Data and analytics for today's digital business competition and innovation. Written by an academic, the book has nonetheless the main goal to provide a toolbox suitable to be useful to business practice and know-how. To this end Vincenzo as in his former books has structured the content into three parts that guide the reader through how to control and govern the innovation potential of Big Data and Analytics. First, the book focuses on *Strategy* (Part I), analyzing how Big Data and analytics impact on private and public organizations, thus, examining the implications for competitive advantage as well as for government and education. The last chapter provides an overview of Big Data business models, creating a bridge to the content of Part II, which analyzes the managerial challenges of Big Data and analytics governance and evaluation. The conclusive chapter of Part II introduces the reader to the challenges of managing change required by an effective use and absorption of Big Data and analytics, actually trying to complement IT and non-IT managers' perspective. Finally, Part III discusses through structured and easy to read forms a set of cases of Big Data and analytics initiatives in practice at a global level in 2014.

Use this book as a guide to design your modern analytics-enabled organization. Do not be surprised if it resembles a large-scale real-world laboratory where employees design and conduct experiments and collect the data needed to obtain answers to a variety of questions, from peer influence effects, the influence of dynamic ties, pricing of digital media, anonymity in online relationships, to designing next-generation recommender systems and enquiries into the changing preference structures of Generation Y and Z consumers. This is a bold new frontier and it is safe to say we ain't seen nothing yet.

Ravi Bapna

Preface

Notwithstanding the interest and the hype that surround Big Data as a key trend as well the claimed business potentiality that it may offer the coupling with a new breed of analytics, the phenomenon has been yet not fully investigated from a strategic and organizational perspective. Indeed, at the moment of writing this book, apart from a series of articles that appeared on the Harvard Business review by McAfee and Brynjolfsson (2012) and on MIT Sloan Management Review by Lavalle et al. (2011) and Davenport et al. (2012), most of the published monographic contributions concern technical, computational, and engineering facets of Big Data and analytics, or oriented toward high-level societal as well as general audience business analyses.

An early joint academics-practitioners effort to provide a unified and comprehensive perspective has been carried out by the White Paper resulting from joint multidisciplinary contributions of more than 130 participants from 26 countries at the World Summit on Big Data and Organization Design held in Paris at the Université Panthéon-Sorbonne during May 16–17, 2013 (Burton et al. 2014). However, it is worth to be mentioned that since 2013 new editorial initiatives have been launched such as, e.g., the Big Data journal (Dumbill 2013). Thus, following up the insights discussed in (Morabito 2014), the present book aims to fill the gap, providing a strategic and organizational perspective on Big Data and analytics, identifying the challenges, ideas, and trends that may represent "food for thought" to practitioners. Accordingly, each topic considered will be analyzed in its technical and managerial aspects, also through the use of case studies and examples. Thus, while relying on academic production as well, the book aims to describe problems from the viewpoints of managers, adopting a clear and easy-to-understand language, in order to capture the interests of top managers and graduate students. Consequently, this book is unique for its intention to synthesize, compare, and comment on major challenges and approaches to Big Data and analytics, being a simple yet ready to consult toolbox for both managers and scholars.

In what follows we provide a brief overview, based on our previous work as well (Morabito 2014), on Big Data drivers and characteristics suitable to introduce their discussion also with regard to analytics in the further chapters of this book, whose outline concludes this introduction.

Big Data Drivers and Characteristics

The spread of social media as a main driver for innovation of products and services and the increasing availability of unstructured data (images, video, audio, etc.) from sensors, cameras, digital devices for monitoring supply chains and stocking in warehouses (i.e., what is actually called *internet of things*), video conferencing systems and voice over IP (VOIP) systems, have contributed to an unmatched availability of information in rapid and constant growth in terms of volume. As for these issues, an interesting definition of "Big Data" has been provided by Edd Dumbill in 2013:

> Big data is data that exceeds the processing capacity of conventional database systems. The data is too big, moves too fast, or doesn't fit the structures of your database architectures. To gain value from this data, you must choose an alternative way to process it (Dumbill 2013).

As a consequence of the above scenario and definition, the term "Big Data" is dubbed to indicate the challenges associated with the emergence of data sets whose size and complexity require companies to adopt new tools and models for the management of information. Thus, Big Data require new capabilities (Davenport and Patil 2012) to control external and internal information flows, transforming them into strategic resources to define strategies for products and services that meet customers' needs, increasingly informed and demanding.

However, Big Data computational as well as technical challenges call for a radical change to business models and human resources in terms of information orientation and a unique valorization of a company information asset for investments and support for strategic decisions. At the state of the art the following four dimensions are recognized as characterizing Big Data (IBM; McAfee and Brynjolfsson 2012; Morabito 2014; Pospiech and Felden 2012):

- **Volume**: the first dimension concerns the unmatched quantity of data actually available and storable by businesses (terabytes or even petabytes), through the Internet: for example, 12 terabytes of Tweets are created everyday into improved product sentiment analysis (IBM).
- **Velocity**: the second dimension concerns the dynamics of the volume of data, namely the time-sensitive nature of Big Data, as the speed of their creation and use is often (nearly) real-time.
- **Variety**: the third dimension concerns type of data actually available. Besides, structured data traditionally managed by information systems in organizations, most of the new breed encompasses semi-structured and even unstructured data, ranging from text, log files, audio, video, and images posted, e.g., on social networks to sensor data, click streams, e.g., from Internet of Things.
- **Accessibility**: the fourth dimension concerns the unmatched availability of channels a business may increase and extend its own data and information asset.
- It is worth noting that at the state of the art another dimension is actually considered relevant to Big Data characterization: **Veracity** concerns quality of data and trust of the data actually available at an incomparable degree of volume,

velocity, and variety. Thus, this dimension is relevant to a strategic use of Big Data and analytics by businesses, extending in terms of scale and complexity the issues investigated by information quality scholars (Huang et al. 1999; Madnick et al. 2009; Wang and Strong 1996), for enterprise systems mostly relying on traditional relational database management systems.

As for drivers, (Morabito 2014) identified cloud computing as a relevant one, besides social networks, mobile technologies, and Internet of Things (IoTs). As pointed out by Pospiech and Felden (2012), at the state of the art, cloud computing is considered a key driver of Big Data, for the growing size of available data requires scalable database management systems (DBMS). However, cloud computing faces IT managers and architects the choice of either relying on commercial solutions (mostly expensive) or moving beyond relational database technology, thus, identifying novel data management systems for cloud infrastructures (Agrawal et al. 2010, 2011). Accordingly, at the state of art *NoSQL* (Not Only SQL)[1] data storage systems have been emerging, usually not requiring fixed table schemas and not fully complying nor satisfying the traditional ACID (Atomicity, Consistency, Isolation, and Durability) properties. Among the programming paradigms for processing, generating, and analyzing large data sets, *MapReduce*[2] and the open source computing framework Hadoop have received a growing interest and adoption in both industry and academia.[3]

Considering *velocity*, there is a debate in academia about considering Big Data as encompassing both data "stocks" and "flows" (Davenport 2012). For example, at the state of the art Piccoli and Pigni (2013) propose to distinguish the elements of *digital data streams* (DDSs) from "big data"; the latter concerning static data that can be mined for insight. Whereas *digital data streams* (DDSs) are "dynamically evolving sources of data changing over time that have the potential to spur real-time action" (Piccoli and Pigni 2013). Thus, DDSs refer to streams of real-time information by mobile devices and IoTs, that have to be "captured" and analyzed real-time, provided or not they are stored as "Big Data". The types of use of "big" DDSs may be classified according to those Davenport et al. (2012) have pointed out for Big Data applications to information flows:

---

[1] Several classifications of the NoSQL databases have been proposed in literature (Han et al. 2011). Here we mention *Key-/Value-Stores* (a map/dictionary allows clients to insert and request values per key) and *Column-Oriented databases* (data are stored and processed by column instead of row). An example of the former is *Amazon's Dynamo;* whereas *HBase, Google's Bigtable*, and *Cassandra* represent *Column-Oriented databases*. For further details we refer the reader to (Han et al. 2011; Strauch 2010).

[2] MapReduce exploit, on the one hand, (i) a *map function*, specified by the user to process a key/value pair and to generate a set of intermediate key/value pairs; on the other hand, (ii) a *reduce function* that merges all intermediate values associated with the same intermediate key (Dean and Ghemawat 2008). MapReduce has been used to complete rewrite the production indexing system that produces the data structures used for the Google web search service (Dean and Ghemawat 2008).

[3] See for example how IBM has exploited/integrated Hadoop (IBM et al. 2011).

- *Support customer-facing processes:* e.g., to identify fraud or medical patients' health risk.
- *Continuous process monitoring:* e.g., to identify variations in customer sentiments toward a brand or a specific product/service or to exploit sensor data to detect the need for intervention on jet engines, data centers machines, extraction pump, etc.
- *Explore network relationships* on, e.g., Linkedin, Facebook, and Twitter to identify potential threats or opportunities related to human resources, customers, competitors, etc.

As a consequence, we believe that the distinction between DDSs and Big Data is useful to point out a difference in scope and target of decision making, and analytic activities, depending on the business goals and the type of action required. Indeed, while DDSs may be suitable to be used for marketing and operations issues, such as customer experience management in mobile services, Big Data refer to the information asset an organization is actually able to archive, manage, and exploit for decision making, strategy definition, and business innovation (McAfee and Brynjolfsson 2012).

Having emphasized the specificity of DDS, we now focus on Big Data and analytics applications as also discussed in (Morabito 2014).

As shown in Fig. 1 they cover many industries, spanning from finance (banks and insurance), e.g., improving risk analysis and fraud management, to utility and manufacturing, with a focus on information provided by sensors and IoTs for improved quality control, operations or plants performance, and energy management. Moreover, marketing and service may exploit Big Data for increasing customer experience, through the adoption of social media analytics focused on sentiment analysis, opinion mining, and recommender systems.

As for public sector (further discussed in Chap. 2), Big Data represents an opportunity, on the one hand, e.g., for improving fraud detection as tax evasion control through the integration of a large number of public administration databases; on the other hand, for accountability and transparency of government and administrative activities, due to the increasing relevance and diffusion of *open data* initiatives, making accessible and available for further elaboration by constituencies of large public administration data sets (Cabinet Office 2012; Zuiderwijk et al. 2012), and participation of citizens to the policy making process, thanks to the shift of many government digital initiatives towards an open government perspective (Feller et al. 2011; Lee and Kwak 2012; Di Maio 2010; Nam 2012).

Thus, Big Data seem to have a strategic value for organizations in many industries, confirming the claim by Andrew McAfee and Brynjolfsson (2012) that data-driven decisions are better decisions, relying on evidence of (an unmatched amount of) facts rather than intuition by experts or individuals. Nevertheless, we believe that management challenges and opportunities of Big Data need further discussion and analyses, the state of the art currently privileging their technical facets and characteristics. That is the motivation behind this book, whose outline follows.

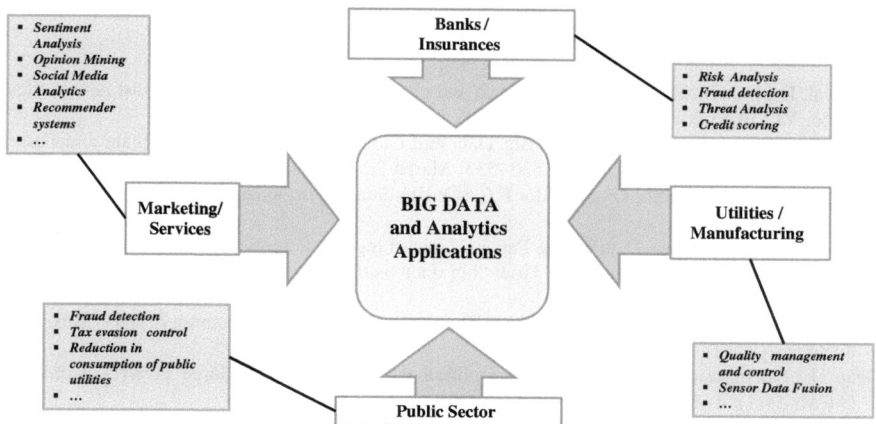

Fig. 1 Big Data Applications. Adapted from (Morabito 2014)

Outline of the Book

The book argument is developed along three main axes, likewise. In particular, we consider first (Part I) *Strategy* issues related to the growing relevance of Big Data and analytics for competitive advantage, also due their empowerment of activities such as, e.g., consumer profiling, market segmentation, and new products or services development. Furthermore, the different chapters will also consider the strategic impact of Big Data and analytics for innovation in domains such as government and education. A discussion of Big Data-driven Business Models conclude this part of the book. Subsequently, (Part II) considers *Organization*, focusing on Big Data and analytics challenges for governance, evaluation, and managing change for Big Data-driven innovation. Finally (Part III), the book will present and review case studies of Big Data *Innovation Practices* at the global level. Thus, Chap. 8 aims to discuss examples of Big Data and analytics applications in practice, providing fact-sheets suitable to build a "map" of 10 interesting digital innovations actually available worldwide. Besides an introduction to the factors considered in the choice of each innovation practice, a specific description of it will be developed. Finally, the conclusion will provide a summary of all arguments of the volume together with general managerial recommendations.

Vincenzo Morabito

References

Agrawal, D., Das, S., El Abbadi, A.: Big data and cloud computing: new wine or just new bottles? Proc. VLDB Endow. 3, 1647–1648 (2010)

Agrawal, D., Das, S., El Abbadi, A.: Big Data and Cloud Computing: Current State and Future Opportunities. EDBT, ACM. pp. 530–533. March 22–24, Sweden (2011)

Burton, R.M., Mastrangelo, D., Salvador F.(eds.): Big data and organization design. J. Organ. Des. 3(1), (2014)

Cabinet Office UK: Open Data White Paper—Unleashing the Potential. (2012)

Davenport, T.H., Barth, P., Bean, R.: How "big data" is different. MIT Sloan Manag. Rev. 54(1), 43–46 (2012)

Davenport, T.H., Patil, D.J.: Data scientist: The sexiest job of the 21st century. Harv. Bus. Rev. October, (2012)

Dean, J., Ghemawat, S.: MapReduce: Simplified data processing on large clusters. Commun. ACM. 51(1), 1–13 (2008)

Di Maio, A.: Gartner open government maturity model. Gartner (2010)

Dumbill, E.: Making sense of big data (editorial). Big Data. 1(1), 1–2 (2013)

Feller, J., Finnegan, P., Nilsson, O.: Open innovation and public administration: Transformational typologies and business model impacts. Eur. J. Inf. Syst. 20, 358–374 (2011). doi: 10.1057/Ejis.2010.65

Han, J., Haihong, E., Le, G., Du, J.: Survey on NoSQL database. 6th International Conference on Pervasive Computing and Applications (ICPCA). pp. 363–366 (2011). doi: 10.1109/ICPCA.2011.6106531

Huang, K.T., Lee, Y., Wang, R.Y.: Quality, information and knowledge. Prentice-Hall, Inc (1999)

IBM, Zikopoulos, P., Eaton, C.: Understanding Big Data: Analytics for Enterprise Class Hadoop and streaming data, 1st edn. McGraw-Hill Osborne Media (2011)

IBM: What is big data?, http://www-01.ibm.com/software/data/bigdata/what-is-big-data.html. Accessed 7 Jan 2015

Lavalle, S., Lesser, E., Shockley, R., Hopkins, M.S., Kruschwitz, N.: Big Data, Analytics and the Path From Insights to Value. MIT Sloan Manag. Rev. 52(2), (2011)

Lee, G., Kwak, Y.H.: An open government maturity model for social media-based public engagement. Gov. Inf. Q. 29(4), 492–503 (2012)

Madnick, S.E., Wang, R.Y., Lee, Y.W., Zhu, H.: Overview and Framework for Data and Information Quality Research. J. Data Inf. Qual. 1, 1–22 (2009). doi: 10.1145/1515693.1516680

McAfee, A., Brynjolfsson, E.: Big data: The management revolution. Harv. Bus. Rev. 61–68 (2012)

Morabito, V.: Big data. Trends and Challenges in Digital Business Innovation, pp. 3–21 Springer, Cham Heidelberg New York Dordrecht London (2014)

Morabito, V.: Trends and Challenges in Digital Business Innovation. Springer (2014)

Nam, T.: Citizens' attitudes toward open government and government. Int. Rev. Adm. Sci. 78(2), 346–368 (2012)

Piccoli, G., Pigni, F.: Harvesting external data: The potential of digital data streams. MIS Q. Exec. 12(1), 143–154 (2013)

Pospiech, M., Felden, C.: Big data—A State-of-the-Art. AMCIS 2012. (2012)

Strauch, C.: NoSQL databases. Lect. Notes Stuttgart Media. 1–8 (2010)

Wang, R.Y., Strong, D.M.: Beyond accuracy: what data quality means to data consumers. J. Manag. Inf. Syst. 12(4), 5–33 (1996)

Zuiderwijk, A., Janssen, M., Choenni, S.: Open Data Policies: Impediments and Challenges. 12th European Conference on eGovernment (ECEG 2012). pp. 794–802, Barcelona, Spain (2012)

Acknowledgments

This book is the result of the last two years of research, where several people are worth to be acknowledged for their support, useful comments and cooperation. A special mention to Prof. Vincenzo Perrone at Bocconi University, Prof. Vallabh Sambamurthy, Eli Broad Professor at Michigan State University, and Prof. Franco Fontana at LUISS University as main inspiration and mentors.

Moreover, I acknowledge Prof. Giuseppe Soda, Head of the Department of Management and Technology at Bocconi University, and all the other colleagues at the Department, in particular Prof. Arnaldo Camuffo, Prof. Anna Grandori, Prof. Severino Salvemini, and Prof. Giuseppe Airoldi, all formerly at the Institute of Organization and Information Systems at Bocconi University, who have created a rich and rigorous research environment where I am proud to work.

I acknowledge also some colleagues from other universities with whom I've had the pleasure to work, whose conversations, comments, and presentations provided precious insights for this book: among others, Prof. Anindya Ghose at New York University's Leonard N. Stern School of Business, Prof. Vijay Gurbaxani at University of California Irvine, Prof. Saby Mitra at Georgia Institute of Technology, Prof. Ravi Bapna at University of Minnesota Carlson School of Management, George Westerman at MIT Center for Digital Business, Stephanie Woerner at MIT Center for Information Systems Research, Prof. Ritu Agarwal at Robert H. Smith School of Business, Prof. Lynda Applegate at Harvard Business School, Prof. Omar El Sawy at Marshall School of Business, Prof. Marco de Marco at Unversità Cattolica del Sacro Cuore di Milano, Prof. Tobias Kretschmer, Head of Institute for Strategy, Technology and Organization of Ludwig Maximilians University, Prof. Marinos Themistocleous at the Department of Digital Systems at University of Piraeus, Prof. Chiara Francalanci at Politecnico di Milano, Wolfgang König at Goethe University, Luca Giustiniano at LUISS University, Prof. Zahir Irani at Brunel Business School, Prof. Sinan Aral at NYU Stern School of Business, Prof Nitham Mohammed Hindi and Prof. Adam Mohamedali Fadlalla of Qatar University, Antonio de Amescua and Román López-Cortijo of Universidad Carlos III de Madrid and Ken and Jane Laudon.

Furthermore, I want to gratefully acknowledge all the companies that have participated to the research interviews, case studies, and surveys.

In particular, for the Financial Institutions: Agos Ducato, Banca Carige, Banca Euromobiliare, Banca Fideuram, Banca d'Italia, Banca Mediolanum, Banco Popolare, Banca Popolare dell'Emilia Romagna, Banca Popolare di Milano, Banca Popolare di Sondrio, Banca Popolare di Vicenza, Banca Popolare di Bari, Banca Sistema, Barclays, BCC Roma, BNL-BNP Paribas, Borsa Italiana, Cariparma Credit Agricole, CACEIS Bank Luxemburg, Carta Si, Cassa Depositi e Prestiti, Cassa di Risparmio di Firenze, Cedacri, Che Banca!, Compass, Corner Bank, Credito Emiliano, Deutsche Bank, Dexia, HypoVereinsbank, Istituto Centrale delle Banche Popolari Italiane, ING Direct, Intesa SanPaolo, Intesa SanPaolo Servitia, Istituto per le Opere Religiose, Luxemburg Stock Exchange, JP Morgan Chase, Key Client, Mediobanca, Monte Titoli, Banca Monte dei Paschi, Poste Italiane, SEC Servizi, Société Européene de Banque, Standard Chartered, Royal Bank of Scotland, UBI Banca, Unicredit, Unicredit Leasing, Veneto Banca and WeBank.

For the Insurance sector: Allianz, Assimoco, Aspe Re, Cardif, Coface, Ergo Previdenza, Europe Assistance, Assicurazioni Generali, Groupama, Munich RE, Poste Vita, Reale Mutua, Novae, Sara Assicurazioni, UnipolSai, Vittoria Assicurazioni and Zurich.

For the Industrial Sector: ABB, Accenture, Acea, Aci Informatica, Acqua Minerale S. Benedetto, Adidas, Alpitour, Alliance Boots, Amadori, Amazon, Amplifon, Anas, Angelini, ArcelorMittal, Armani, Astaldi, ATAC, ATM, AstraZeneca, Arval, Auchan, Audi, Augusta Westland, Autogrill, Autostrade per l'Italia, Avio, Baglioni Hotels, BMW, BASF, Barilla, Be Consulting, Benetton, Between, Business Integration Partners, Brembo, Bravo Fly, BskyB, BSH, BOSH, Boeing Defence, Cementir, Centrica Energy, Cerved, Chiesi Farmaceutici, CNH Industrial, Coca Cola HBC, Coop Italia, Costa Crociere, D'Amico, Danone, Daimler, De Agostini, Diesel, Dimar, Dolce and Gabbana, General Electric, Ducati, Elettronica, Edipower, Edison, Eni, Enel, ENRC, ERG, Fastweb, Ferservizi, Fincantieri, Ferrari, Ferrovie dello Stato, FCA, Finmeccanica, GlaxosmithKline, GE Capital, GFT Technologies, Grandi Navi Veloci, G4S, Glencore, Gruppo Hera, Gruppo Coin, Gruppo De Agostini, Gtech, Gucci, H3G, Hupac, Infineon, Interoll, Il Sole24Ore, IREN, Istituto Poligrafico e Zecca dello Stato, ITV, Kuwait Petroleum, La Perla, Labelux Group, Lamborghini, Lavazza, Linde, LBBW, Levi's, L'Oréal, Loro Piana, Luxottica, Jaguar Land Rover, Lucite International, MAN, Magneti Marelli, Mapei, Marcegaglia, Mediaset, Menarini, Messaggerie Libri, Miroglio, Mondelez International, Mossi & Ghisolfi, Natuzzi, Novartis, Oerlikon Graziano, OSRAM, Piaggio, Perfetti, Pernod Ricard, Philips, Pirelli, Porsche, ProSiebenSat1, Procter & Gamble, Prysmian, RAI, Rexam, Rolex, Roche, Retonkil Initial, RWE, Saipem, Sandoz, SEA, Seat PG, Selex, Snam, Sorgenia, Sky Italia, Schindler Electroca, Pfizer, RFI, Telecom Italia, Telecom Italia Digital Solution, Telecom Italia Information Technology, Tenaris, Terna, Trenitalia, Tyco, TuevSued, Telefonica, Unilever, Unicoop Firenze, Virgin Atlantic, Volkswagen, Vodafone and Wind.

For the Public Sector: Agenzia per l'Italia Digitale, Comune di Milano, Regione Lombardia and Consip.

Acknowledgments

I would especially like to acknowledge all the people that have supported me during this years with insights and suggestions. I learned so much from them, and their ideas and competences have inspired my work: Silvio Fraternali, Paolo Cederle, Massimo Milanta, Massimo Schiattarella, Diego Donisi, Marco Sesana, Gianluca Pancaccini, Giovanni Damiani, Gianluigi Castelli, Salvatore Poloni, Milo Gusmeroli, Pierangelo Rigamoti, Danilo Augugliaro, Nazzareno Gregori, Edoardo Romeo, Elvio Sonnino, Pierangelo Mortara, Massimo Messina, Mario Collari, Giuseppe Capponcelli, Massimo Castagnini, Pier Luigi Curcuruto, Giovanni Sordello, Maurizio Montagnese, Umberto Angelucci, Giuseppe Dallona, Gilberto Ceresa, Jesus Marin Rodriguez, Fabio Momola, Rafael Lopez Rueda, Eike Wahl, Marco Cecchella, Maria-Louise Arscott, Antonella Ambriola, Andrea Rigoni, Giovanni Rando Mazzarino, Silvio Sperzani, Samuele Sorato, Alberto Ripepi, Alfredo Montalbano, Gloria Gazzano, Massimo Basso Ricci, Giuseppe De Iaco, Riccardo Amidei, Davide Ferina, Massimo Ferriani, Roberto Burlo, Cristina Bianchini, Dario Scagliotti, Ettore Corsi, Luciano Bartoli, Marco Ternelli, Stewart Alexander, Luca Ghirardi, Francesca Gandini, Vincenzo Tortis, Agostino Ragosa, Sandro Tucci, Vittorio Mondo, Andrea Agosti, Roberto Fonso, Federico Gentili, Nino Lo Banco, Fabio Troiani, Federico Niero, Gianluca Zanutto, Mario Bocca, Marco Zaccanti, Anna Pia Sassano, Fabrizio Lugli, Marco Bertazzoni, Vittorio Boero, Carlo Achermann, Stefano Achermann, Jean-Claude Krieger, Reinhold Grassl, François de Brabant, Maria Cristina Spagnoli, Alessandra Testa, Anna Miseferi, Matteo Attrovio, Nikos Angelopoulos, Igor Bailo, Stefano Levi, Luciano Romeo, Alfio Puglisi, Gennaro Della Valle, Massimo Paltrinieri, Pierantonio Azzalini, Enzo Contento, Marco Fedi, Fiore Della Rosa, Dario Tizzanini, Carlo Capalbo, Simone Battiferri, Vittorio Giusti, Piera Fasoli, Carlo di Lello, Gian Enrico Paglia, George Sifnios, Francesco Varchetta, Gianfranco Casati, Fabio Benasso, Alessandro Marin, Gianluca Guidotti, Fabrizio Virtuani, Luca Verducci, Luca Falco, Francesco Pedrielli, Riccardo Riccobene, Roberto Scolastici, Paola Formaneti, Andrea Mazzucato, Nicoletta Rocca, Mario Breuer, Mario Costantini, Marco Lanza, Marco Poggi, Gianfranco Ardissono, Alex Eugenio Sala, Daniele Bianchi, Giambattista Piacentini, Luigi Zanardi, Valerio Momoni, Daniele Panigati, Maurizio Pescarini, Ermes Franchini, Francesco Mastrandrea, Federico Boni, Mauro Minenna, Massimo Romagnoli, Nicola Grassi, Alessandro Capitani, Mauro Frassetto, Bruno Cocchi, Marco Tempra, Martin Brannigan, Alessandro Guidotti, Gianni Leone, Stefano Signani, Domenico Casalino, Fabrizio Lugoboni, Fabrizio Rocchio, Mauro Bernareggi, Claudio Sorano, Paolo Crovetti, Alberto Ricchiari, Alessandro Musumeci, Luana Barba, Pierluigi Berlucchi, Matthias Schlapp, Ugo Salvi, Danilo Gismondi, Patrick Vandenberghe, Dario Ferri, Claudio Colombatto, Frediano Lorenzin, Paolo Trincianti, Massimiliano Ciferri, Danilo Ughetto, Tiberio Strati, Massimo Nichetti, Stefano Firenze, Vahe Ter Nikogosyan, Giorgio Voltolini, Andrea Maraventano, Thomas Pfitzer, Guido Oppizzi, Alessandro Bruni, Marco Franzi, Guido Albertini, Massimiliano De Gregorio, Vincenzo Russi, Franco Collautti, Massimo Dall'Ora, Fabio De Ferrari, Mauro Ferrari, Domenico Solano, Pier Paolo Tamma, Susanna Nardi, Massimo Amato, Alberto Grigoletto, Nunzio Calì, Gianfilippo Pandolfini, Cristiano Cannarsa, Fabio Degli Esposti, Riccardo

Scattaretico, Claudio Basso, Mauro Pianezzola, Marco Zanussi, Davide Carteri, Giulio Tonin, Simonetta Iarlori, Marco Prampolini, Luca Terzaghi, Christian Altomare, Pasquale Tedesco, Michela Quitadamo, Dario Castello, Fabio Boschiero, Aldo Borrione, Paolo Beatini, Maurizio Pellicano, Ottavio Rigodanza, Gianni Fasciotti, Lorenzo Pizzuti, Angelo D'Alessandro, Marcello Guerrini, Michela Quitadamo, Dario Castello, Fabio Boschiero, Aldo Borrione, Paolo Beatini, Pierluigi De Marinis, Fabio Cestola, Roberto Mondonico, Alberto Alberini, Pierluca Ferrari, Umberto Stefani, Elvira Fabrizio, Salvatore Impallomeni, Dario Pagani, Marino Vignati, Giuseppe Rossini, Alfio Puglisi, Renzo Di Antonio, Maurizio Galli, Filippo Vadda, Marco De Paoli, Paolo Cesa, Armando Gervasi, Luigi Di Tria, Marco Gallibariggio, David Alfieri, Mirco Carriglio, Maurizio Castelletti, Roberto Andreoli, Vincenzo Campana, Marco Ravasi, Mauro Viacava, Alessio Pomasan, Salvatore Stefanelli, Roberto Scaramuzza, Marco Zaffaroni, Giuseppe Langer, Francesco Bardelli, Daniele Rizzo, Silvia De Fina, Paulo Morais, Massimiliano Gerli, Andrea Facchini, Massimo Zara, Luca Paleari, Carlo Bozzoli, Luigi Borrelli, Marco Iacomussi, Mario Dio, Giulio Mattietti, Alessandro Poerio, Fabrizio Frustaci, Roberto Zaccaro, Maurizio Quattrociocchi, Gianluca Giovannetti, Pierangelo Colacicco, Silvio Sassatelli, Filippo Passerini, Mario Rech, Claudio Sordi, Tomas Blazquez De La Cruz, Luca Spagnoli, Fabio Oggioni, Luca Severini, Roberto Conte, Alessandro Tintori, Giovanni Ferretti, Alberta Gammicchia, Patrizia Tedesco, Antonio Rainò, Claudio Beveroni, Chiara Manzini, Francesco Del Greco, Lorenzo Tanganelli, Ivano Bosisio, Alessandro Campanini, Giovanni Pietrobelli, Pietro Pacini, Vittorio Padovani, Luciano Dalla Riva, Paolo Pecchiari, Francesco Donatelli, Massimo Palmieri, Alessandro Cucchi, Riccardo Pagnanelli, Raffaella Mastrofilippo, Roberto Coretti, Alessandra Grendele, Davide Casagrande, Lucia Gerini, Filippo Cecchi, Fabio De Maron, Alberto Peralta, Massimo Pernigotti, Massimo Rama, Francisco Souto, Oscar Grignolio, Mario Mella, Massimo Rosso, Filippo Onorato, Stefan Caballo, Ennio Bernardi, Aldo Croci, Giuseppe Genovesi, Maurizio Romanese, Daniele Pagani, Derek Barwise, Guido Vetere, Christophe Pierron, Guenter Lutgen, Andreas Weinberger, Luca Martis, Stefano Levi, Paola Benatti, Massimiliano Baga, Marco Campi, Laura Wegher, Riccardo Sfondrini, Diego Pogliani, Gianluca Pepino, Simona Tonella, José González Osma, Sandeep Sen, Thomas Steinich, Barbara Karuth-Zelle, Ralf Schneider, Rüdiger Schmidt,Wolfgang Gärtner, Alfred Spill, Lissimahos Hatzidimoulas, Marco Damiano Bosco, Mauro Di Pietro Paolo, Paolo Brusegan, Arnold Aschbauer, Robert Wittgen, Peter Kempf, Michael Gorriz, Wilfried Reimann, Abel Archundia Pineda, Jürgen Sturm, Stefan Gaus, Andreas Pfisterer, Peter Rampling, Elke Knobloch, Andrea Weierich, Andreas Luber, Heinz Laber, Michael Hesse, Markus Lohmann, Andreas König, Herby Marchetti, Rainer Janssen, Frank Rüdiger Poppe, Marcell Assan, Klaus Straub, Robert Blackburn, Wiebe Van der Horst, Martin Stahljans, Mattias Ulbrich, Matthias Schlapp, Jan Brecht, Enzo Contento, Michael Pretz, Gerd Friedrich, Florian Forst, Robert Leindl, Wolfgang Keichel, Stephan Fingerling, Sven Lorenz, Martin Hofmann, Nicolas Burdkhardt, Armin Pfoh, Kian Mossanen, Anthony Roberts, John Knowles, Lisa Gibbard, John Hiskett, Richard Wainwright, David Madigan, Matt Hopkins, Gill Lungley, Simon Jobson, Glyn

Acknowledgments

Hughes, John Herd, Mark Smith, Jeremy Vincent, Guy Lammert, Steve Blackledge, Mark Lichfield, Jacky Lamb, Simon McNamara, Kevin Hanley, Anthony Meadows, Rod Hefford, Stephen Miller, Willem Eelman, Alessandro Ventura, David Bulman, Neil Brown, Alistair Hadfield, Rod Carr and Neil Dyke.

I would especially like to gratefully acknowledge Gianluigi Viscusi at College of Management of Technology (CDM)-École polytechnique fédérale de Lausanne (EPFL), Alan Serrano-Rico at Brunel Univeristy, and Nadia Neytcheva Head of Research at the Business Technology Outlook (BTO) Research Program who provided me valuable suggestions and precious support in the coordination of the production process of this book. Furthermore, I acknowledge the support of Business Technology Foundation (Fondazione Business Technology) and all the bright researchers at Business Technology Outlook (BTO) Research Program that have supported me in carrying out interviews, surveys, and data analysis: Florenzo Marra, Giulia Galimberti, Arianna Zago, Alessandro De Pace, Matteo Richiardi, Ezechiele Capitanio, Giovanni Roberto, Alessandro Scannapieco, Massimo Bellini, Tommaso Cenci, Giorgia Cattaneo, Andrada Comanac, Francesco Magro, Marco Castelli, Martino Scanziani, Miguel Miranda, Alice Brocca, Antonio Attinà, Giuseppe Vaccaro, Antonio De Falco, Matteo Pistoletti, Mariya Terzieva and Daniele Durante.

A special acknowledgement goes to the memory of Prof. Antonino Intrieri who provided precious comments and suggestions throughout the years.

Finally I acknowledge my family whose constant support and patience made this book happen.

Vincenzo Morabito

Contents

Part I Strategy

1 Big Data and Analytics for Competitive Advantage 3
- 1.1 Introduction 3
- 1.2 Competitive Advantage Definition: Old and New Notions 4
  - 1.2.1 From Sustainable to Dynamic 5
  - 1.2.2 From Company Effects to Network Success 6
- 1.3 The Role of Big Data on Gaining Dynamic Competitive Advantage 6
  - 1.3.1 Big Data Driven Target Marketing 6
  - 1.3.2 Design-Driven Innovation 8
  - 1.3.3 Crowd Innovation 9
- 1.4 Big Data Driven Business Models 10
- 1.5 Organizational Challenges 11
  - 1.5.1 Skill Set Shortages 12
  - 1.5.2 Cultural Barriers 12
  - 1.5.3 Processes and Structures 13
  - 1.5.4 Technology Maturity Levels 13
  - 1.5.5 Organizational Advantages and Opportunities ... 13
- 1.6 Case Studies 14
- 1.7 Recommendations for Organizations 17
  - 1.7.1 Ask the Right Questions 17
  - 1.7.2 Look Out for Complementary Game Changing Innovations 18
  - 1.7.3 Develop Sound Scenarios 18
  - 1.7.4 Prepare Your Culture 18
  - 1.7.5 Prepare to Change Processes and Structure 19
- 1.8 Summary 19
- References 20

2	**Big Data and Analytics for Government Innovation**.............		23
	2.1	Introduction...	23
		2.1.1 New Notions of Public Service: Towards a Prosumer Era?.....................	24
		2.1.2 Online Direct Democracy	25
		2.1.3 Megacities' Global Competition.................	25
	2.2	Public Service Advantages and Opportunities...............	26
		2.2.1 New Sources of Information: Crowdsourcing........	26
		2.2.2 New Sources of Information: Internet of Things (IoTs).......................	27
		2.2.3 Public Talent in Use.........................	29
		2.2.4 Private–Public Partnerships	31
		2.2.5 Government Cloud Data	31
		2.2.6 Value for Money in Public Service Delivery	32
	2.3	Governmental Challenges	33
		2.3.1 Data Ownership............................	33
		2.3.2 Data Quality	34
		2.3.3 Privacy, Civil Liberties and Equality..............	34
		2.3.4 Talent Recruitment Issues	35
	2.4	Case Studies	36
	2.5	Recommendations for Organizations......................	39
		2.5.1 Smart City Readiness	39
		2.5.2 Learn to Collaborate.........................	40
		2.5.3 Civic Education and Online Democracy	41
		2.5.4 Legal Framework Development	41
	2.6	Summary..	42
	References		42
3	**Big Data and Education: Massive Digital Education Systems**		47
	3.1	Introduction...	47
		3.1.1 From Institutionalized Education to MOOCs	49
	3.2	MOOC Educational Model Clusters	51
		3.2.1 University-Led MOOCs	51
		3.2.2 Peer-to-Peer MOOCs	52
	3.3	The Role of Big Data and Analytics......................	54
	3.4	Institutional Advantages and Opportunities from MOOCs	55
	3.5	Institutional Challenges from MOOCs.....................	57
	3.6	Case Studies	60
	3.7	Recommendations for Institutions........................	62
	3.8	Summary..	62
	References		63

4	**Big Data Driven Business Models**		65
	4.1	Introduction	65
	4.2	Implications of Big Data for Customer Segmentation	69
	4.3	Implications of Big Data as a Value Proposition	69
	4.4	Implications of Big Data for Channels	70
	4.5	The Impact of Big Data on Customer Relationships	71
	4.6	The Impact of Big Data on Revenue Stream	72
	4.7	The Impact of Big Data on Key Resources and Key Activities	73
	4.8	The Impact of Big Data on Key Partnerships	74
	4.9	The Impact of Big Data on Cost Structures	75
	4.10	Organizational Advantages and Opportunities	76
	4.11	Organizational Challenges and Threats	77
		4.11.1 Creativity and Innovation Capability Deficit	77
		4.11.2 Interrogating Big Data	77
		4.11.3 Plug and Play Architectures	78
	4.12	Summary	78
	References		79

Part II Organization

5	**Big Data Governance**		83
	5.1	Introduction to Big Data Governance	83
		5.1.1 Big Data Types	85
		5.1.2 Information Governance Disciplines	87
		5.1.3 Industries and Functions	90
	5.2	Big Data Maturity Models	91
		5.2.1 TDWI Maturity Model	91
		5.2.2 Analytics Business Maturity Model	93
		5.2.3 DataFlux Data Governance Maturity Model	94
		5.2.4 Gartner Maturity Model	95
		5.2.5 IBM Data Governance Maturity Model	96
	5.3	Organizational Challenges Inherent with Governing Big Data	97
	5.4	Organizational Benefits of Governing Big Data	99
	5.5	Case Studies	100
	5.6	Recommendations for Organizations	101
	5.7	Summary	102
	References		103
6	**Big Data and Digital Business Evaluation**		105
	6.1	Introduction	105
	6.2	Digital Business Evaluation Using Big Data	106

	6.3	Organizational Advantages and Opportunities	108
		6.3.1 Customer Value Proposition	109
		6.3.2 Customer Segmentation	110
		6.3.3 Channels	111
		6.3.4 Customer Relationship	111
	6.4	Organizational Challenges	113
		6.4.1 Key Resources	113
		6.4.2 Privacy and Security	114
		6.4.3 Cost Structure	115
	6.5	Cases Studies	116
	6.6	Recommendations for Organizations	121
		6.6.1 Hardware	121
		6.6.2 Software	122
	6.7	Summary	122
	References	122
7	**Managing Change for Big Data Driven Innovation**	125
	7.1	Introduction: Big Data—The Innovation Driver	125
	7.2	Big Data—The Key Innovative Techniques	126
		7.2.1 Integration of Data Platforms	127
		7.2.2 Testing Through Experimentation	128
		7.2.3 Real-Time Customization	128
		7.2.4 Generating Data-Driven Models	128
		7.2.5 Algorithmic and Automated-Controlled Analysis	129
	7.3	Big Data: Influence on C-Level Innovative Decision Process	129
		7.3.1 Stimulating Competitive Edge	130
		7.3.2 Predictive Analytics: Data Used to Drive Innovation	130
	7.4	The Impact of Big Data on Organizational Change	132
		7.4.1 An Incentivized Approach	133
		7.4.2 Creating a Centralized Organizational 'Home'	133
		7.4.3 Implementing the Changes—First Steps	135
	7.5	Methodologies for Big Data Innovation	135
		7.5.1 Extending Products to Generate Data	135
		7.5.2 Digitizing Assets	135
		7.5.3 Trading Data	136
		7.5.4 Forming a Distinctive Service Capability	136
	7.6	New Big Data Tools to Drive Innovation	137
		7.6.1 The Hadoop Platform	137
		7.6.2 1010DATA Cloud Analytics	137
		7.6.3 Actian Analytics	138
		7.6.4 Cloudera	138
	7.7	Models of Big Data Change	139
		7.7.1 Big Data Business Model	139
		7.7.2 The Maturity Phases of Big Data Business Model	139
		7.7.3 Examples of the Business Metamorphosis Phase	142

7.8	Big Data Change Key Issues		143
	7.8.1	Storage Issues	143
	7.8.2	Management Issues.	144
	7.8.3	Processing and Analytics Issues	144
7.9	Organizational Challenges		145
	7.9.1	Data Acquisition	145
	7.9.2	Information Extraction	146
	7.9.3	Data Integration, Aggregation, and Representation	146
7.10	Case Studies		147
7.11	Recommendation for Business Organizations		149
7.12	Summary.		150
References			150

Part III Innovation Practices

8 Big Data and Analytics Innovation Practices 157
- 8.1 Introduction. 157
- 8.2 Sociometric Solution. 158
  - 8.2.1 Developer 158
  - 8.2.2 Applications 159
- 8.3 Invenio 160
  - 8.3.1 Developer 160
  - 8.3.2 Applications 161
- 8.4 Evolv 161
  - 8.4.1 Developer 162
  - 8.4.2 Applications 163
- 8.5 Essentia Analytics 163
  - 8.5.1 Developer 164
  - 8.5.2 Applications 164
- 8.6 Ayasdi Core 165
  - 8.6.1 Developer 165
  - 8.6.2 Applications 166
- 8.7 Cogito Dialog 167
  - 8.7.1 Developer 167
  - 8.7.2 Applications 168
- 8.8 Tracx 168
  - 8.8.1 Developer 169
  - 8.8.2 Applications 169
- 8.9 Kahuna. 170
  - 8.9.1 Developer 170
  - 8.9.2 Applications 171

- 8.10 RetailNext 172
  - 8.10.1 Developer 172
  - 8.10.2 Applications 173
- 8.11 Evrythng 173
  - 8.11.1 Developer 173
  - 8.11.2 Applications 174
- 8.12 Summary 175
- References 175

9 **Conclusion** 177
- 9.1 Building the Big Data Intelligence Agenda 177
- References 180

Index 181

Acronyms

ACID	Atomicity, Consistency, Isolation, and Durability
AI	Artificial Intelligence
API	Application Programming Interface
B2B	Business to business
B2G	Business to government
BI	Business Intelligence
BM	Business Model
BMI	Business Model Innovation
BS	Bachelor of Science
CD	Compact disc
CEO	Chief Executive Officer
CIO	Chief Information Officer
CMO	Chief Marketing Officer
CRM	Customer Relationship Management
CSFs	Critical Success Factors
CTO	Chief Technology Officer
CxO	C-level Manager
DDS	Digital data stream
DG	Data Governance
ERP	Enterprise Resource Planning
EU	The European Union
GPS	Global Positioning System
HR	Human Resources
ICT	Information and Communication Technology
IoTs	Internet of Things
IP	Intellectual Property
IP address	Internet Protocol address
IPO	Initial public offering
IT	Information technology
KPIs	Key performance indicators
MIS	Management Information Systems

MOOCs	Massive open online courses
MS	Master of Science
NoSQL	Not Only SQL
OER	Open educational resources
OLAP	Online analytical processing
P2P	Peer 2 Peer
PC	Personal computer
QR code	Quick Response Code
R&D	Research and Development
RFID	Radio-frequency identification
ROI	Return on investment
SMEs	Small and medium enterprises
SQL	Structured Query Language
UK	The United Kingdom
UN	The United Nations
US	The United States of America
VOIP	Voice over Internet Protocol

Part I
Strategy

Big Data and Analytics for Competitive Advantage

Abstract
The role of this chapter is to introduce the reader to the utilization of big data for achieving competitive advantage. It begins by clarifying current notions of competitive advantage in strategic literature and highlights the current organizational challenges in taking advantage of the big data trend, as well as the possible advantages and opportunities. Finally, a case study discussion provides insights from practice and highlights points of attention, for those pursuing big data-driven competitive advantage.

1.1 Introduction

The concept of competitive advantage has created kaleidoscope of perspectives about its sources and mechanisms of generating it and destructing it, about what influences it and how can companies plan for it. Yet, the very theories of competitive advantage have been products of their times, explaining rather than predicting what made companies successful during the era of their development. Understanding the strategic role of IT has been even more challenging, as strategic literature ignored its importance as strategic asset until recently. Also, Management Information Systems (MIS) literature on the organizational value of IT has been confused amidst multitude issues of analysis, methodology, and measurement or simply distinguishing between causal relationships and correlation (Drnevich and Croson 2013).

However, e-commerce has changed our perception about the strategic importance of IT for the going concern of organizations and with the advent of big data, another era of strategic game playing is likely, as rules of competition may change yet again and so will our understanding of competitive advantage. Concurrent social changes, for example, new ways of funding and valuing organizations as well as virtual money such as bitcoin, may even change our understanding of the link of competitive advantage to monetization.

Before we discuss, however, the potential implication of big data on business strategy and competitive advantage, let's briefly review the key strategic perspectives thus far.

1.2 Competitive Advantage Definition: Old and New Notions

As popularized by Michael Porter's back in the 80s, competitive advantage denotes a company's profit making superiority over its competitors (Porter 1985). Such superiority was determined by a company's *position* in its sector and its ability to defend its position against challenges from competitors, new entrants, suppliers and even changes in customers' preference. In response, companies' strategies aimed at controlling every aspect of business activity and even plan to ensure that the industry was safeguarded from new entrants. Long-term or exclusive contracts with suppliers, covert price fixing, heavy advertising to orient consumer preferences, heavy capital investments were few of the moves open to companies in the competition chest board (Drnevich and Croson 2013). For example, the fierce competition between car manufacturers in the 90s leading to the concentration of the sector into few large car manufacturing groups is characteristic of that era (KPMG 2010).

Others suggest that competitive advantage can be obtained by efficient management of resources, including ones' employees, or by reducing transaction costs within the value chain. Anyway, successful *governance* required its own IT tools. All types of Enterprise Resource Planning (ERP) systems are prime examples of IT investments oriented to help managers at all levels attain resource efficiency; while IT-assisted, vertical business models that 'cut out the middleman' was a great example of reducing transaction costs. E-commerce phenomenal success over brick and mortar organizations was based on this simple principle, enabling people to shop for the best price product from the convenience of home at zero extra cost.

For those advocating *competence* as the source a competitive advantage, companies should decide and focus on developing their key capabilities, a set of valuable, rare, imperfectly imitable, non-substitutable resources, which could propel a business to such an advantageous position (Wu 2013). This set comprised anything from exclusive or discriminatory access to capital resources (raw materials or even expertise) to business process superiority (such as procurement, innovation or marketing) to combinations of the above (KPMG 2010; Taylor and LaBarre 2008). This required companies to predict customers' behaviors in the long-term and commit in the development and retention of such key capabilities. Process efficiency and knowledge management were considered particularly important from this perspective as it was the combination of resources in particular ways that gave companies an advantage over its competitors, and that requires *know-how*. The role of IT from this perspective is to assist people to take more effective decisions and do so efficiently.

1.2 Competitive Advantage Definition: Old and New Notions

With the advent of e-commerce and the rise of the "maverick" entrepreneur, business ethos towards control vis à vis openness changed and *flexibility* as the source of competitive advantage came to the forefront (Taylor and LaBarre 2008). Yet, it is rooted in Schumpeter's theories on creative destruction, where the industries evolve as new companies come up with new ways of doing things, thus, pushing old ones who cannot adapt out of the market (Schumpeter 1934). Hence, for a company to survive or to success should build in the capability to renew itself. From this perspective, companies with great operational flexibility that can quickly respond to challenges coming from shifting customer preferences, new entrants' changes of industry norms, and unpredicted competitors' moves will survive. Even better, innovative companies that can challenge the status quo and gain the profits of first mover's advantage and move on as market's mature or cut down their loses if ventures don't prove successful.

Thus, the strategic game changed from a slow careful positioning on the competition chessboard, to a fast action game, where speed is a crucial factor. Big data driven business models will exacerbate this trend. Already, real-time, location-based offers—the likes of Groupon—have proliferated and are now part of most inner city dwellers' life (Raice and Woo 2011).

Big data however poses technical challenges of storage and processing, and while the load of necessary inflexible capital investments is now over, matters of repurposing, sharing or turning infrastructure into a shared public good arise. The recent trend of Shared services and Shared Clouds are typical examples of infrastructure sharing and perhaps the same principle will be the norm for big data storehouses, e.g., by Pharmaceuticals, where companies, academics and public sector will openly utilize for common good (Schultz 2013).

Before we discuss the influence of big data on companies' efforts to achieve competitive advantage, we will briefly summarize the trends of our conceptions of competitive advantage.

1.2.1 From Sustainable to Dynamic

Globalization and e-commerce are radically changing consumer preferences and a flood of young Internet entrepreneurs that is driving discontinuous change business environment has emerged. This change is becoming more ambiguous and difficult to predict and plan for. For example Facebook has transformed the online retail market as Skype has transformed telecommunications. Sure enough a key shift in recent strategy theories is that competitive advantage is neither something a company owns nor something that it can safeguard. Emphasis has moved away from controlling in strategic orientation (Schumpeter 1934) to position game-changer innovation as key to business success.

1.2.2 From Company Effects to Network Success

Such unpredictably changing market conditions were defined by Williamson as turbulent environments (O'Brien 1976), demand networking strategies to navigate them successfully (Raice and Woo 2011; Schultz 2013). While collaboration always had a position in business, the nature of it is ever-changing (Morabito 2014). Conglomeration, lobbying, contractual and gentlemen agreements amongst large group of companies dominated business life in the past; nowadays, a shift towards open networks of suppliers, employees, customers has blurred the boundaries of companies, shared value amongst networks or produced public goods. Interdependence between companies and the public has intensified, as customers, suppliers or simple product evangelists nurture and propagate company information and referential credibility. For example, open source software has spread its paradigm becoming the norm for certain domains: nowadays people advertise product or services for free to their friends by clicking the share button, or recommend a friend for a job on LinkedIn at your spare time, and all this creates business value for free. It, of course, creates a lot of social-media-derived big data about our social behavior that companies are eager to understand the workings of, whether to nurture and reward us or to control and manipulate us, will depend on their strategic perspective (Morabito 2014).

1.3 The Role of Big Data on Gaining Dynamic Competitive Advantage

The overarching disruptive power of big data demands that organizations engage with it at a strategic level. However, how organizations will utilize this technology trend with their existing business model will depend on their orientation. While, consultants at A.T. Kearney argue that big data would have positive effects across strategy and operations (Hagen et al. 2013). In summary, the advantages of utilizing big data to obtain competitive advantage has been discussed into relation to big data driven target marketing, design-driven innovation, and crowd innovation, all of which will be discussed in detail in the following sections.

1.3.1 Big Data Driven Target Marketing

Big data can change the way companies identify and relate to their customer base. Undoubtedly, companies can boost the old marketing strategies using new big data tools and expertise. Market penetration strategies can leverage big data to feed marketers information on how to keep existing customers and improve repetitive sales. Likewise, new customer engagement techniques, like gamification, promise improved loyalty levels (Paharia 2013).

Cross-selling, for example, leverages a company's affinity and knowledge of its market to sell different products to the same people. Banks, for example, have started not only to analyze vast amounts of their clients' transactions in relation to social media to understand their customer preferences, but also to create new offerings to their clients. Citi, for example aggregates data from its global customer base, to help corporate clients identify market trends (Lesk 2013).

Identifying, however, new market niches must be the real power of big data and its real challenge. Companies no longer need to approach the market in large demographic chunks. They can instead use emerging analytics to identify new niches or even subdivide existing target markets into smaller more coherent groups to unlock their potential (Adamson et al. 2012). Targeting becomes a matter of aggregating multiple small niches. Combined with advancements in automated marketing communications, we are heading towards the era of mass customization.

Thus, the ultimate big data promise for marketers is that of mass customization. big data collection, synthesis and analysis promises to provide businesses with real insight about its customers' behaviors based on actual past and real-time, step-by-step behaviors. Much like in virtual ethnography (Hine 2000), that seeks to understand online communities through participation, social media data is collected covertly. Because most of us post spontaneous opinions and views in social media, information is free from response biases often encountered in surveys or under focus group conditions. This gets rid of the cost of ineffective market research, which can then mislead sales efforts, marketing plans and company strategies. Sentiment analysis on what we post about areas of our lives on social media unveils our attitudes and can lead to discovery about new product and service requirements (Morabito 2014; LaValle et al. 2011). Fine grained behavioral analysis aspires to feed predictive analytics, enabling marketers to spot deviations in our purchasing patterns. An initial issue was corresponding social media views and opinions to demographics, so one can understand who says what to profile information and improve targeting. The ability to correlate social media data, for example tweets with Facebook and LinkedIn profiles, has mitigated our doubts about the source of information.

Thus, big data gives Marketing Relationship Managers an excellent tool to feed us the right information, to influence us at the right moment towards making that final decision to buy. There is now a whole sector of social media analytics dedicated at eliciting these insights. Mashable.com alone offers 20 Application Programming Interface (API) that can help people scan different channels, like Facebook and Twitter or even texts in newspaper articles and blogs, for what people want. In the same way, they can also get real-time feedback about how promotions and other promotional activities are received (Provost and Fawcett 2013).

But data has also changed the way we can target people. We don't need to group people into large or even small target groups, we can target people directly based on the electronic trails of our computer's IP address about our lifestyle choices, from what we buy to what we vote for to what we are interested in, where we are located, what our demographic characteristics are.

While social media, however, dominate current discussions about the potential of big data to provide companies with a competitive advantage, it is likely that really differentiated business models will take advantage of design-driven innovation relating, for example, to the Internet of Things (IoT), see also (Morabito 2014).

1.3.2 Design-Driven Innovation

The combination of big data sources with other emerging technologies can inspire design-driven innovations. These innovations are disruptive game changers that manage innovations that customers do not expect but they eventually love. Design, in its etymological essence, means "marking sense of things" and design-driven innovations are the R&D process for meanings (Verganti 2009).

For example Apple did not change how we make calls from our mobile, but what we do with our mobile and how we think of it. For everything you want to do, there is now an app for that, from designing color schemes for your baby's room to passing time playing angry birds to checking the news to watching a film to measuring the dimensions of your rooms. An iPhone is not a phone anymore, it is a multiple purpose tool (Verganti 2009) and Apple is not a phone-making company, it's the company that has changed our lives and most people love it for it. Products are not seen as outputs of some faceless industrial process anymore, they are symbols of the ethos and caliber of the people who designed it. Buying a product is also a representation of who you are and who you favor. Hence, product innovation is not just about products, it is the strategy of sharing common meanings with your customers and being part of the community.

The same way product innovation is not just about products, but also about sharing common meanings, business model design is also about sharing meanings about what an organization stands for. For example, Asos.com is a fashion retailer though is not just about cloths (Asos 2012). The company has invested in a marketplace site which is not *just* about fashion it is about fashion Democracy, enabling anyone, anywhere in the world to sell fashion, to anyone, anywhere in the world and for a 10 % commission per sale, it is a self-sustained business model as well (Asos 2012).

What will constitute big data Design driven Innovations then? To date, "Big data = Social Data" in most people's minds, yet really transformative innovations are likely to be inspired by the Internet of Things (IoT). Intelligent systems equipped with sensors and decision support systems promise autonomous, rather than automated, innovations. Such intelligent systems change our paradigm, the very core assumptions about what is possible, what is right and what is wrong. They promise an "always-on, always-aware, always-connected, always-controllable" (Paharia 2013) machine-to-machine coordinated world. This will affect almost every aspect of infrastructure as we know it. Such technologies will turn mundane everyday things into novel offerings. Commuting, for example, may change dramatically over the next few decades. Your future car may be more of a driverless taxi you pay for on demand. You will be able to call it to pick you up and drive you to work as technology allows cars to communicate with other cars and the road infrastructure in a safe way, and, of course, self-regulate their own green energy consumption and storage as they will most like run by solar or hydrogen power (Neiger 2014; Griggs 2014). And perhaps, you won't even have to own it! You will be able to hire it from city stations, from companies such as, e.g., www.Car2go.com.

Since 2008 more things are connected to the internet than people, making it a huge business opportunity. According to the UK government's Department for Business, Innovation and Skills (BIS) the global market for smart city solutions will be at more than $400 billion annually by 2020. This may sound huge to some but it is still a fraction of global infrastructure spending (Townsend 2013). Though, an increasing movement of civic hackers, open-source technologies and open government data are still working together in order to demonstrate the value of smart technology to make cities more efficient, democratic, safer and sociable (Townsend 2013). And while this may be a challenge for organizations who strive for profit, it is extremely valuable to societies and possibly to social entrepreneurs who strive for social impact and social change, rather than money.

Perhaps ideas for innovations won't even come from within organizations and institutions; perhaps we have entered an era of peer-to-peer innovation where ideas and even solutions are crowdsourced and crowdfunded. The following section describes how the locus of innovation has shifted over the years from an internal process to becoming the creative engagement of communities of users, and how thus its ownership and directions shifts from the organization to the community (Morabito 2014).

1.3.3 Crowd Innovation

Big data can not only change how we approach the market with a product or service, but also how we design the product to start with. Open innovation was based on the premise that innovation ideas that can be useful for organizations may lie outside the organization and companies should not restrict themselves from harnessing these ideas for the sake of control (Chesbrough 2003). This perspective suggests some very different principles about how a successful organization should behave. For example, it abolishes the "non-invented here" notion to recognize talent with useful ideas wherever these may come from (universities, suppliers, customers, other companies, the public). Intellectual Property (IP) is a trading asset to be bought and sold for profit. And IP can be a matter of co-creating with outsiders for mutual benefit (Chesbrough 2003). Big data can take this conception into a whole new level. Seen as product requirements, social media can be scanned for customer complaints and product related wish lists. But it is not only that we can get better insight into the market, we can also respond rapidly.

Open innovation is now facilitated by innovation intermediaries, like *Innocentive* platform which match makes 'solvers' and companies with a problem seeking a solution. Big companies can take advantage of these developments to outsource such expertise, and they do. For example AstraZeneca, has set up an innovation pavilion that hosts their challenges on Innocentive. As part of this, it has set up a $100,000 innovation fund to source a solution for a Targeted Delivery of Oligonucleotides that will improve their therapeutic effectiveness on tumors cells (Innocentive 2014). But such outsourced expertise is available to smaller companies too. While this is a good thing, outsourcing expertise is a great leveler between large and small companies, and big data has given small organizations a leg up.

In the big data era, not only data and opinions are open, but so are ideas, even business ideas! Innovation hubs pop up across the globe to provide support to people with ideas to incubate new businesses offering, mentoring, and avenues to funding. Crowdfunding sites have broadened the funding avenues and the funding base even more, by enabling consumers to support these creative business ideas directly. For example Kickstarter.com is a community of people working together that is a crowdfunding platform to enables people to donate, pre-order or get a stake in a company of their liking (Kickstarter 2014).

Anything from Art and Comic design to Food and Technology business ideas are included. *Lix*, for example, a pen-like 3D printer idea has pledged for £30,000 only to collect £485,249 from 5,388 backers in 26 days, most of them early adopters who pre-ordered the pen (LIX 2014).

Social media and big data feed off each other. Identified ideas, prototypes, products and scenarios are discussed, developed and constantly updated in collaboration within communities, and tested using against historical and real-time data to predict market reactions (Choi and Varian 2012; Hafkesbrink and Schroll 2011). Using predictive analytics, for example innovators can get insights about best case scenarios and comparisons of different alternatives (Kearney 2014).

1.4 Big Data Driven Business Models

The emergence of mobile phones is a potentially lucrative media platform for marketers. Mobile devices have enabled context-specific, real-time marketing communications for new types of middlemen, like daily deal sites, and take advantage of these technological advancements. Groupon location-based services, are an example of just that, aspiring to becoming the ultimate virtual marketplace, where local people can find local deals on anything, anytime, anywhere (Styles 2014). They monitor the location of millions of their subscribers across the globe to match them with local deals in their area based on their interests. With the proliferation of such sites, deal aggregator sites, like Yipit offer one-stop shop of all daily deal sites to customers (Raice and Woo 2011).

However, we have not yet become really creative with big data. So far, the aspirations of most people are driven by old conceptions of adding value, still seeking to use big data to do old things perhaps more efficiently and more effectively, and certainly more flexibly, yet the same. With big data changing the rules favoring those with technical and analytical skills, it is inevitable that technology companies will diversify, entering traditional sectors whether on their own or by acquiring smaller and aspiring companies in the market. Data storage and analysis capability give a competitive advantage to companies who want to make an inroad into other sectors.

In the sphere of retailing for example, online advertising and cross-selling seems to be the key drivers for utilizing big data. It will not be surprising however if game changing business models in the retail sector are driven by big technology companies. IBM on April 2014 announced the acquisition of Fluid to develop a virtual personal shopper mobile app, based on its intuitive Watson technology that can interact with people in natural language (Dignan 2014). It does not take a big stretch of imagination to understand the transformative potential of combining Artificial Intelligence (AI) with big data analytics.

Furthermore, Google has made inroads into the travel market, ironically enough partly funded by travel agencies themselves through online advertising expenditure. Nearly 70 % of travel bookings are done online. Some 70–90 % of advertising by online Tour Agencies is spent on Google. Google know how the competition performs, owns the channel of reaching customers, employs the right caliber analysts, has the culture to keep them, immense data storage capability and a loyal audience. With a capabilities storehouse like this, Google can make inroads into every retail market it pleases (Brumley 2014).

Perhaps more impressive and overarching will be smart city innovations relating to the "Internet of Things" (IoT). Data can be generated by sensors integrated into anything we know, from garbage bins and bike wheels to water pipes and traffic lights, combined with Artificial Intelligence (AI) technologies can form a network of self-managing city infrastructure. No wonder IBM, Microsoft and Cisco are all into the race of winning smart city pilot projects (Ratti 2014). It is the role of big data in designing these disruptive innovations that will transform the way we live.

Do big companies have an advantage in this competitive space? Perhaps or perhaps not. A competing paradigm is emerging that is more in line with 'open' conceptions of the prosumer, i.e. a customer that produce their own products or services. And this is the conception of Service Mashups–compositions of service modules put together by consumers themselves. Hence, the role of companies is to put together the service modules in a way that can be easily combined with other modules to form a service. Already businesses are working towards developing web and cloud based interactivity environments where IoT services can be put together (Im et al. 2013; Guinard and Trifa 2009).

1.5 Organizational Challenges

While businesses across industries recognize the imperative of big data, there are many challenges that face the research and evolution in this field. The most prevalent are skill set shortages, cultural barriers, processes and structures, and technology maturity levels. These issues are discussed in what follows.

1.5.1 Skill Set Shortages

One commonly referred problem with respect to big data is having the right people. Data scientists are often PhD graduates who combine mathematical and programming skills, able to interrogate the databases to uncover trends and build predictive models to check different scenarios (Kearney 2014; Davenport and Patil 2012). Unlike large online retailers, such as Amazon, technology companies, such as Google and Financial institutions, most organizations had not invested in such expertise. While Data scientists are a rare commodity and very likely to be highly pricey, assess to it may not be impossible, as outsourcing companies are popping up. For example, Exerfy.com is a Harvard spin off, that specializes in resourcing Data Scientists for organizations or undertake Analytics projects on their behalf (Harvard Innovation Lab 2014). Perhaps, even the pool of expertise is not that small. Big data opens a new employment avenue for mathematicians and data modeling people working for financial institutions and perhaps students with strong mathematical skills are likely to be drawn to this new field. Perhaps even open source coders will create ever so user-friendly, predictive analytics freeware that can be interrogated by none experts, in natural language. After all, some freeware tools already exist for those who are statistically inclined.

1.5.2 Cultural Barriers

While market-driven innovations require insight, design-driven innovations call for foresight! Strategic and Technology foresight go hand-in-hand. For company boards who long viewed IT as a support function, the struggle to change their attitude, attract and keep the right talent will be even harder. Spencer Stuart's 2011 Index shows that the average age of the Standard and Poor's 500 board members is 62.4 years (Bricker and Eckler 2014). C-level management in the US may have a hard time shedding old assumptions and wholeheartedly fostering new ways of conducting businesses.

In addition, in a world where competitive advantage is created and depleted quickly, capability may be a matter of sourcing, investments, and alliances rather internal evolution and development; thus, patterns of capability development may be common in start-ups as well as technology giants (Fine et al. 2002).

Organizations that have learned to collaborate, they will now be more able to compete. Innovation 3.0 (Hafkesbrink and Schroll 2011), for example, is based on collaborative practices, where it is not companies but communities of interest and communities of practice, with wide participation for suppliers, customers, even competitors who seek a benefit in creating a common purpose. Still many organizations are struggling with internal animosities, silo mentalities and professional territories. Big data has become a new reason to fight about, as marketing compete against IT departments for big data ownership, and of course for the investment budgets that go with it (Gardner 2014).

1.5.3 Processes and Structures

For big data driven strategies to succeed they need to be implemented, and they need to be implemented rapidly. This fundamentally means changing processes and possible structures and architecture, with knock on effects on business and technical architecture.

Particular after years of pursuing process standardization to affect operational efficiencies, people and departments are now stuck in their ways. Job descriptions are tight down to particular roles and so are reward systems and remuneration. Departmental and directorial kudos depends on the budget allocate to them. Big data driven innovations demand enterprise-wide collaboration, flexibility and knowledge sharing. Inevitably this will require organizations to take a modular approach to their structure, to enable them to mix and match accordingly. It will also mean that company policies, remuneration and leadership orientation will have to change or perish.

1.5.4 Technology Maturity Levels

To enter a field still in development, particularly one that depends a lot on emerging technologies, one need to plan for the technology obsolescence and technological skills renewal. The big data sphere both in terms of data collection, quality controls and analysis is still in development and inevitably investments in any platform run an inherent risk of becoming outdated or disrupted by new technologies. For example, innovations on database infrastructure, such as orthogonal frequency-division multiplexing (OFDM) (Werbach and Mehta 2014), can facilitate real-time analytics, in ways that is not currently possible. Advances in in-memory computing capability, such as Non-volatile memory (NVM) devices (Lankhorst et al. 2005), can address energy consumption concerns and analytics speed (Chen et al. 2014). Adoption of ubiquitous applications will transform not only what we can do with technology but our attitude towards it, with implications on company, public policy, and the organization of social life (Lesk 2013; Adamson et al. 2012).

1.5.5 Organizational Advantages and Opportunities

Much like with most disruptive innovations, embarking on big data utilization projects will accrue a number of organizational benefits. Those benefits are discussed below:

a. *Improve decision making* by lowering the cost of better quality information analysis
b. *Improve business performance* by disseminating information more effectively across the organization

c. *Improve collaboration* by developing a common, enterprise-wide business intelligence, integrating views on identified business opportunities
d. *Generate and pre-test value propositions* utilizing advanced and discovery analytics.

Others focus more on new opportunities that arise from the utilization of big data and big data analytics. For example, Michael and Miller (2013) are arguing for the opportunities that will arise from mining non-text data, such as videos, pictures, and voice, as well as humans—machines and machine-to-machine interactions (LaValle et al. 2011). We've also assisting at the steadily increasing of the amount of data captured in bidirectional interactions, both people-to-machine and machine-to-machine, by using telematics and telemetry devices in systems of systems. Particularly, interesting is the impact of big data on Health-related industries. Integrating and sharing different forms of biological information, from high-resolution imaging such as X-rays, Computed Tomography (CT) scans, and Magnetic Resonance Imaging (MRIs) to health records and lifestyle choices, expert communities can get a better understanding of what makes us ill and what keeps us healthy. According to Adrian Usher, Chief Information Security Officer of the of the Skype division at Microsoft, particularly interesting for the sector will be the integration of nanotechnology embedded in people, that will be utilized as a monitoring and diagnostics tool (Shah 2013).

While big data visionaries talk about business advantages and opportunities, others warn about its risks, particularly those of infringing on our privacy and abusing our civil liberties, as well as being discriminated against (Lerman 2013). Data breaches and security concerns are pertinent both in decentralized, ubiquitous and in centralized cloud conditions; also concerns about privacy and confidentiality are not characteristics about big data, but on social data utilization in general (see digital business identity issues discussed in Morabito (2014)).

The real "elephant in the room" is that big data analysis seeks to make inferences about who we are based on our online behavior as if this is the whole picture. In addition, predictive analytics are modeled based on human theories about cause and effect attributing perhaps the wrong labels to people. For example, Jeffrey Zaslow gives an account of how he 'wrestled' with his Tivo machine algorithms to avoid inaccurate stereotyping based on his TV recordings (Zaslow 2014). While in entertainment this makes a funny account, things could get more serious in healthcare.

1.6 Case Studies

In 2008, Groupon was the first organization to offer prepaid discount vouchers for a variety of services, restaurant discounts, Spa experiences, and museum visits at discounted prices of 50 % or more. Given its wide appeal, companies in the business to consumer (B2C) sector used Groupon to reach new customers at introductory prices and to create online buzz.

On the basis of its popularity, Google offered Groupon $6 billion and eventually it was valued at $12.7 billion. Meanwhile, 400 similar websites began to copy the business model. By February 2013, the company has failed twice to meet their own earning predictions, thus, not translating revenues into profits, and their CEO is fired (Lappin 2013). In year 2014, their share trades 40 % down from last year at $7 a piece almost a third its $20 Initial Public Offering price (Lappin 2011). Yet, it has 44 million customers and increasing sales. Selling local stuff seems to be its more profitable segment with profit margins around 30 %. So how can big data help Groupon ramp up its profits? In 2013, Groupon loses his Chief data scientist.

The Groupon team has been using open source data analysis software that was appropriate for predictive analytics from a personal computer. Although, it could not be used for Groupon's total set of dataset information. This made responses to be disconnected, slow and cumbersome, yet one Groupon analysts have spent too much time configuring to their needs to let go.

Another, grappling issue for Groupon's business model is cutting down on overhead costs, i.e. management and administrative costs, which are around 50 %. Fine grained, internal performance analysis of its operational costs can identify where savings can be made to optimize operations at a global scale.

> **Point of Attention:** Adopting big data and big data analytics does not translate into competitive advantage as such. You need to have a clear strategy, in the face of anticipated competition from copycats, whether to protect your advantage or to utilize next generation technologies to better adapt in changing market conditions.

Groupon invests in serving its most profitable market better. Taking advantage of its large customer base, it has now invested in real-time, location-based services to match customers' position with nearby deals and offers.

Will that offer Groupon a distinctive competitive advantage? How long before such technology can be copied by competitive sites, like Living Social (2014), or deal aggregators, like Yipit (2014)? And what would stop, the likes of Amazon, to enter the push market of geolocated deals to its own customer base?

Let's consider now the case of pharmaceuticals. MIT professor Natasha Dow Schull wrote in MIT Technology Review that technology companies are betting that the affordable care Act's mandate to cut costs will boost use of gadgets that let people monitor their own conditions (Schüll 2014).

In a recent Digital Health Summit she noted that it was featured: "smart scales and water bottles, digital pedometers, electronic skin patches, heart-rate-detecting earphones, and an impressive collection of wristbands packed with sensors to log a person's steps, heart rate, sleep phases, and more.... The pitch was that a person needing guidance on daily lifestyle decisions such as what to eat, when to sleep, and how much to exercise could simply consult the data dashboard" (Schüll 2014).

These are only some of the wearable sensors that will be collecting data on our health and provide biofeedback, transforming, thus, the end-to-end healthcare supply chain and even the kind of therapeutic interventions available to people. While these promise to change the competition landscape, western medicine is still very much drug based and pharmaceuticals are getting into the big data game early.

A big collaboration project amongst pharmaceutical giants was announced in 2013, it is named '*Project Data Sphere*' (LSC 2014). This platform allows researchers to combine trials to create larger more helpful data sets, something they have wished for a very long time. A goal of the *Project Data Sphere* is to spark innovation through access to comparator arm data from historical cancer clinical trials. The data can allow for more efficient research through improved trial design and statistical methodology, reduced duplication and smaller trial sizes, as well as the development of broader data standards (LSC 2014). Astrazeneca, Bayer, Celgene, Johnson and Johnson, Pfizer, Memorial Sloan Kettering Cancer Center and Sanofi committed to pulling together information resources to accelerate cancer drug discovery (Comer 2014).

The idea is simple, pull together all information resources about clinical data and make it available to the international community of clinical researchers. The target is to beat them in the drug obsolescence race, constantly improving the offerings to cancer patients.

SAS provides the platform and Sinequa the capability to index and analyze data in different languages. The reason behind the collaboration is simple: improve the rate of bringing new cancer medicine in the market and doing it while lowering costs. What is the motivation of each of the big pharmaceutical to collaborate? To understand this we need to understand the structure, current dynamics, and future of the industry and where competitive advantage is coming from now and in the future. To sell cancer medicine is consider as a business to business (B2B) and business to government (B2G) activity. While the medicine is used by the public it is actually governments and private insurers who decide which medicine they will subsidize and avail to the public.

Cancer patients themselves have no knowledge and no say in this process, and of course cancer medicine is not sold over the counter. Hence, price competition happens at a B2B level. In most countries, insurers differentiate their offerings too (Schultz 2013). Low paying customers get a lower contribution and highly paying customers a higher contribution to drugs. Pharmaceuticals incentivize the inclusion of their branded prescription drugs in insurer and government lists, with rebates, i.e. money back discounts for quantity purchases, in order to compete with generics. Generics are low cost, non-branded, copy cut medicine with the same or similar therapeutic effects (Provost and Fawcett 2013).

With most governments shifting towards cutting down on healthcare costs, generics have now 70 % of the market in most areas, pushing revenue growth of the top pharmaceuticals down to 2–4 % in 2011–2012 from 11 to 14 % in 2003–2007 (Kaplan et al. 2013). While this is true in most areas, it is not for cancer treatment. Why? Generic cancer drugs have low profit margins, hence there are only a few companies producing them, leading to drug shortages when production issues arise. So there is a market gap for cheap cancer medicine (Pellegrino Blog 2014).

In addition, the dominance of pharmaceuticals in health care may change. Advances in other areas, such as high-end medical nanotechnology and biologics, and a shift in focus from treatment to prevention will enable new types of entrants will take away market share of the healthcare budget. Hence, it is in the interest of pharmaceuticals to collaborate in order to compete, not only amongst themselves but very likely with up and coming technology companies too.

> **Point of Attention:** Big data and analytics can help industries redefine themselves and the value of product offerings to their customers. Big data may enable traditional industries to make big leaps forward, but it will shift competition within the sector to competitors outside the traditional industry boundaries.

Big data analytics in the sphere of bioinformatics can make collaboration between companies in order to possible. To give you an example, the cost of reading a human genome in 2001 was $95 m. In the near future, it will probably cost $1,000 and it will be a matter of hours. Moreover, as wearable biosensors are increasingly adopted, vast amounts of day to day contextualized biological data can be aggregated. Such data can now be easily aggregated and correlated not only to understand diseases better, but also to personalize treatments.

1.7 Recommendations for Organizations

Several recommendations arise regarding strategy in the big data era. Whilst, these are neither new nor unique to big data-driven business modeling, they are however accentuated in this era. Recommendations arise in the whole spectrum of strategy development, from strategy formulation questions to synthesizing insights to implementing strategic decisions, to ensuring the existence of contingency planning. Big data (Junqué de Fortuny et al. 2013).

1.7.1 Ask the Right Questions

The big data era favors organizations with foresight and collaborative skills and public good orientation. Big data can provide answers to many questions, so many in fact that one can get lost in them. To this end, a focus on skills and education is relevant to have a competitive exploitation of the opportunity coming from big data and big data analytics. Companies with PhD level people in their boards are likely to have a differential advantage over companies with good administrators. Why? Simply because PhDs are trained to turn problems into relevant questions, design different methods to answer them, understand the bias in these methodologies, understand a plethora of data analysis and finally can turn such insights into persuasive reports. Yet, some classic, strategic questions should be asked:

1. Does big data change your business model by creating new business opportunities or change your relationship with suppliers and customers?
2. Can big data improve the value added to your customers by your offering?
3. Can big data help you identify new target customers and keep them?

1.7.2 Look Out for Complementary Game Changing Innovations

Big data technologies do not develop in isolation. Other technologies develop in parallel that will have synergistic effects with big data. Companies who want to take advantage of the big data revolution will have to keep an eye on such technologies and how they can combine to add value to their business model. For example, embedding sensors into humans and animals will give a new meaning to ubiquitous computing. Also transform the potential of industries, such as bioinformatics, pharmaceuticals, health services, and even insurance.

Researchers at the University of Washington have now managed to establish brain-to-brain communication via computer interfaces, where 'person A' was able to send a brain signal via the Internet to control the hand motions of a 'person B' (Armstrong and Ma 2014). Which industries might be disrupted by combining big data analytics with brain-to-brain interface communications might be a question for organizations in the learning and health fields, for example, to envision.

1.7.3 Develop Sound Scenarios

Now more than ever, competitive analysis should be centered on customer needs. As new business models arise, companies should be constantly on the lookout for emerging competitive offering arising in unexpected fields. Sound scenario planning will require not only an analysis of political, economic, social, technological, legal and environmental factors, but also of paradigm shifts occurring by the interplay of these factors. Big data discovery analytics can expose us to indications of such changes, but it will be fundamentally our own open mindedness that will determine whether we are able to synthesize them into comprehensive views of the future.

1.7.4 Prepare Your Culture

Cultural barriers have always been hurdles to major changes. Turning a company to be data centric is a big change in its own right, particularly when we talk about discovery. Discovery requires a bottom-up, inductive thinking. It requires people to observe in order to develop hypotheses to test and this demands that they shed their preconceptions, stereotypes and need for clarity. Most organizations have selected and conditioned their management to be otherwise; good efficient administrators, some with better interpersonal skills and a flair for 'big-picture' thinking, yet not many with the new skills required. In addition, employee assessments are structured around productivity and efficiency, perhaps also relational skills, but certainly not around innovativeness. If we want this paradigm shift, we need to review how old systems work contrary to it.

1.7.5 Prepare to Change Processes and Structure

Discovering a new strategic choice will not lead to any advantage unless organizations can act upon it. Making strategic units data-driven requires embedding data analysts at the core of the team. And this alone is a big change. In addition, big data can give first movers advantage to organizations only if they have the capability to review their processes and restructure accordingly. Designing a modular enterprise IT architecture that can be easily reconfigured will be fundamental. Doing so, within a dedicated community of practice including the whole value chain, will be even more profitable.

1.8 Summary

In this chapter we have discussed how big data can be utilized to achieve competitive advantage. We opened this discussion by reviewing the evolution of our understanding of competitive advantage and highlighted two advancements: on one hand competitive advantage is a dynamic ever evolving effort, as opposed to a sustainable asset. On the other hand shift from organizational to community ownership of competitive advantage.

Then we illustrated how big data can affect different aspects of a business model that offer add-on capabilities to organizations. In particular, we discussed the effects of big data on marketing, innovation and business model design (Kearney 2014), touching upon the different forms of collaborative organization upstream and laterally to provide value added offerings.

Current challenges for existing organizations were highlighted as well as organizational advantages from embracing big data and business opportunities that open up in the new era. Two case studies were discussed: Groupon and the Pharmaceuticals big data consortium, from different points of view. We highlighted the importance of scenario planning and the monetization of big data driven business models, as well as the role of big data to set into gear big changes in different sectors.

The question as to whether big data will provide a differential advantage to one company over another is still open. Whole sectors seem to embrace big data concurrently leaving their weakest links behind to perish. In addition, technology companies seem to have an advantage over others, as they have ample expertise to deploy in data analysis. This leads to big technology providers making inroads to previously traditional sectors, such as, e.g., travel and retail. Thus, big data is fussing out industry boundaries and competition, perhaps even our understanding of what competitive advantage is.

References

Adamson, B., Dixon, M., Toman, N.: The end of solution sales. Harv. Bus. Rev. **90**, 60–70 (2012)

Armstrong, D., Ma, M.: Researcher controls colleague's motions in 1st human brain-to-brain interface. http://www.washington.edu/news/2013/08/27/researcher-controls-colleagues-motions-in-1st-human-brain-to-brain-interface/ (2014). Accessed 15 Nov 2014

Asos: Asos discover fashion online. https://marketplace.asos.com/ (2012)

Innocentive: AstraZeneca Challenge: Targeted delivery of oligonucleotides. https://www.innocentive.com/ar/challenge/9933013 (2014). Accessed 15 Nov 2014

Bricker & Eckler: Board Demographics: compare your board's composition in terms of age, gender, and ethnicity. http://www.acredula.com/details.aspx?id=105 (2014). Accessed 15 Nov 2014

Brumley, J.: Google just became a real problem for online travel agents. http://investorplace.com/2014/04/goog-stock-google-travel-booking/#.VCPn_Pl_veg (2014). Accessed 15 Nov 2014

Chen, M., Mao, S., Liu, Y.: Big data: a survey. Mob. Netw. Appl. **19**, 171–209 (2014)

Chesbrough, H.: Open Innovation: The New Imperative for Creating and Profiting from Technology Xerox Parc: The Achievements and Limits of Closed Innovation, pp. 1–10. Harvard Business School Press, Boston (2003)

Chesbrough, H.W.: The era of open innovation. MIT Sloan Manag. Rev. **44**, 9 (2003)

Choi, H., Varian, H.: Predicting the Present with trends. Econ. Rec. **88**, 2–9 (2012)

Comer, B.: After delays, project datasphere rolls out. http://blog.pharmexec.com/2014/04/09/after-delays-project-datasphere-rolls-out/ (2014). Accessed 15 Nov 2014

Davenport, T.H., Patil, D.J.: Data scientist: the sexiest job of the 21st century. Harv. Bus. Rev. **90**, 70–76 (2012)

Dignan, L.: IBM's watson unit invests in fluid, eyes personal shopping applications. http://www.zdnet.com/ibms-watson-unit-invests-in-fluid-eyes-personal-shopping-applications-7000028580/ (2014). Accessed 15 Nov 2014

Drnevich, P.L., Croson, D.C.: Information technology and business-level strategy: toward an integrated theoretical perspective. MIS Q. **37**, 483–509 (2013)

Fine, C.H., Vardan, R., Pethick, R., El-hout, J.: Rapid-response capability in value-chain design. Sloan Manag. Rev. **43**, 69–75 (2002)

Gardner, J.: Who owns big data: The CMO or CIO?. http://www.wired.com/2013/06/who-owns-big-data-the-cmo-or-cio/ (2014). Accessed 15 Nov 2014

Griggs, B.: The CNN 10: future of driving (2014)

Guinard, D., Trifa, V.: Towards the web of things: web mashups for embedded devices. In: International world wide web conferences, pp. 1–8 (2009)

Hafkesbrink, J., Schroll, M.: Innovation 3.0: embedding into community knowledge—collaborative organizational learning beyond open innovation. J. Innov. Econ. **7**, 55 (2011)

Hagen, C., Ciobo, M., Wall, D., Yadav, A., Khan, K., Miller, J., Evans, H.: Big data and the Creative Destruction of Today's Business Models, pp. 1–18. Kearney Publishing, Chicago (2013)

Harvard Innovation Lab: What is experfy?. https://www.experfy.com/ (2014). Accessed 15 Nov 2014

Hine, C.: Virtual ethnography. In: Fielding, N., Lee, R.M., Blank, G. (eds.) The Sage Handbook of Online Research Methods, p. 179. Sage, London (2000)

References

Im, J., Kim, S., Kim, D.: IoT mashup as a service: Cloud-based mashup service for the internet of things. In: Proceedings—IEEE 10th international conference on services computing, SCC 2013, pp. 462–469 (2013)

Junqué de Fortuny, E., Martens, D., Provost, F.: Predictive modeling with big data: is bigger really better? Big Data. **1**, 215–226 (2013)

Kaplan, W.A., Wirtz, V.J., Stephens, P.: The market dynamics of generic medicines in the private sector of 19 low and middle income countries between 2001 and 2011: a descriptive time series analysis. PLoS ONE **8**, e74399 (2013)

Kearney, A.: Big data and the creative destruction of today's business models—strategic IT article —A.T. Kearney (2014)

Kickstarter.: http://www.kickstarter.com (2014). Accessed 15 Nov 2014

KPMG: Brand and ownership concentration in the European automotive industry (2010)

Lankhorst, M.H.R., Ketelaars, B.W.S.M.M., Wolters, R.A.M.: Low-cost and nanoscale non-volatile memory concept for future silicon chips. Nat. Mater. **4**, 347–352 (2005)

Lappin, J.: Groupon, Down 40 % in 2014, finally does something for shareholders. http://www.forbes.com/sites/joanlappin/2014/05/05/groupon-down-40-in-2014-finally-does-something-for-shareholders/ (2013). Accessed 15 Nov 2014

Lappin, J.: Deduced reckoning is assembling the mosaic! http://www.forbes.com/sites/joanlappin/2011/02/04/deduced-reckoning-is-assembling-the-mosaic/ (2011). Accessed 15 Nov 2014

Lavalle, S., Lesser, E., Shockley, R., Hopkins, M.S., Kruschwitz, N.: Big data, Analytics and the Path From Insights to Value. MIT Sloan Manag. Rev. **52**(2), 21–31 (2011)

Lerman, J.: Big data and its exclusions. Stanf. Law Rev. **55**, 55–63 (2013)

Lesk, M.: Big data, big brother, big money. IEEE Secur. Priv. **11**, 85–89 (2013)

Life Sciences Consortium (LSC): Project data sphere, project data sphere. Accessed 15 Nov 2014

Living Social: Livingsocial https://www.livingsocial.com (2014). Accessed 15 Nov 2014

lixpen.com: LIX—The smallest 3D printing pen in the world. https://www.kickstarter.com/projects/lix3d/lix-the-smallest-3d-printing-pen-in-the-world (2014). Accessed 15 Nov 2014

Michael, K., Miller, KW.: Big data: new opportunities and new challenges. Computer **46**, 22–24. Long Beach, California (2013)

Morabito, V.: Trends and Challenges in Digital Business Innovation. Springer International Publishing, New York (2014)

Neiger, C.: 5 Future car technologies that truly have a chance. http://auto.howstuffworks.com/under-the-hood/trends-innovations/5-future-car-technologies.htm#page=0 (2014). Accessed 15 Nov 2014

O'Brien, D.P.: Markets and hierarchies: analysis and antitrust implications (book review). Econ. J. **86**, 619–621 (1976)

Paharia, R.: Loyalty 3.0: How to Revolutionize Customer and Employee Engagement with Big Data and Gamification. McGraw Hill Professional, New York (2013)

Pellegrino Blog: Generic drug shortage limits affordable cancer treatment options. http://www.pellegrinoandassociates.com/generic-drug-shortage-limits-affordable-cancer-treatment-options/ (2014). Accessed 15 Nov 2014

Porter, M.E.: Competitive Advantage: Creating and Sustaining Superior Performance. The Free Press, New York (1985)

Provost, F., Fawcett, T.: Data science and its relationship to big data and data-driven decision making. Data Sci. Big Data. **1**, 51–59 (2013)

Raice, S., Woo, S.: Groupon's Boston problem: copycats. http://online.wsj.com/news/articles/SB10001424052702303763404576420090000910026 (2011). Accessed 15 Nov 2014

Ratti, C.: Forget flying cars. Smart cities just need smart citizens. http://www.archdaily.com/author/carlo-ratti/ (2014). Accessed 15 Nov 2014

Schüll, N.D.: Obamacare meets wearable technology. http://m.technologyreview.com/view/526576/obamacare-meets-wearable-technology/ (2014)

Schultz, T.: Turning healthcare challenges into big data opportunities: a use-case review across the pharmaceutical development lifecycle. Bull. Am. Soc. Inf. Sci. Technol. **39**, 34–40 (2013)

Schumpeter, J.A.: The Theory of Economic Development: An Inquiry Into Profits, Capital, Credit, Interest, and the Business Cycle. Harvard University Press, Cambridge (1934)

Shah, S.: Big data will go mainstream when nanotechnology is embedded into humans, says Skype CISO. In: Computing, 26 Apr 2013, http://www.computing.co.uk/ (2013). Accessed 7 Jan 2015

Styles, K.: Groupon adds location-based deals for mobile users. http://mobilemarketingmagazine.com/groupon-adds-location-based-deals-mobile-users/ (2014). Accessed 15 Nov 2014

Taylor, W.C., LaBarre, P.G.: Mavericks at Work: Why the Most Original Minds in Business Win. HarperCollins, New York (2008)

Townsend, A.: A manifesto for smart city development. http://www.theeuropean-magazine.com/anthony-townsend-2/8244-a-manifesto-for-smart-city-development (2013)

Verganti, R.: Design driven innovation. Harv. Bus. Sch. **40**, 288 (2009)

Werbach, K., Mehta, A.: The spectrum opportunity: sharing as the solution to the wireless crunch. Int. J. Commun. **8**, 22 (2014)

Wu, M.: Towards a stakeholder perspective on competitive advantage. Int. J. Bus. Manag. **8**, 20–29 (2013)

Yipit: Yipit has every deal in your city. http://www.yipit.com (2014). Accessed 15 Nov 2014

Zaslow, J.: If TiVo thinks you are gay, here's how to set it straight. http://online.wsj.com/articles/SB1038261936872356908 (2014). Accessed 15 Nov 2014

Big Data and Analytics for Government Innovation

Abstract

This chapter discusses the transformation of the public service provision model due to big data, and in particular due to public engagement in the context of open government initiatives. We outline the changing role of governments in societies, and the technological enablement towards direct online democracy and active citizen engagement, as well as the utilization of big data enabled governance as a competitive advantage for attracting resources and talent to maintain a global smart megacity status. To this end, this chapter discusses the utilization of (a) new sources of data, such as Crowdsourcing, Internet of Things, (b) engage public talent, (c) institutionalize private–public partnerships and (d) seeks for new models of value-for-money public provision, but also the challenges that big data present us with respect to data ownership, data quality, privacy, civil liberties, and equality, as well as public sector's ability to attract big data analyst talent. We demonstrate different aspects of this discussion through two case studies: Barcelona Smart City and Haiti's emergency support during the 2010 earthquake disaster.

2.1 Introduction

This chapter discusses the impact of big data in the public sphere on public service provision and new opportunities for public service organization and structure that may transform the role of governments in societies.

The utilization of ICT to improve public sector services has started with the whole e-government discussion. Transforming government services using ICTs has been a complex and costly task, often associated with the automation of public services and business systems integration. While e-government projects focused on operational efficiency, initiatives such as Open Government efforts sought to foster public service transparency, civic participation, and inter-departmental collaboration. This could be achieved by sharing public sector infrastructure, seamless information sharing with other agencies, bundling core competencies to improve service delivery and engaging external entities, such as universities and businesses (Executive Office of the President of USA 2014).

While these changes definitely seek to effect efficiencies, they are also qualitative in nature, changing fundamentally the nature of the relationship between governments and citizens. Big data initiatives come to underpin their progress. Since 2012, both EU and the US are seeking ways, though legislative and policy changes, to remove obstacles in the use of big data which promise greater effectiveness with lower costs in the public sector (Nagy-Rothengass 2013). Civic participation via social media, for example, can also reduce the cost of public service delivery. Crowdsourcing information on potholes, for example, can cut down on inspection costs. Big data also promise clockwork provision of public service. Intelligent assets, such as intelligent traffic lights can notify a central asset management system about their state of maintenance ahead of time and larking issues in their working condition, so repair work can be streamlined without disruption of service (Thomas 2013).

Before we go on to elaborate on the role of big data in civil life, it is important to understand some underlying shifts in the role of Governments and its relationship citizens.

2.1.1 New Notions of Public Service: Towards a Prosumer Era?

Everything about civil service, even its very naming "service", has emphasized the transactional relationship between citizens and government. The relationship is simple. Civilians pay taxes and in exchange they are served in various fields, health, education, road maintenance and the like.

Recently, however, a new understanding of public provision put citizens in the role of partners. The key idea is that the pursuit of public ends is the responsibility of everybody—private and nonprofit entities, the public, and government. Partnership with citizens and community involvement was a big part of the 2010 Manifesto of the Conservative party in UK under the auspices of the "Big Society" program (Conservative Party 2010). The US Open Government initiative, announced only a year before in 2009 also seeks foster civic participation (McDermott 2010). Both are premised on the idea of enabling people to take care of themselves and of each other. Social media and smartphones can facilitate the interaction between citizens and governments on the go. They can also amplify the communication and engagement of public though communities of interest. To combat crime, for example, citizens need to coalesce with police in monitoring and reporting suspicious activities. Recently, this is also happening in other areas too of civic responsibility.

Application developers, such as Citysourced.com have developed applications enabling citizens and residents to report and provide information to local government about all sorts of civic issues, from potholes to graffiti, fly tipping, broken pavements or street lights. People can do so anonymously or not, they can upload photos, and pin them on a street map. The report is sent to councils and there is a tracking of progress on the issue online (CitySourced Inc. 2014). This is a typical example of how technology has facilitated citizens to play the role of council inspectors and this is a free service to the community and to the government too, as it minimizes inspection costs. Charities and interest groups work together to amplify the message. Cyclist communities, for example, have a big interest in potholes as it is a big nuisance for them, so pothole reporting is promoted by cycling charities and associations (The National Cycling Charity 2014).

2.1.2 Online Direct Democracy

And even more fundamental change might take place due to social changes and technology advancements; one that aspires to give citizens decision making power on social issues, much like the type of direct democracy of ancient Greece. PartyX (Nelson et al. 2015), is such an initiative. They seek to take advantage of developments in online collective decision making, to involve every stakeholder in political decision making. As this is currently on beta version and used only at local level for local issues, it does not fall under the big data agenda as yet. Should this kind of technology however go into adoption phase and used to debate global issues, then we can start seeing big data making inroads into the political and legislative sphere. Real-time, big volume, unstructured information aside, global political debating will add another dimension of interest in our discussion of big data; that of 'multilingualism'. Dealing with multilingualism is a dimension already high in EU agenda (Nagy-Rothengass 2013).

2.1.3 Megacities' Global Competition

Since 2011, more people live in cities than in rural areas for the first time in human history. Megacities, i.e. cities larger than 10 million people, are an emerging phenomenon. According to the UN, the number of megacities will have grown from five in 1975 to 26, with 24 of them located in the developing world (United Nations Department of Economic and Social Affairs 2006). Megacities are not a local or national issue. They will affect the future prosperity and stability of the entire world as they will shape the balance of power of national economies in a global world, affect population mobility and configuration of talent, and will influence the social and political dynamics of the world (United Nations Department of Economic and Social Affairs 2006). Megacities have a functional and a symbolic role. What would UK be without London? And what would The Emirates be without Dubai?

Megacities are not just key instruments of social and economic development at all fronts but also harbors of social innovation for the private and public sector due to their unique dynamics. Megacities are an attractive proposition for those seeking a better quality of life in terms of a higher standard of living, better jobs, fewer hardships, and better education. In a globally competitive environment Megacities compete for capital resources including global talent. They typically face a 5 % population growth rate, which challenges the quality of living indices (such as security, cost of living, mobility, employment, environmental) that put pressure on urban infrastructure and public policy. To raise their attractiveness, megacities need to improve on those indices (United Nations Department of Economic and Social Affairs 2006; Mostashari et al. 2011). Hence, Megacity Mayors face unique dilemmas, primarily on how to raise standards of living across a number of well-being indices in the face of high population growth rates, while compete in the global environment.

Smart city infrastructure, the bundle of Internet of Things solutions for city infrastructure management and intelligent infrastructure-citizen interfaces are considered to provide a way forward. The quantity of data produced and the criticality of infrastructure management will raise the bar for big data analytics and management. We will discuss this opportunity as part of the content in the next section.

2.2 Public Service Advantages and Opportunities

2.2.1 New Sources of Information: Crowdsourcing

Crowdsourcing is becoming an increasingly common term and opens new avenues for creating free public value, civic engagement, and transparency. It can take many forms. 'Crowdreporting', for example, is a common form of crowdsourcing in the public sphere, at the moment, and in line with the new conception of citizen as a partner. The "SeeClickFix.com" is a typical example (SeeClickFix 2014). It is an online service designed to help citizens report non-emergency issues in their neighborhood, via a web interface, Facebook or smartphone apps. The issue handling process is tracked online. After the issue is reported, it is tracked online the same way logistics companies track the delivery of packages to their destination, only that information is published via Twitter and Facebook to inform the public (SeeClickFix 2014). "Nothing new" one might say, reporting issues like this could be done in the past using other means, like calling the council or writing a letter. What is so different after all? I guess the answer should be immediacy and transparency, and perhaps non-evasiveness.

The public does not need to go out of their way to report such issues anymore. There is an app for that or they can just log into Facebook. There is no wait on the telephone to reach an operator, there is no time consuming writing of memo. The process is blended into our everyday social life. Now everybody with a smartphone can go around and report civic issues. In addition, direct feedback and traceability can give people satisfaction and a sense of achievement that they have contributed to common good. In the past, reported information was not acknowledged and follow-up information was non-existent. So, direct interaction between public and government agencies in this civic reporting encapsulated three governmental goals:

(i) to engage the public into civic life, as citizens actively engage in the process; (ii) to decrease the cost of civil service, as citizen engagement is voluntary and free of charge; and (iii) to improve transparency of public service processes, as the issue handling process is now traceable online at par with private organizations (Vicini and Sanna 2012).

The creation of public goods via crowd reporting is not, however, the sole privilege of government agencies. Weather underground, for example, combines crowd-sourced human observation with weather station data to establish a new level of accuracy within weather reporting. Weather data is assimilated from 2,000 weather stations maintained by the Federal Aviation administration, 26,000 stations part of the Meteorological Assimilation Data Ingest System (MADIS) and a 16,000 of personal weather stations adhering to quality controls and standards. Coupled with crowd observations and meaning scientific analysis from meteorologists provide valuable insights for the co into the science behind the data and the relationship between weather and climate change (The Weather Channel Inc. 2014). This blend of human insight with private and public sensor systems, gives rise to the idea of the *Internet of Everything* (Danova 2014), the merge of structured and unstructured data in a variety of forms, from textual to pictures, videos and audio material.

Crowdreporting can also take the form of feedback. For example, the "Did You Feel it" service in the US surveys people on a number of earthquake parameters regarding their experience of particular earthquake incidents. Enriching numerical descriptors with empirical data can enrich knowledge of qualitative descriptors such as intensity (USGS 2014). Using crowd feedback to train intelligent Internet of Things (IoTs) technology utilizes the wisdom of the crowds in artificially intelligent public systems. We discuss this idea of public organization in the subsequent section, when we introduce the concept of *Cognitive city* as a potential domain for big data analytics application.

2.2.2 New Sources of Information: Internet of Things (IoTs)

While there is not a commonly agreed definition, the Internet of Things (IoTs) refers to the network of intelligent devices which include sensors to measure the environment around them, actuators which physically act back into their environment such as opening a door, processors to handle and store the vast data generated, nodes to relay the information and coordinators to help manage sets of these components (Zhang and Mitton 2011).

IoTs have made way into utilities, smart homes, healthcare and wellbeing applications, and they are expected to proliferate into other areas, such as commuting and transport (as shown in Fig. 2.1).

IoTs will push our data storage, connectivity and architecture limits to a new high. The socio-economic implications for how will live our lives might be huge. For example, McKinsey Global Institute (Manyika et al. 2011) reports a 300 %

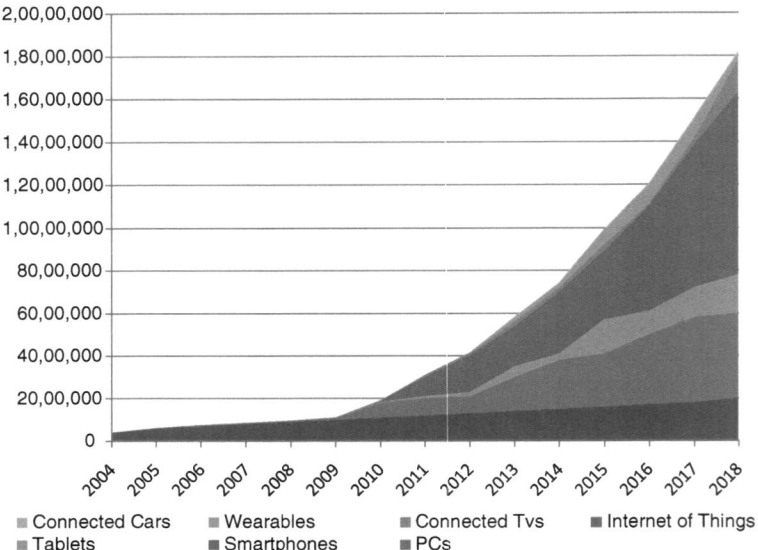

Fig. 2.1 The internet of everything adapted from Danova (2014). The number of devices in use globally are shown on the y-axis

increase in connected machine-to-machine devices over past 5 years and a sheer 80–90 % decline in microelectronics pricing which is anticipated to lead in 1 trillion more 'things' connecting to the Internet across industries such as manufacturing, health care, and mining with a potential $36 trillion cost saving in operating costs (Manyika et al. 2011).

While big emphasis is given currently into the development of intelligent assets by equipping them with sensors that beam information about their properties and conditions, what really makes up the internet of things is their distributed, purposeful collaboration, and this requires architecture, i.e. organization and structure, in line with the ethics of transparency (Bentley et al. 2014). Hence most of such technologies are clustered around common purpose for example smart city technologies, or smart car technologies to denote what drives the logic of their architecture. One of the trendiest such clusters is, of course, Smart City, which suggests an advanced connectivity through a highly networked city infrastructure via intelligent assets. The promise of course is a fertile foundation and over time capable to attract new businesses and investments and further urban growth and socio-economic development (URBACT 2012).

While the Internet of things can provide efficient use of resources, it nevertheless lacks in responsiveness and agility. To instill responsiveness into city management, we may be required to take a step further into developing cognitive city systems. Decisions about cities need to be based on principles, values, and thereby qualitative metrics as to how people want to live their lives, and what well-being means

2.2 Public Service Advantages and Opportunities

to them. Hence, a smart city is as different to a cognitive city, as a robotic arm is to social anthropoid. A platform that can combine citizens' active engagement into decision making about local government's decisions and community well-being.

Given that architecture is central to our notion of the Internet of things, we can view cognitive cities as providing the principles for humanizing their design. Not only sense and perceive but also learn, memorize, recall relevant experiences in order to adapt their responses accordingly. Almost like biofeedback, people can provide real-time feedback teaching the system how to behave. After all, cities seek to improve their quality of life of their citizens; and quality is in the eye of the beholder. People can train machines to include feature extraction, classification and clustering, all of which they can then be perfected through successive optimization of their algorithm (Warner 2011).

Smart city sensors can therefore be trained by people to learn, memorize, recall relevant experiences, who teaches them and who makes the final value judgment on things? This is an area of debate still in its infancy, but one that breeds big legal, political, and ethical questions about the future of social life. EU for example, supports initiatives that foster social innovation and inclusiveness together with economic innovation and environmental sustainability to engage citizens in public service co-creation and local authority support. Most critical to crowdsourcing success is the feeling by participants that their efforts were considered and that results came from the initiative (Evans-Cowley 2011). This requires moderators who are competent social networkers, able to used crowdsourcing tools that link and provide feedback easily, as well as a change in processes used to develop governmental services (Brabham 2009).

2.2.3 Public Talent in Use

Consultation is nothing new in public life. In developed nations it is actually institutionalized. City and regional planners are always looking for ways to engage the public in the process of planning. As a consequence Crowdsourcing of ideas and solutions has emerged as a web-based model to help in solving difficult challenges. This Section explores the use of crowdsourcing to support problem solving in planning. A case study of designing a planning curriculum using crowdsourcing is highlighted. In this case, crowdsourcing was a successful model for generating creative ideas to support curriculum revision (Evans-Cowley 2011).

The study discussed in Evans-Cowley (2011) that people chose to participate for altruistic reasons, such as an opportunity to contribute to the community, to contribute their knowledge, and that they wanted to be part of a conversation on the topic. Thus, public involvement is a central concern for urban planners. Considering the difficulties inherent in the typical public involvement process, the challenge for planners is how best to implement such programs. The Web can be used to exploit collective intellect among a population in ways one-to-one meetings (Brabham 2009).

Consequently, at the state of the art, for example, (Brabham 2009) argues that the crowdsourcing model is appropriate for enabling citizen participation in public planning projects. Starting with an exploration of the challenges faced by public participation in urban planning projects, (Brabham 2009) supports the argument of the Web as an appropriate technology for harnessing far-flung genius. Then, it concludes with an exploration of crowdsourcing in a hypothetical neighborhood planning example, together with a description of the challenges of implementing crowdsourcing.

Also, governments gradually use the Internet to aid in transparency, accountability, and public participation activities, and there is growing interest in innovative online problem-solving to serve the public good. The crowdsourcing model influences the collective intelligence of online communities for particular purposes. To develop better tools that engage the public, it is important to understand how and why people participate in these kinds of activities. In 2009, for example, the Federal Transit Administration in US used crowdsourcing for public participation in transit planning (The Next Stop Design project). Based on interviews with 23 participants, they analyzed the motivations of those participants to engage the project (OGP 2014).

Taking the above issues into account, it is worth noting that while data is the raw material of knowledge, it is really the interpretation of such data that can be acted upon by providing insights, foresight, knowledge or skill, etc. Interpretation of information requires a schema, a way of looking at data and drawing conclusions. In modern societies this was traditionally the job of experts. In the digital era, this is changing! Printing empowers individual ownership of ideas, the digital era empowers co-ownership. Wikipedia is a prime example of how data and information is organized and interpreted in a collaborative way online to provide an understanding on each subject matter through a constant ever evolving debate. The idea is premised on Marshall McLuhan motto that "the medium is the message", in that a certain medium facilitates certain interpretations that other media do not (Bentley et al. 2014).

To this end, online communities have become an important source for knowledge and new ideas. Making "big data" available to a large number of analysts means that more ideas can converge on how to mine such data. A platform for doing so is Kaggle (2014), a world's leading an online platform, which operates as a knowledge broker between companies aiming to outsource predictive modeling competitions and a network of over 100,000 data scientists (Kaggle Inc. 2014). Currently, clients include companies such as General Electric (GE), Ford, Facebook and Microsoft, and health service organizations, such as Heritage Provider Network, in California who seeks to develop a predictive algorithm that can identify patients who will be admitted to a hospital within the next year. Such predictive analytics in the service of health care provision can inform the development of more accurate Public health budgets and cost cutting plans (Pinsent Masons LLP 2013).

2.2.4 Private–Public Partnerships

Private–Public partnerships can be seen to emerge in almost every aspect of public service. With the privatization of most utilities and the trend towards outsourcing, much of the public sector in advanced societies is run by the private organizations. Countries in the periphery of Europe, such as Greece are going through the teething pains of making this transition now. With global competition on public service management, we are entering of course a new phase of relations between public and private organizations. That of partnership; the pursuit of a long standing mutually beneficial and loyal relation that will ensure long-term planning and prosperity (Miller 2013).

Big Data management has a core role to play in supporting decisions on all of these partnerships, which is why progressive governments are aiming to mobilize and support in the field. The event organized by the World Resource Institute on "Public–Private Partnerships for Open Government" in London 2013 is characteristic. It sought to share the task of mobilizing citizen engagement, developing more transparent and accountable governments (Stefan and Kisker 2011). This has implications for data ownership and data management at all public service fronts from healthcare and natural resources to publicizing data on contracting, government expenditure infrastructure, and government aid to third parties. One aspect that deems these partnerships fundamental is the lack of expertise within the public sector and the ability to vet and support them. Another, of course, is the upfront investment in infrastructure, big data clouds for example, that large organizations can afford with the view to recoup them though long-term government contracts. Yet another reason is the ability and urge of private companies to experiment with new technologies in less sensitive contexts and provide governments with 'safe' technology options that are not like to raise public criticism.

Due to the power to profile people and triangulate information about individuals, big data analytics offers deals with some fundamental concerns of public services. Identity management, for example, is a big issue for most public services, from tax collection to health provision to parking ticket collection. Big data analytic technologies may make it possible for public service organizations to combat fraud, improve data breach monitoring and authentication (Zhang and Chen 2010). On the other hand, getting it wrong may have some serious repercussions. We discuss this in more details in Sect. 2.3.

2.2.5 Government Cloud Data

Governments have slowly embarked on Cloud computing to tackle the much to be desired transparency, participation, and collaboration amongst its agencies but also with the public. The idea, the concept, and the term, that is cloud computing, have passed into common currency in an ambiguous manner. The very concept characterized by three main entities—Software, Hardware and Network to describe the fusion of Virtualization, Grid computing, Utility computing and Web technologies that result in new models of IT service delivery (Clark et al. 2013).

Cloud computing permits central governments to uniformly cover the whole country with e-government solutions, independently of divergence of local administrative units that may be better or worse prepared to provide e-services. Service-oriented architecture facilitates provision of compound services covering whole customer processes, where a customer may be a citizen or an enterprise. The roll out of such systems can happen simultaneously and cost efficiently, as licensing and support can be negotiated on the whole.

By now consumers, corporations, and governments are used to store their data to "the cloud" so they can be accessed from any device, anywhere anytime. According to Lerman (2013) over 69 % of Americans now use webmail services, store data online, and utilize online applications. This trend is only going to continue, with industry analysts predicting clouds to be $40 and $160 billion over the next few years, not accounting for the internet of things applications (Lerman 2013). With the wider adoption of cloud computing, the term C-Government was coined to connote agility due to its virtualization, scalability due to grid computing and the simplicity of Web 2.0. Clouds need to be interconnected to make it easier for users to switch between cloud service providers as well as the providers to supply infinite resources (Yiu 2012).

While the relevance of clouds for governments and their potential, e.g., for voting information systems has been greatly welcomed, enthusiasm has been curbed by identify vulnerabilities involved in the digitalization of government transactions and the electoral process, thus surfacing issues with trust and transparency (Manyika et al. 2011; Al-khouri 2012). The issues will be dealt with in later sections.

2.2.6 Value for Money in Public Service Delivery

The whole move from paper-filling to e-government services was to facilitate cost cutting partially though integration across public services. Big Data offers Governments the possibility to do so without going through the pains of Business systems integration.

The UK alone, according to the Head of Digital Government Unit, Chris Yu, estimates that some 16–33 billion per year can be saved by taking advantage of big data in the public sector, which can lead to £250–£500 per capita gains. This is calculated based on a number of initiatives having to do with performance management to improve the overall efficiency of government operations, reduce fraud and error, and tax collection alone (Laney 2014). McKinsey Global Institute estimates the potential savings at a European level to mount up to €150–€300 billion a year (Yiu 2012).

A number of analytical tools can also mine data regarding citizen sentiment towards public services to provide feedback and highlight opportunities to customize service delivery by helping employees better understand the needs of each citizen. This is no different to how commercial organizations use it to customize their service to paying customers. Providing quality service to citizens has been government agenda for most developed nations and in particular those who want to attract international talent. For example, predictive analytics in the area of health informatics, particularly epidemiology, can also be a huge help for governments who need to gear up for crisis management. The more accurately people can predict the spread of disease the more cost effective prevention and treatment is expected to be, the less the disruption to public life.

Such benefits accrue without further changes in the current public service structures, yet even more benefits may accrue if we consider the potential of adopting predictive analytics to advance crime prevention and reduce policing resources or introducing smart grid technology to improve the efficient use of utility resources, (gas, electricity and water).

2.3 Governmental Challenges

2.3.1 Data Ownership

With data ownership come great responsibility for its management, storage, use and misuse. But in the age of open (public) data who really bears such responsibility? Who is the legal guardian of it and what is written in the implicit contract between civilians and government regarding its use and protection? In one sense all public data is private data in that it is either civilians personal or lifestyle information or relates to the functioning of the public service which is nevertheless accountable to the public, at least in democratic settings. In that sense, governments and public organizations are custodians of our data, granted permission to use it in exchange of providing us with public services and promote public good (Gudipati et al. 2013). Take the United States Patent and Trademark Office online database, for example, which contains over 8 million patents and 16 million filings dating back to Samuel Hopkins's 1790 and receives 200,000 patent applications and 100,000 trademark applications each year (Hoffman and Podgurski 2013). Who does this information belong too? Obviously, the patent holders and submitters. Yet, such information would be useless for both the person and the country unless the US government safeguards its existence and integrity. Indeed, personal data can be created by a variety of sources from people, machines, devices, and the rightful owner of such data is the authority which can verify its veracity as being the 'True Owner' of the data (Al-khouri 2012).

This will bear interesting questions when devices will monitor our behavior and condition beaming information about our whereabouts and state. While devices are susceptible to error, people are susceptible to deception and self-deception. Governments and public agencies will have to make rules to decide how to handle the inconsistencies.

2.3.2 Data Quality

Big Data can amplify the repercussions and implications of poor data quality, and is a particularly important issue for governments and civilians alike. Recorded data can be flawed (erroneous, miscoded, fragmented, or incomplete) due to workload pressures and user interface workarounds (Junqué de Fortuny et al. 2013). Data should be checked for completeness, conformity, consistency, accuracy, duplication, and integrity, and good practices around data quality do exist. In private organizations, non-quality data can be ignored from consideration, without compromising the integrity of analysis or affecting the user. For example, if a retailer does their analysis only on the 'clean' data of their customers to profile and predict future sales, the customer is not greatly affected (Crawford 2013). The same cannot be true for the health service, for example, particularly if 'unclean' data are characteristic of a locality (e.g. a local hospital). Poor data quality can result from integrating data sources. Data issues can also emerge from the integration, federation or conglomeration of data, and given the variety and volume of big data, testing this data can be a big task. Various big data testing procedures have started to emerge, using grid processing technologies, such as Hadoop, to support a timely processing (Crawford 2013).

While, data stewardship and data testing procedures can deal with the "Garbage in" problem, another issue is lurking in the seams of public sector decision-making; and this is all forms bias [selection bias, confounding bias, and measurement bias (Kerr and Earle 2013)]. Confounding occurs when we correlate two phenomena, which has been studied independently (Howarth 2014; IQ Analytics 2014). For example, pulling together smoking habits from Facebook profiles and associating this with youth diabetes statistics, might erroneous speak of causal relationship that could be mediated by another factor, for example unemployment or heredity or the family's economic status. Selection bias can come from all possible sources and most importantly due to differential devise use amongst different countries, ages and socioeconomic groups. Kate Crawford principle research in Microsoft and Visiting professor of MIT, gives brilliant accounts on the hidden biases in big data in Harvard Business Review blog (Crawford 2013). Given the sensitivity of public services that can bear life threatening and legal implications, treating information with utmost rigor is fundamental. Thus, we need to outline and progress the conversations on regulatory and other interventions to address data analysis difficulties that could result in invalid conclusions and unsound public health policies (Microsoft 2014).

2.3.3 Privacy, Civil Liberties and Equality

Privacy and civil liberties are the two sides of the same coin. User profiling is the process of collecting information about a user in order to construct their profile. The information in a user profile may include various attributes of a user such as

2.3 Governmental Challenges

geographical location, academic and professional background, membership in groups, interests, preferences, opinions, etc. More, ominous applications include cell-phone tracking and the proposed creation of a national biometric database.

As Kerr and Earle (2013) argue profiling individuals on the basis of their health, location, electricity use, and online activity raise risks of discrimination, exclusion and loss of control. When these involve access to public services, repercussions are exacerbated. The promise of big data is based on prediction with the view to preempt possible threats. If, for example, one can predict increased burglaries in an area, local government can increase policing of this area to preempt such incidents (Barcelona City Council 2014).

Preemptive action is based on prediction and prediction on predictive algorithm based on social information and this curtails civil liberties replacing proof with risk estimates. With increased predictive capability comes increased responsibility to avoid such threats that can make governments more conservative in how they approach social risks. To what extent can governments afford to let unemployed youth roam the streets freely, once we have established that it is highly probable to commit petty theft or drug dealing? On the other hand, shall we detain or curtail the freedom of youth to meet and socialize and lead them to isolation and depression? To what extent policemen should be informed about such correlations and would that lead to discrimination of every unemployed youth, who treated with suspicion may even turn to crime as self-fulfilling prophesy theory would predict?

Also, Professor Lerman (2013), for example, raises another issue; the issue of equality regarding public treatment of people and groups who do not fully participate in the information society, because they don't have the means, time or appetite for. Statistics about the digital divide show great variation in digital engagement from country to country, age group participation, socio-economic class, urban or rural living and, of course, between countries (Lerman 2013). Some interesting 2014 statistics about the global internet and social media use can be found at the social media community blog hub (Kemp 2014). The risk here is that governments may come to rely so much on big data that they forget to ensure that they engage people to understand their needs and considered these during decision-making.

2.3.4 Talent Recruitment Issues

Given the scarcity of data analysts talent in the market, the public sector will have a hard time attracting such talent as permanent stuff. In the UK, for example, public sector organizations are obliged to recruit below market going rates to justify Human Resource (HR) expenses (PageGroup 2014). In addition, the once upon the time job security and fringe benefits of working for the public sector increasingly disappear, making public sector organizations even less attractive. With large organizations such as banks, insurances, large online retailers and consultancies competing for such resources, governments will have a hard time attracting and keeping such talent. On the other hand, governments could use University talent.

A resource much underutilized particularly in Europe, despite the depth and breadth of skills relevant to the public sector (Campos 2008).

On the other hand, there is always training as an option to up skilling public sector staff. In February 2014, for example, the UK government announcement that £150,000 of government funding would be dedicated to Open data training of more than 150 Public Sector employees (Gangadharan 2013).

2.4 Case Studies

Barcelona embarked on the smart city journey 10 years ago in an informal fashion resulting in many smart city projects now dispersed in various departments across the city, currently being collated under a single program. The 22@ Barcelona region, once in need of redevelopment, has been transformed into a living test site for piloting new technologies (Department for Business Innovation and Skills 2013).

Xavies Trias, mayor of Barcelona since 2011, has recognized the importance of digital technologies for the future prosperity of the city. In his words in outlining his commitment states that Barcelona "…should not waste the opportunity we have to apply these new technologies to improving people's quality of life, by generating a new "economy of urban innovation" based around smart cities. This is another of our future commitments" (Department for Business Innovation and Skills 2013).

To progress this agenda he formed Urban Habitat, a government wide management structure to promote collaboration across water, energy, human services and environment agencies. Whereas, housing and urban planning were also grouped together. To further cement cross agency collaboration, the Smart City Personal Management Office, oversaw all projects with a smart city aspect. While there are over 100 projects with a smart city angle, 13 are highlighted as strategic for the smart future of Barcelona, tackling the necessary infrastructure to support smart city applications, kit out city assets with intelligent sensors, and define smart city public services. To this end, the telecommunications network is revamped to integrate fiber optic networks, and Wi-Fi networking, public and a centralized management system enabling the interoperability and prioritization of mobility, public transport and urban infrastructure, applying concepts such as priority and intermodality to make more efficient and sustainable mobility in cities. This is underpinned with intelligent data project collating information from smart assets and public service organizations with the view to opening these up to the public. New public services are progressed such as energy projects relating to the urban lighting of Barcelona, creating microgrids to create local generation and consumption of green energy, telemanagement of irrigation urban green spaces and electric car mobility options, as well as, smart parking options to enable speedy parking avoiding unnecessary city traffic. Citizens will have contactless and mobile apps to use city services. Some projects focus more generally on a mentality change around smart city agendas. The O-Government project, for example, seeks to gain support for Open Government, strategy and roadmaps and improve transparency, open data and civic participation. The "Citizen compromise to sustainability 2012–2022" seeks to gain definition and traction for a city roadmap that can provide a more equitable, prosperous and self-sufficient environment to its people (Department for Business Innovation and Skills 2013).

The regeneration of the 22@ Barcelona region was a public-private partnership were companies, universities, research, and communities work in close proximity with municipal leaders to exchange knowledge and streamline innovation, but also ensure inviting and engaging urban planning by subsidizing housing and developing green spaces. Local and international, private and public funding was used for infrastructure development and the testing of new public services. The government facilitated access to public funds by institutionalizing InnoActiva, a consultancy agency which to supports private companies to make their case to public authorities and institutions. Following the Silicon Valley cluster model, it is setting up clusters in areas that they can develop a competitive advantage. Hence, 22@ is oriented to attracting talent and expertise in Media, Information and Communication Technologies, medical technologies, energy and design.

As to big data and analytics issues, open data is actually a core part of Barcelona's smart city event. Public and business access to information such as election results, population, public facilities, or economy sits in a public repository called Open Data BCN. Microsoft for example utilized data relating to a town festival called "La Merce" as a pilot to providing improved crowd management solutions. To this end, data feeds from social media, credit card transactions, web site visits, customer service inquiries, GPS data, traffic status, weather data, and parking was collected and analyzed. These data sought to gain insights about people's perceptions of the festival's entertainment and food venues, citizen interests, people mobility patterns, and medical and crime incidents that can help the planning and management of the next event (Vienna University of Technology 2014).

The city also pilots the provision of services based on mobile identification technologies. Through a smartphone app, citizens can access information about parking tickets and car towing destinations, request public subsidies for nonprofit activities, and the like, providing a proof of concept and of technology and getting the necessary public engagement to move to the next level (Davenport and Prusak 1997). Consequently, public transport smart apps are ahead of their generation due to popular demand.

In Barcelona transport information is based on a hyper-reality app. Anyone can obtain information on bus stop locations, location, lines and even be directed to it by simply pointing a smartphone camera in any direction, working wonders for citizens new to an area, tourists and even blind people who can be oriented towards their target destination using voice directions or Microsoft (2014).

Public engagement also manifest in developmental work for the smart city. Sentilo, for example, is an open source sensor and actuator platform sponsored by the Barcelona City Council, and designed by an open community.

> **Point of Attention:** Barcelona's open-source, smart city platform, engages local talent in smart city development, ensures technology and provider independence and data stewardship and remains with the public, under its stewardship and safeguards civil liberties.

With the view to establish the city's reputation as a smart city, Barcelona also drives the Smart City Protocol initiative which seeks to connect global cities in pilot projects to address common challenges (Bain and Sentilo 2014). Barcelona is a small cosmopolitan city with the vision to grow and an exemplar for smart city development that remains open, transparent, and democratic through an exchange of all capital resources from capital and infrastructure to knowledge and talent.

While for most, smart city applications are still considered a nice-to-have feature in our city life, crisis management is the acid test for any smart application. All emergency services share a common requirement, when it comes to information management. They need to accurately analyze life critical, real-time information from diverse sources, in order to deploy and manage emergency service workflows (Gangadharan 2013).

During the Haiti earthquake in 2010, emergency services needed to be dispatched to the area to support the government cope with the circumstances. InStedd, a company specializing in technology design for emergency services such as natural disasters and diseases, offered support to the emergency services and people. Within 48 h the company has set up the telecoms infrastructure and gain buy in for setting up an emergency response number. The company offered a message-integrated communications from two mobile network companies; incoming aid requests were received in Haitian Creole. These were routed to Riff/EIS for analysis (Alehegn 2010).

Riff has the capability to automatically extract features, classify data and tag data and their metadata (e.g. source and target geo-location, time, route of transmission) and before it can process it via algorithms. The analytics module can detect relationships between these extracted features within a collaborative space or across different collaborative spaces. Riff can also combine information from GeoChat, a collaboration tool geolocating human comments, observations and reports to make information richer and relevant. Riff then shared information with Crowdflower another workflow provider, handling the distribution of tasks to a bilingual volunteer workforce for translation, tagging, and geocoding. Information was then forwarded to Ushahidi, a website initially developed to map reports of violence in Kenya now turned a global crowdsourcing platform with humanitarian goals. 'Ushahidians', as a community of interest helped to map, accurately geotag information to provide accurate coordinates to the search and rescue team on the ground (Meier 2012).

> **Point of Attention:** Smart apps and open collaboration platform can become the critical infrastructure platform for the application of big data and analytics to disaster recovery.

The value of swarm intelligence-based approaches for workflow-based emergency management systems has been outlined as far back as 2007 (Bentley et al. 2014). This was an example par excellence for a bundle of crowdsourcing services combined to provide an emergency response information architecture working with the added complication of bilingualism. Data quality is of paramount importance to prioritize calls and minimize erroneous dispatching of scarce rescue resources. Timely and accurate information processing was life critical. International crowds of volunteers were utilized and important safety critical decisions had to be taken on the fly by the government and participating companies alike. The venture's success was based on companies' technical capability and social responsibility, and openness to collaboration with other companies and volunteers for the same cause.

2.5 Recommendations for Organizations

Governments will have to find their feet and strike the right balance between progress and the challenges of the big data era and redefine its relationship to the public and to private capital in a world of global competition. Smart city has become perhaps a pillar of competitive advantage for those who can grasp the opportunity, while others will lag behind. As to these issues, in what follows we point out some key factors for an effective application and exploitation of big data and analytics in public sector digitalization, particularly, for smart cities and service oriented initiatives.

2.5.1 Smart City Readiness

Each country will have to access the readiness of its cities to become and its positioning in a smart cities global landscape. The European Smart Cities initiatives, audits cities on the basis of the six factors shown in Table 2.1 (Vienna University of Technology 2014).

Smart city strategy at a national level is likely to be faced with budgetary tensions between rural and urban development and a nation should have a vision and a view of how to engage its people and private investors in the conversation. Moreover, both local and central governments will have a 'good cop, bad cop' role to play between role modeling the opening up information and effecting transparency and ensuring that information is safeguarded from abuse by involved parties.

In addition, smart cities will divulge responsibility for city services to machines, partnerships with private companies and the public and this requires not only educated citizens but also a change in mentality about civic responsibility from all these parties.

Table 2.1 Factors for smart cities initiatives audit

Factors	Description
Smart economy	Innovative spirit and entrepreneurship, productivity, workforce flexibility, ability to transform and international embeddedness
Smart mobility	Local and international accessibility, availability of ICT infrastructure, innovative transport systems
Smart environment	Attractive natural conditions, pollution, environmental protection and sustainable resource management
Smart people	Level of qualification, affinity to life-long learning, social and ethnic plurality, creativity, flexibility, cosmopolitanism and open-mindedness
Smart living	Cultural facilities, health conditions, individual safety, housing quality, education facilities, touristic attractively and social cohesion
Smart Governance	Participation in decision making, public and social services, transparent governance, political strategies and perspectives

2.5.2 Learn to Collaborate

Like most sociotechnical changes, to realize the benefits of big data and smart city initiatives we need to change the way we do things. In particular, these technologies require the diverse stakeholders collaborate. Government agencies and departments have been traditionally separated by internal rivalries and financial competition developing into an embedded silo mentality and culture. Information has been seen as power and it has been hoarded to make people indispensable in the face of downsizing, cost cutting, and other modernization attempts. Davenport and Prusak highlighted such issue as far back as 1997 (Davenport and Prusak 1997).

Focus on efficiency and years of recruiting people and managers focusing on cost cutting exercises have stripped the public sector from innovative human resources and know-how and practices (Parker 2014). Public sector practices in terms of renewing their staff and policies about paying their staff at the low end of market prices makes it difficult for them to attract human talent, or indeed to manage external associates who recruit such talent.

The public sector will need to rethink its internal recruitment processes to employ smart people who will focus on creating successful partnerships with the private sector and the public. If governments are to show the way of developing smarter cities, they should orient themselves to attracting people with high qualifications, affinity to life-long learning, social and ethnic plurality, creativity, flexibility, cosmopolitanism and open-mindedness. In addition, managing successful collaborations will require new managerial skills. High partnering skills involve:

1. creating rapport via openness and self-disclosure and feedback,
2. trust building through actions and words,
3. creative conflict resolution and problem solving,
4. appetite for change, and
5. welcoming interdependence (Dent 2006).

Furthermore, partnering in the sphere of emerging technologies will also require reviewing public sector procurement policies to allow wider participation in the supplier pool and perhaps even participation of newly established technology ventures that might be considered risky (Uyarra et al. 2014).

Finally, for Governments to continue to be relevant in a big data world, with limited resources, they need to become smarter and this means fostering public participation in decision making, public and social services, and making governance, political strategies and perspectives transparent and lean.

2.5.3 Civic Education and Online Democracy

The key aspirations of open government are the engagement of the public in the political processes and their involvement in self-service public services. This will require heightened levels of interest, knowledge, and maturity from the public, as well as new modes of participation by governments. One means to achieve the former is education. A United Nations review of such program in the US, showed that such program had changed both people's engagement levels and feeling of adequacy to engage in the political process, but not people's respect for different political viewpoints, social cohesion and trust (United Nations Publication 2010).

Online participation in democratic processes can provide an affordable ways to consult governments and take part in decision making in ways that it was not possible before. Relevant initiatives spring up slowly in different countries. In January 2014, California, for example, institutionalized the California Report Card, mobile-friendly web-based platform that encourages citizens to engage in the deliberative process via chat rooms where they would enter their own suggestions but also rate others' suggestions (Newsom and Goldberg 2014).

2.5.4 Legal Framework Development

Legal frameworks lag behind technological developments at all fronts of virtually enabled living. The persistence and rise of Cyberbulling is a testament to that. Big data profiling raises many issues regarding privacy, civil liberties, and equality, as they were described above. With on demand public services via smart applications entering the mix, such issues, particularly those of inclusion and exclusion from this virtual world, can achieve another level of inequality. Thus, Governments need to define new legal frameworks to regulate life and perhaps they even need to do so at a global level, as internet engagement is a global phenomenon. Big data analytics can be used as the tool to help international government bodies to analyze people's sentiments but also integrate best practices on such matters, but also to make law more understandable by its law enforcement groups and the public (Morabito 2014).

2.6 Summary

This chapter discussed the impact of big data in the context of public service provision and new opportunities for public service organization and structure that may transform the role of governments in societies. We started our analysis by discussing developments in public service provision, which treats citizens as *prosumers* (proactive consumers) of public service delivery, moves towards direct online democracy, and finally, to active engagement and a global smart megacities competition for resources and talent.

In this context, governments seek to gain an advantage by utilizing a) new sources of data, such as Crowdsourcing, Internet of Things, b) engage public talent, c) institutionalize private–public partnerships and d) seeks for new models of value-for-money public provision. Despite its potential, the adoption of big data and analytics are not without challenges, particularly for central governments. Of particular interest are the challenges regarding data ownership, data quality, privacy, civil liberties, and equality, as well as public sector's ability to attract big data analyst talent.

We showcased two case studies demonstrating how new forms of public service provision. Barcelona Smart City provides an example par excellence of collaboration between the private and public sector for regional redevelopment. Haiti's emergency support during the 2010 earthquake disaster demonstrates how big data in the hands of passionate volunteers can organize and support with life-critical emergency services, providing a life example as to what can be achieved through the blend of human intuition and available big data integration and advanced analytics. Like most sociotechnical changes, challenges reside in the social sphere of technology acceptance and use, as well as with the regulation of such technology, hence our recommendations are directed towards auditing readiness for Smart City development, reskilling public servants with partnership management skills, developing public's mentality of civic participation and updating legal frameworks to cope with developments in the big data area.

References

Alehegn, T.: Crisis mapping and collaboration between Western and African ICT developers for Haiti quake. http://www.tadias.com/01/19/2010/crisis-mapping-and-collaboration-between-western-and-african-ict-developers-for-haiti-quake-response/ (2010). Accessed 15 Nov 2014

Al-khouri, A.M.: Data ownership: who owns "my data"? Int. J. Manag. Inf. Technol. **2**, 1–8 (2012)

Bain, M.: Sentilo—sensor and actuator platform for smart cities. https://joinup.ec.europa.eu/community/eupl/document/sentilo-sensor-and-actuator-platform-smart-cities (2014). Accessed 15 Nov 2014

Bentley, R.A., O'Brien, M.J., Brock, W.: A: mapping collective behavior in the big-data era. Behav. Brain Sci. **37**, 63–76 (2014)

Brabham, D.C.: The public participation process for planning projects. Plan. Theor. **8**, 242–262 (2009)

City Council: Mobile digital ID for Barcelona citizens. http://www.mobileid.cat/en (2014). Accessed 15 Nov 2014

Clark, B.Y., Brudney, J.L., Jang, S.-G.: Coproduction of government services and the new information technology: investigating the distributional biases. Public Adm. Rev. **73**, 687–701 (2013)

CitySourced Inc.: Citysourced. http://www.citysourced.com (2014). Accessed 15 Nov 2014

Conservative Party: Building a big society. London, UK (2010)

Crawford, K.: The hidden biases in big data. http://blogs.hbr.org/2013/04/the-hidden-biases-in-big-data/ (2013). Accessed 15 Nov 2014

Danova, T.: The internet of everything. http://www.businessinsider.com/the-internet-of-everything-2014-slide-deck-sai-2014-2?op=1 (2014). Accessed 15 Nov 2014

Davenport, T.H., Prusak, L.: Information Ecology: Mastering the Information and Knowledge Environment. Oxford University Press, New York (1997)

de Campos, A.: Literature on university-industry links: towards an integrated approach in the study of influencing factors. Merit. Unu. Edu. **44**, 0–32 (2008)

Dent, S.M.: Partnership Relationship Management (2006)

Department for business innovation and skills: global innovators: international case studies on smart cities smart cities study (2013)

Evans-Cowley, J.: Crowdsourcing the curriculum: public participation in redesigning a planning program. Soc. Sci. Res. Netw. Work. Pap. Ser. (2011)

Executive Office of the President of USA: Big data. Seizing Opportunities. Washington, D.C. (2014)

Gangadharan, S.P.: How can big data be used for social good? http://www.theguardian.com/sustainable-business/how-can-big-data-social-good (2013)

Gudipati, B.M., Rao, S., Mohan, N.D., Gajja, N.K.: Big data: testing approach to overcome quality challenges structured testing technique. Infosys Labs Briefings **11**, 65–73 (2013)

Hoffman, S., Podgurski, A.: The use and misuse of biomedical data : is bigger really better? Am. J. Law Med. **39**, 497–538 (2013)

Howarth, B.: Big data: how predictive analytics is taking over the public sector. http://www.theguardian.com/technology/2014/jun/13/big-data-how-predictive-analytics-is-taking-over-the-public-sector (2014)

IQ Analytics: big data training a priority for the public sector. http://www.itqanalytics.com/community/blog/big-data-training-a-priority-for-the-public-sector#.VDJhABbILcs (2014). Accessed 15 Nov 2014

Junqué de Fortuny, E., Martens, D., Provost, F.: Predictive modeling with big data: is bigger really better? Big Data **1**, 215–226 (2013)

Kaggle Inc.: The home of data science. http://www.kaggle.com (2014). Accessed 15 Nov 2014

Kemp, S.: Social, Digital and mobile around the world. http://wearesocial.sg/blog/2014/01/social-digital-mobile-2014/ (2014). Accessed 15 Nov 2014

Kerr, I., Earle, J.: Prediction, preemption, presumption how big data threatens big picture privacy. Stanf. Law Rev. **66**, 65 (2013)

Laney, D.: Who owns (really owns) "Big Data". http://blogs.gartner.com/doug-laney/who-owns-really-owns-big-data/ (2014). Accessed 15 Nov 2014

Lerman, J.: Big data and its exclusions. Stanford Law Rev. Online. **66**, 55–63 (2013)

Manyika, J., Chui, M., Brown, B., Bughin, J., Dobbs, R., Roxburgh, C., Byers, A.H.: Big Data: The Next Frontier for Innovation, Competition, and Productivity. McKinsey Global Institute, Washington, DC (2011)

McDermott, P.: Building open government. Gov. Inf. Q. **27**, 401–413 (2010)

Meier, P.: How crisis mapping saved lives in Haiti. http://newswatch.nationalgeographic.com/2012/07/02/crisis-mapping-haiti (2012). Accessed 15 Nov 2014

Microsoft: City deploys big data bi solution to improve lives and create a smart-city template. http://www.microsoft.com/casestudies/Microsoft-Excel-2010/City-of-Barcelona/City-Deploys-Big-Data-BI-Solution-to-Improve-Lives-and-Create-a-Smart-City-Template/710000003415 (2014). Accessed 15 Nov 2014

Miller, H.E.: Big-data in cloud computing: a taxonomy of risks. Inf. Res. **18**, 571 (2013)

Morabito, V.: Trends and Challenges in Digital Business Innovation. Springer International Publishing, New York (2014)

Mostashari, A., Arnold, F., Maurer, M., Wade, J.: Citizens as sensors: the cognitive city paradigm. International Conference & Expo on Emerging Technologies for a Smarter World, pp. 1–5. IEEE (2011)

Nagy-Rothengass, M.: European Activities in the Area of Big Data. META-Forum, p. 27. Berlin (2013)

Nelson, S., Milberry, K., Richardson, J., Martin, M., Thomson, K.: PartyX. http://partyx.ca/ (2015). Accessed 8 Jan 2015

Newsom, G., Goldberg, K.: Let's amplify California's collective intelligence. http://citris-uc.org/lets-amplify-californias-collective-intelligence-op-ed-ken-goldberg-gavin-newsom-california-report-card/ (2014). Accessed 15 Nov 2014

OGP: Open Government Partnership. http://www.opengovpartnership.org (2014). Accessed 15 Nov 2014

PageGroup: Public sector salary survey: insight and trends. http://www.michaelpage.co.uk/salary-survey/public-sector.htm#salary-results (2014). Accessed 15 Nov 2014

Parker, L.: Cuts mean a smaller public service must be smarter. http://www.governmentnews.com.au/2014/06/cuts-mean-smaller-public-service-must-smarter (2014). Accessed 15 Nov 2014

Pinsent Masons LLP: Calls for EU public private "Big Data" partnership. http://www.out-law.com/articles/2013/november/calls-for-eu-public-private-big-data-partnership/ (2013). Accessed 15 Nov 2014

SeeClickFix: Report neighborhood issues and see them get fixed. www.SeeClickFix.com (2014) Accessed 15 Nov 2014

Stefan, R., Kisker, H.: Sizing the cloud. http://www.forrester.com/Sizing+The+Cloud/fulltext/-/E-RES58161 (2011). Accessed 15 Nov 2014

The National Cycling Charity: Fill that hole. http://www.fillthathole.org.uk (2014). Accessed 15 Nov 2014

The Weather Channel Inc: Weather underground. http://www.wunderground.com (2014). Accessed 15 Nov 2014

Thomas, J.C.: Citizen, customer, partner: what should be the role of the public in public management. Public Adm. Rev. **73**, 786–796 (2013)

United Nations Department of Economic and Social Affairs: World Urbanization Prospects: The 2005 Revision (2006)

United Nations Publication: e-Government and New Technologies: Towards better citizen engagement for development. Geneva, Switzerland (2010)

URBACT: Smart cities: Citizen innovation in smart cities. http://urbact.eu/en/projects/innovation-creativity/smart-cities/homepage/ (2012). Accessed 15 Nov 2014

USGS: DYFI background—the science behind the maps. http://earthquake.usgs.gov/research/dyfi/ (2014). Accessed 15 Nov 2014

Uyarra, E., Edler, J., Garcia-Estevez, J.: Barriers to innovation through public procurement: a supplier perspective. Technovation **34**(10) 631–645 (2014). doi: 10.1016/j.technovation.2014.04.003

Vicini, S., Sanna, A.: How to co-create Internet of things-enabled services for smarter cities. The First International Conference on Smart Systems, Devices and Technologies, pp. 55–61. Stuttgart, Germany (2012)

Vienna University of Technology: European smart cities 3.0. http://www.smart-cities.eu/ (2014). Accessed 15 Nov 2014

Warner, J.: Next steps in e-government. In: Proceedings of the 12th Annual International Digital Government Research Conference on Digital Government Innovation in Challenging Times—dg.o '11, p. 177. ACM Press, New York, USA (2011)

Yiu, C.: The big data opportunity-making government faster, smarter and more personal, Policy exchange. London, UK (2012)

Zhang, L., Mitton, N.: Advanced Internet of things. 2011 International Conference on Internet of Things and 4th International Conference on Cyber, Physical and Social Computing, pp. 1–8 (2011)

Zhang, W., Chen, Q.: From E-government to C-government via cloud computing. 2010 International Conference on E-Business and E-Government, pp. 679–682. IEEE (2010)

Big Data and Education: Massive Digital Education Systems 3

Abstract

This chapter discusses how massive digital education systems like MOOCs, facilitate the distance learning aspects of formal education institutions and enable a peer-to-peer learning. It discusses how MOOCs open new income streams for traditional institutions through employment recruiting services, syndication, and sponsoring, as well as by advertising income, selling student information to potential employers or advertisers. To this end, this chapter first explains MOOC educational models (peer-to-peer and institutional) and the role that big data and analytics are playing in this context, highlighting institutional advantages, opportunities and challenges. It then explains two cases studies where big data and analytics played essential roles in the design and delivery of the curricula.

3.1 Introduction

Distance learning has always been designed for those who did not have access to formal learning institutions. Open Universities around the world have made such markets their primary focus. Pedagogical material was adapted to reach students with different socioeconomic backgrounds, learning habits, and studying patterns, at remote areas or even close to home but limited in free time or incompatible working schedules with those of institutions. Originally distance learning programs employed a variety of audiovisual, information dissemination means, such as television programs, CDs and the like but there was still lacking student-tutor and peer-group interaction. It was really online social platforms that could re-instill the social aspect of learning (Marques 2013).

Over the past 20 years, an academic revolution has taken place, unprecedented in their global scope and diversity of institutions and people they affect, due to advancements in information and communications technologies (ICTs) (Executive 2014; Yuan and Powell 2013). Education is a key factor to economic development for nations and social mobility for the individual. Two factors have accentuated the need for global demand in education. The skills currently required to compete in a global environment are changing due to shifts in the economic model and competition from emerging developing markets. ICT's have given nations and institutions the opportunity to resource highly skilled people anywhere in the world and individuals the opportunity to move up socially. This journey is not without challenges. Developing countries for example have low digital technology penetration. Africa, the Middle East, and Latin America/Caribbean constitute just 17.2 % of the world's Internet users (Miniwatts Marketing Group 2014). Basic technology education and affordability hold people back from developing necessary technological skills. On the other hand, initiatives such as Negroponte's One Laptop Per Child (OLPC) project which sought to provide each child in the development world with a low-budget computer slowly change this dynamic.

The use of ICT technologies in education has come under different guises. Guri-Rosenblit (2010) mentions more than 20 different relevant terms, each connoting slight different implementations of a fundamentally same thing ICT-enabled distance learning:

- Internet mediated teaching,
- technology-enhanced learning,
- web-based education,
- online education,
- computer-mediated communication (CMC),
- telematics environments,
- e-learning,
- virtual classrooms,
- I-Campus,
- electronic communication,
- information and communication technologies (ICTs),
- cyberspace learning environments,
- computer-driven interactive communication,
- open and distance learning (ODL),
- distributed learning,
- blended courses,
- electronic course materials,
- hybrid courses,
- digital education,
- mobile learning,
- technology-enhanced learning.

Massive Open Online Courses (MOOCs) have recently come to be added to this long list of different implementations of ICT-enabled distance learning. While MOOCs facilitated the distance learning aspects of formal education institutions, they also introduced an even more fundamental educational change; they opened up participation to education by enabling a peer-to-peer learning. They offer the possibility to thousands of people to voluntarily share knowledge with each other

3.1 Introduction

through open access to courses. Hence, they practically provide to anyone interested fast-track, accessible, flexible, free or affordable courses, at different levels from higher education to vocational training courses. Not only the courses themselves add to the content variety of big data, but big data can have a leading role to play in the production and delivery of MOOCs educational material.

In doing so, they are a key game changer in the education sector with pervasive global implications, about nations' economic capabilities, international relations and global social mobility and welfare.

This chapter begins by discussing the implications of MOOCs in the educational sphere and the role of big data in the design and implementation of MOOCs. It is structured as follows.

3.1.1 From Institutionalized Education to MOOCs

MOOCs were an offshoot of formal education. MOOCs is rooted within the ideology of open access to education without demographic, economic, and geographical constraints which dates back in the early 20th century (Yuan and Powell 2013). Figure 3.1 outlines the historical development of MOOCs thus far.

In 2001, MIT established the Open Courseware initiative (Massachusetts Institute of Technology 2014). The priority was to disseminate knowledge far and wide where people can interact to learn and support each other in their journey to knowledge. By 2007, MIT has put all their courses online and available to the public. In the original announcement of the program to New York Times, MIT's president Dr Vest had predicted

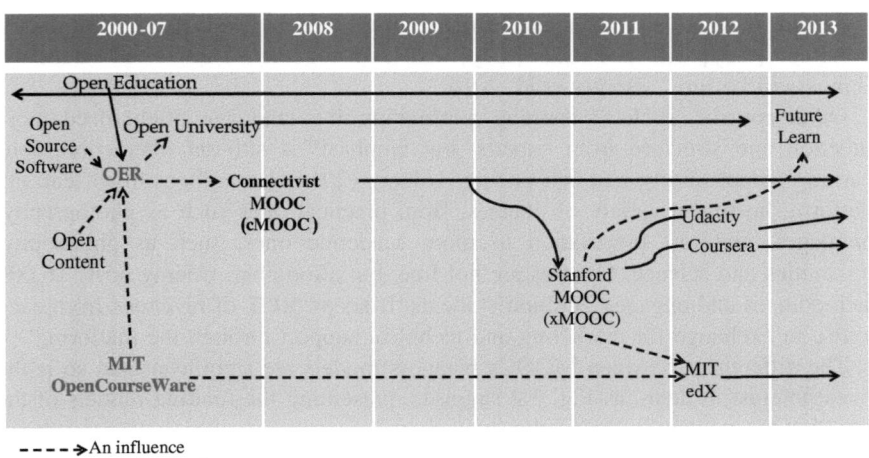

Fig. 3.1 MOOCs and open education timeline. adapted from Yuan and Powell (2013)

I also suspect, in this country and throughout the world, a lot of really bright, precocious high school students will find this a great playground. [...] there will probably be a lot of uses that will really surprise us and that we can't really predict (Goldberg 2001).

Indeed, open courseware was a stepping stone to a much larger scale change. Since then we have a proliferation of MOOC platforms and a number of highly regarded institutions that have embarked on the very same journey. Coursera (2014), for example, established in 2013 is a partnership between Stanford University and 61 well-regarded universities. EdX (2014) is established by Massachusetts Institute of Technology, École Polytechnique Fédérale de Lausanne, The Hong Kong University of Science and Technology. Udacity (2014), Peer 2 Peer (P2P) University, and FutureLearn (the UK Open University's MOOC platform) are other related platforms are just but a few other offshoots of institution-led MOOCs.

However a number of community-based, open learning platforms have started to pop-up with significant differences in their pedagogic approach and philosophy. Peer 2 Peer University (2014), for example, is a grassroots initiative. It creates a model for lifelong learning by facilitating learners to interrogate Internet material to co-create their curriculum and in doing so taking responsibility for their own and their teams learning.

According to the website of Peer 2 Peer University, openness, community and peer learning are the key drivers and nothing falls beyond the agency of the learner. Even the technology and process of learning can be open to change should the learners wish to. The idea is to leave behind the hierarchical and role separation of academics and students. Materials such as readings, videos and panel discussions seek to provoke discovery, rather than transmit knowledge. They are designed in self-contained modules to be consumed on demand, rather than follow a discipline. Their motto stir away from institutional conventions, to create an environment of "No judgment" where you "Put in what you want" and "Take what you can" an environment where educators and learners accept that they will experiment and in doing so "[they] will take risks. [they] will learn together. Things will be messy. Things will be fun." (Berger et al. 2014).

Other courses, such as learning a programming language might need more direction and structure from experts, but emphasis is still on interaction, self-learning responsibility and self-pacing. Udemy (2014) is another online learning platform, hosting a variety of courses, from practical ones such as photography, languages, and test preparation to more academic ones, such as philosophy, humanities and science. Courses are not free, but affordable. Udemy hosts 16,000 such courses and engages 3million students. It keeps 50 % of revenues from each course in exchange for marketing and technical support through the platform.

The differences between MOOCs business models are significant and so is the invest interest in them, as Fig. 3.2 suggests, presenting the funding models of the key MOOCs players in the market nowadays.

MOOCs are in search for business model validity and sustainability. For Coursera for example, the business principles resemble those of Amazon. Create a

3.1 Introduction

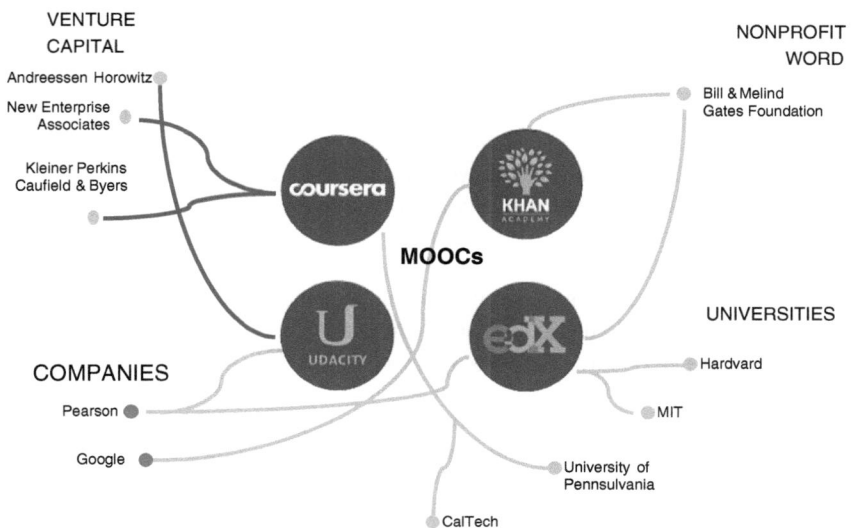

Fig. 3.2 MOOCs platforms and investor interests. Adapted from (Davidson 2014)

hub of suppliers to attract a large number of students who will be attracted in finding whatever they want in one place. For others, such as Simon Nelson of FutureLearn (Wilby 2014), the name of the game remains to be seen, as the potential of the technology has not been envisioned let alone realized. Udacity focuses on employment and employ training teaming up with companies such as Google, AT&T to offer degrees that are of interest (Udacity 2014). EdX is steering its model away from course provision to becoming the manager of the technology platform hosting MOOCs, and providing their platform management expertise as a service to universities.

Not only is their market focus different, but so is their funding models too. Venture Capitalists, philanthropists and national and educational institutions are all happy to part with their funds to support the MOOCs agenda. Coursera (2014) has accepted some $65 million, while Udacity (2014) another $15 million from venture capitalists, and this bears a risk in terms of the openness of their business models as their investors may demand the commercialization of courses for business profit (Watters 2012; The Economist explains 2014).

3.2 MOOC Educational Model Clusters

3.2.1 University-Led MOOCs

University led MOOCs, also characterized as xMOOCs, represent the latest innovation in formal education. Accredited institutions are now accepting MOOCs as part of a degree, yet a wholly free online degree is not in effect. Tuition fees are driven down because, while students still have to pay to certify for their degree, they don't pay for the operational costs of running the academic process, such as supervision expenses, classroom and facilities maintenance and the like. When MOOCs are able to provide free accredited online degrees, the University business model will have fundamentally changed (Dellarocas 2013).

A feasible economic option for universities is virtualizing traditional teaching, by recording of live lectures and presentations. Nothing new here e-Lectures are then delivered over the Web using a Learning Management System (LMS). While attendance levels may drop, student performance is not necessarily compromised (Ottmann 2013). In addition, reaching student populations around the globe is not only flattering for academics. but also a great way to decrease their face to face teaching load. MOOCs are certainly attractive to both academics and university management due to their ability to attract venture capital and grant money, often linked to academic reward systems. Another source of potential income is advertising. This is perhaps the reason why prestigious institutions have joined forces to offer their modules and degrees from a single platform. The likes of Harvard, MIT, Cornell, Berkeley, and others founded the non-profit edX to offer the option to "...take great courses from the world's best universities" or to "Take the world's best courses online for free" (Ottmann 2013). After all, there seems to be a gap in the market for low cost educational provision. According to Laurillard et al. (2010), professor of learning with digital technologies at the Institute of Education, University of London, student loans are higher than credit card loans in the US, while 40 % of student debt will never be repaid in the UK, and by 2025 demand will double to approximately 200 million students per year as emerging economies demand access to higher education.

Perhaps this also indicates a deeper shift away from government budgets to more self-sustainable forms of funding or to better links between tertiary education and private capital, or even perhaps a shift in the mission and student reach of universities to exploit new technologies in order to educate the global population and, in that way, create common worldviews.

The same process of student-expert can be observed in MOOCs with more practical content where professionals or experts provide training and skills development to novices. Many of the courses in Coursera (2014), are of this type.

3.2.2 Peer-to-Peer MOOCs

University-led, xMOOCs differ from peer-to-peer driven MOOCs, also referred to as cMOOCs [i.e. connectivist MOOCs (Yuan and Powell 2013)]. They differ in philosophy, delivery and intention and a certain 'war' of learning ideology and practice is currently played out. The quickest way perhaps to understand cMOOCs is to juxtapose them against their more traditional counterparts. Table 3.1 outlines some of the basic differences.

Table 3.1 xMOOCs versus cMOOCs

	xMOOCs	cMOOCS
What is the ultimate goal?	Deliver content to larger/new audiences; provide certifications; experiment with new course; increase access to top Northern American universities or provide free access to education	Create a learning community, which can continue to learn together in the future
What learning or instructional theories are informing the instructor's decisions?	Traditional teacher-centered approach: knowledge is transmitted from the instructor to the student	Community approach: the learning process focuses on collaborations between learners
What is the role of the instructor?	Creates course content, pedagogical approach and assessments	Participates and facilitates other learners to create content, learning goals, generate new knowledge, etc.
What role does the learner play?	The learner receives knowledge, participates in small work groups, and responds to tests and assessments	The learner co-creates the pedagogical approach and assessment
How are learners building new knowledge?	Learners view content developed by the instructor and apply it to problems or projects defined by the instructor	Learners create projects relating to course themes; share information and knowledge; help each learn
How is learning assessed?	Learners complete assessments that evaluate comprehension from the instructor's view	Learners share and self-assess their learning paths
Who is creating the content?	The instructor creates the content	The content goal is created by a core group of learners; content is created by all participants
What types of interactions are taking place?	Learners work in small groups to complete assessments based on provide course content	Learners research and share relevant course content to achieve learning goal
How flexible are the course path and the course goals?	Learning path is set in syllabus and curriculum planning material	Learning goals broadly set by core participants during the course, in response to the community, on a week-by-week basis

Source Crowley et al. (2013)

Instead of relying on traditional education models, P2P or cMOOCs seek to motivate learning collaborations amongst students. In some ways, students are not students in that there are not teachers either. cMOOCS are communities of learning of like-minded people taking responsibility for and orchestrating their own learning process. In doing so, they co-define their learning objectives, create content through research, share themes, give feedback, insights, ideas and support. While a core group tends to take more of the coordination activities, course goals and objectives are fluid and determined in response to the community.

The idea of learning through research is not foreign to formal education. There are plenty of Masters in Research usually a stepping stone to a PhD, and, of course, Doctorate programs, the pinnacle of formal education, all using research as the means or path to achieving knowledge. However, achieving a degree is a solitary process where the student takes accountability for his or her own research to which they present to some academic authority in exchange for a certification of their ability. cMOOCs so far do not work like this, at least not yet. Why is this important from a big data point of view? For starts, as there is no curriculum, information from any source can be combined to improve learning. Anything from government information to data generated by the internet of things, social media, academic journals, observations from virtual games, countries statistics bureaus can be blended, or in the speak of big data, mashed to create new knowledge. Such blending might be criticized or supported by one's learning group but inevitably there is no academic authority to bind that search to specific sources, ideas or frameworks. The world of internet is the learners' oyster (Yeager et al. 2013).

At the moment, most cMOOcs are teachers and academics interested in learning per se. P2PU (2014) is such an institution, where a team of experts has come together to explore new ideas in curriculum development and design, research, knowledge sharing, etc. and by doing so develop our knowledge about learning! Will such form go mainstream? It is remained to be seen.

3.3 The Role of Big Data and Analytics

This section seeks to understand the role of big data in this new field of education. It should be evident to the reader by now that cMOOCs make use of mashing disparate sources of open information, whether big or small, to discover and create new knowledge. But what is the role big data in xMOOCs?

Much like any other business, MOOCs need to develop market strategies for attracting new students. Hence, big data can help with the market analytics within the academic sphere. Indeed, such market research services for academic institutions has now reserved its own term: *Academic analytics* (García and Secades 2013). Academic Analytics utilizes large data sets, statistical techniques, and predictive modeling to offer business intelligence to academic institutions to improve on their customer experience. For example, education systems, especially MOOCs with varying degrees of student engagement and completion rate, will require a careful management of resources as well as seek cross selling opportunities of more premium products. This will be particularly true as xMOOCs will try to capitalize on their large student basis to satisfy their investors. Such predictive analytics are likely to be integrated with workflow systems to automate or at least semi-automate administration processes. For example, academic analytics can also inform a decision-support system and a workflow system to automate the admissions process. They can also be used to support students throughout the learning process. Utilizing existing knowledge and models relating to student effort and success, they can monitor students' interaction with the system, alerting administrators when student engagement patterns change in order to initiate communication with the student, or indeed send a predetermined default email communication (Campbell et al. 2007).

Another more fundamental use of big data analytics is its use as a learning tool. This particular use of big data analytics has been defined as *Learning Analytics* (Fournier et al. 2011). Learning analytics utilize individual learner-produced data against known models about successful learner interactions and behaviors. People in the learning analytics community propose six critical dimensions, both soft and hard, along for designing such learning models. Soft issues relate to assumptions about humans or the society, e.g., competences or ethics. Hard challenges on the other hand relate to data and algorithms. In that sense, Learning analytics can be defined as

> ...the area of discovery analytics which model of intelligent and learner-produced data to discover information and social connections for predicting and advising people's learning. (Siemens 2010).

Such analytics have appeal to a number of educational stakeholders. For example, individual learners can be assisted in reflecting on their achievements and patterns of behavior in relation to others, academics can have early warnings about students requiring extra support and attention and plan relevant interventions; management and course leaders can be assisted in developing and marketing attractive academic programs and curricula and promote them (Campbell et al. 2007).

3.4 Institutional Advantages and Opportunities from MOOCs

According to Global Industry Analysts (Report and asp 2014), the global e-learning market will reach $107 billion by 2015. Inevitably institutions want to leverage their operations to capture market share. MOOCs open new income streams for traditional institutions by not only relying on state education subsidies and student tuition, but through employment recruiting services, syndication, and sponsoring, as well as by advertising income, selling student information to potential employers or advertisers (Report and asp 2014).

Traditional institutions, particularly universities, aspire to transform higher education by expanding academic access on an unprecedented scale as means to cut costs in already underfunded public universities. While others propose various forms of 'pay-as-you-learn' teaching provision. One school of thought proposes that MOOCs was an experiment that has served their purpose as a driver for institutions to take a more strategic approach to online learning, which create new opportunities for universities, by

- *Utilizing openness as an online learning approach* through the use of online communities, including models for scalable provision that may generate revenues, and goes beyond institutional boundaries.
- *Inventing new Business models*, such as applying the concepts of freemium and premium offers into online learning, providing institutions with new ways of thinking about marketing and income generation.
- *Enabling Service Disaggregation* that includes unbundling and re-bundling of courses and delivery related services to offer premium educational services such as paying for assessment and/or teaching support.
- *Experimenting with new approaches* for teaching and learning, by utilizing new technologies.
- *Creating new education models* that cater for Learners with various studying patterns across the globe.
- *Developing internal capability* by reviewing their technical infrastructure, academic and support staff working practices (Yuan et al. 2014).

It is also important for academic institutions at all levels to increase learning attainment without increasing their costs. Learning Analytics, along with educational data mining and teaching analytics can all be seen as three aspects of the same solution to raising the education standards of the youth without necessarily increasing the number of educators required, thus making institutions more cost efficient. Learning analytics focus on capturing student behavior and correlating it to achieving learning objectives, educational data mining seek to design predictive analytics models for student attainment while teaching analytics helps educator translate such findings into better course design and student support procedures and interventions. As time goes by more and more online tools are being developed in this area. According to Charlton and Mavrikis (2013), the Course Resource Appraisal Model (CRAM), for example, allows educators to understand the impact of different delivery modes (face-to-face, blended learning and larger-scale delivery) on student learning and hence ease off transition or improve course design. The authors (Charlton and Mavrikis 2013) also argue that the Maths-Whizz can improve maths scores by online tutoring students and assessing score levels. BlikBook focuses on modeling class engagement and substitutes lecturers' student support engagement by assisting students find relevant material. Table 3.2 provides a brief overview of some of the most commonly used learning analytic tools currently available and their impact on learning as presented in Charlton and Mavrikis (2013).

3.4 Institutional Advantages and Opportunities from MOOCs

Table 3.2 Tools and their data

Tools and platforms	Learning analytics perspective	Educational data mining perspective	Teaching analytics perspective
Jenzabar	Strong analytics overall and systemic approach using large-scale data from across the organization	Learning analytics and statistical models are used to create predictive analysis	The tool provides visual representations to lecturers and support staff to inform which students need support and why
CRAM (course resource appraisal model)	Provides visual representation of teaching	Classification system and relationships to support activities across teaching and learning analysis	Automated visual models of the impact on teaching and learning
Maths whiz	Domain-specific analysis that enables different types of insight into the students' learning and relative learning of maths	Uses analysis clustering models of static relative learning points to determine maths age and contextual data	Uses a visual model to provide information of the teachers to use as part of their teaching
BlikBook	Social peer group approach for exchange and group problem solving	Student modeling and profiles for community use	Student feedback to the teachers and more peer-led student groups
MiGen	Social grouping and outcome predictions of students	Rule-based analysis and other computational techniques to analyze task progression	Constant visual analytics of teaching and learning for teachers to instigate immediate intervention on task progression and collaborative activities

Adapted from Charlton and Mavrikis (2013)

A key issue that all educational systems have to solve in society today is young people's motivation to learn. Like many other fields, education may need to seek outside their conventional boundaries for solutions. One area of interest for motivating and maintaining student engagement may come from gamification, which utilized sound game theory and game mechanics, as also mentioned in chapter one. It is a potentially powerful method for driving user engagement, and not very far from educational simulations (see for example, virtonomics (2014)).

3.5 Institutional Challenges from MOOCs

As it stands, MOOCs have a fundamental problem of identity and therefore issues around their monetization efforts. Most MOOC start-ups do not appear to have clear business models and like most ventures nowadays strive for achieving market share and worry about profitability later. This is particularly true of xMOOCs, such as

Coursera, who seek to increase throughput. On the basis of registration numbers, xMOOCs seek revenues for certification fees; recruitment services, sponsorships. Yet, many institutions do not trust the quality of MOOC delivery yet; at least not enough to offer their institutional degrees. Thus, MOOCs are still seen as an interesting branding and marketing activity at present (Yuan 2013).

Indeed the quality of learning through MOOCs is uncertain. To start with there is high dropout rate, often reported as high as 90 % (Liyanagunawardena et al. 2013). For traditional institutions this rate would be alarming, if not fatal for their going concern. Some suggest, however, that the same yardsticks for evaluating MOOCs cannot hold true, simply due to the nature and stage of adoption of the new technology.

Moreover quality issues need to be overcome, as is a certain attachment to 'old ways' of teaching and old ways of evaluating teaching. Nevertheless, certain incidents may harm the relationship between MOOCs, academics, and students. In February 2013, for example, the Coursera/Georgia Tech course "Fundamentals of Online Education" was cancelled, making students lose all their online contributions (Morrison 2013). In the same year, UC Irvine professor Richard McKenzie abandoned his economics MOOC course in the middle due to disagreement over how to best conduct the course. Michigan professor, Gautam Kaul caused waves with his Coursera-run finance class by refusing to give students the correct answers to assignments, "to avoid preparing new sets of questions with multiple versions to allow [students] to attempt each one more than once. Handing out answers will force us to do that." Karen Head, Georgia Institute of Technology professor, raised concerns around the technical functionality of MOOCs to serve her pedagogical requirements (Watters 2013). Quality also suffers when student success rates are measured. For example, while 74 % of students in traditional classes passed, only 51 % of those attended Udacity's MOOCs equivalent program succeeded. To address quality issues, for example, Udacity had turned to corporate training (Watters 2013).

Another threat remains hidden in the potential success of MOOCs; that of pedagogical hegemony. When and if education is concentrated in the hands of few global institutions and driven by few academics who are able to reach out to large numbers of students globally, then we might be creating a world where knowledge is founded on the same principles, ideas and viewpoints, in the exclusion of others. This will not only compromise the financial going concern of institutions but the plurality of knowledge bases and hence the democratization of ideas. This is of course not an issue for collaborative learning environments such as cMOOCs, as the learning agenda is not controlled by an authority but co-created on the way by participants.

cMOOCs, despite being a fundamental departure from existing, instructor-led, educational models, and indeed better positioned to use big data as a tool for knowledge discovery and integration, face their own challenges. They require a degree of student maturity, motivation and responsibility in order for students to take responsibility for their own learning and for that of others, thus, undertaking the level of research and knowledge sharing required and expected by others. This

3.5 Institutional Challenges from MOOCs

may not be feasible at all ages or at least a different kind of socialization and upbringing must precede it for primary and high school students to be able to engage at that level, and national curricula mandate must be able to open up to become compatible. Even in adult education context, people may find themselves in the midst of difficult group dynamics such as conflict, different levels of commitment. Certain skills need to be developed such as conflict resolution, team building, and creative thinking.

Moreover, even web search is biased. The topology of the Web allows us to see only few of the billion documents on a topic, and even when they find less popular information they need the critical skills to evaluate it (Barabási 2003). Boyd (2010) emphasized that information brokers, such as Google, filter information without necessarily taking a critical point of view, and hoped that social media can play a mediating role to balance this out (Kop 2011).

A new perspective seems to emerge, seeking the integration of instruction-led modes of learning with more social forms of peer to peer learning to provide a more holistic experience (see Fig. 3.3) (Crosslin 2014). Such solution might be a safer option, but lacks imagination and still recycles old notions of educating.

Perhaps educators need to look into other aspects of social life to design educational products. We also need to start differentiating MOOCs based on their audience and purpose, which might be a vicious cycle as people have not decided on the business model for MOOCs.

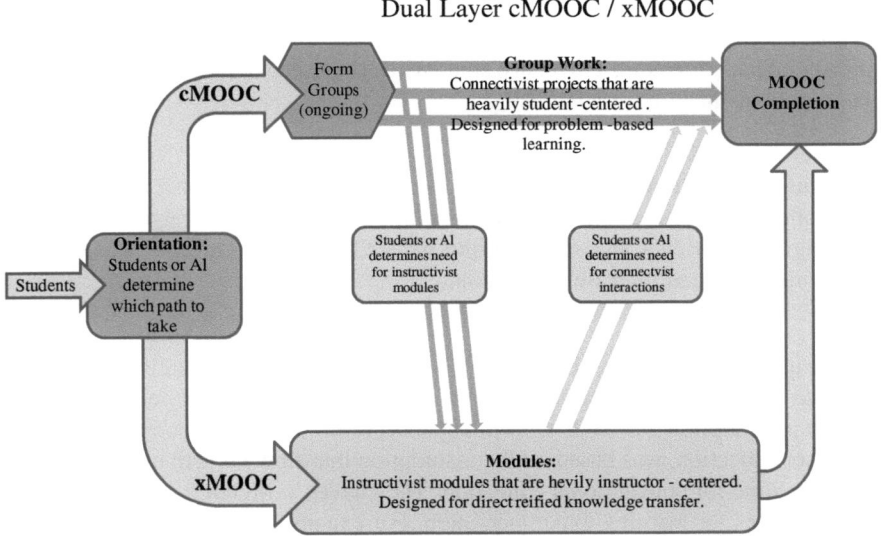

Fig. 3.3 Integrating cMOOC and xMOOC best practices. Adapted from Crosslin (2014)

3.6 Case Studies

HarvardX was formally launched in October 2012 and is co-hosted in EdX platform along with MIT, Duke University and other institutions. Since its launch it had 1,331,043 registrants in 195 countries with various degrees of certification attainment (Harvard University 2014). In its first year alone, over 500,000 students have registered for HarvardX courses, which is larger than the number of Harvard graduates in its 377-year history. Aside US that accounts for 36 % of enrolments, the rest of its student cohort comes from 204 different countries. Amongst them, Nigeria is the most enrolled country of Africa, Spain is the first in Europe, India is the highest-enrolled country in Asia with almost 50,000 students, and Brazil in South America. A potential barrier to global participation in enrolment may be language as most students from global HarvardX enrolment comes from English-speaking countries (Harvard University 2014). In China, for example, only 23,548 students enrolled in spite of its huge population of 1.3 billion. Interestingly certification attainment data do not follow the pattern of enrolment. Despite of accounting for less than 2 % of enrolment each, Burkina Faso, Greece, and Georgia are the countries with the highest rates of certificate attainment, indicating perhaps differences in the culture, educational structure and conditions or personal motivations for attending the course. However, certification is more likely among registrants who enroll near the launch dates, but viewing likelihood is stable through the run of the courses, indicating perhaps a premeditation on achieving a particular educational goal (Harvard University 2014).

It is important also to note that the median age of students is 28 and most of them already have a Bachelors or a Master's degree. So HarvardX course seems to act as an educational 'top-up', rather than a university substitute, and appeal more to the already educated, mature university students as opposed to the uneducated masses its proponents have been advertising.

Point of Attention: MOOCs are not substitutes for conventional universities or other learning institutions. However, the use of big data analytics both in designing curricula and in delivering MOOCs can provide new modes for learning, merited their own attention.

The ultimate question is "Do MOOCs work?" Harvard representatives answer the question with a poignant clarification: "Work for what?" (Summary et al. 2013). So far, the presumption that MOOCs will enhance, replace and disrupt existing models of higher education, was based on the assumption that students will utilize MOOCS as a substitute for conventional education. They haven't. MOOCs seem to be open, virtual spaces for learning experimentation. For example, registrant activity within courses is diverse. Certification attainment is one possible learning pathway and there is an indication that they might benefit from synchronous course schedules and the cohorts that they build. Most, simply watch videos or read text. Some registrants dip into a couple of sessions in the first two weeks and then abandon it either to register to other courses or sign up properly on a later instance of the course. Others focus on self-assessment to test themselves (Summary et al. 2013).

MOOCs success was allegedly based on their adherence to well-established educational and learning models. For these models to be relevant, however to the new context, similar motivations, interactions, norms, expectations, should be present; something not necessarily true when comparing MOOCs to conventional education settings. For example, open enrolment periods and unrestricted use of course resources raise important questions for analysis and design. Perhaps, we need to examine MOOCs in their own right and not as substitute of universities or other institutions. To this end, new metrics, far beyond grades and course certification, would be necessary to capture the diversity of usage patterns and goals (Summary et al. 2013).

The second case study we discuss in this Chapter is the one of Livemocha, which is a free online language learning community, providing instructional materials in 38 languages and a platform for speakers to interact with and help each other learn new languages. It has approximately 12 million registered members from 196 countries, with over 400,000 users visiting the site daily (Livemocha 2014). It was founded in 2007, by Shirish Nadkarni and Krishnan Seshadrinathan and is based on the idea that you best learn a language when you interact with native speakers. By 2010, it was announced as one of the top 50 websites by, the New York Times and the Financial Times, and Time magazine (2010).

Livemocha's online social language learning platform has followed a classic disruptive innovation path through business model innovation, to transfer online the process of learning a foreign language in a foreign country. The business model was simple. Engage native speakers who want to learn another language for free and are willing to help others to learn their own language; hence, native speakers alternate between being students and tutors. Offer a platform of tools and techniques (such as flashcards, quizzes) to help students with learning and memorizing. Maintain fair access and reciprocity in the community with the exchange of virtual tokens and rules often enjoyed by time banks and reciprocal feedback on both student performance and the quality of the reviewer (Gartner 2013).

> **Point of Attention:** Technology-enabled learning communities will generate new types of unstructured big data relating to education and learning. New norms in community education can provide new principles to model learning analytics, based on principles of reciprocity and mutual benefit and gamification.

Income comes mainly from advertising, with approximately 700,000 recurring users each month and approximately 1.85 million users reached within the first 15 months from its launch. In the next phase, Livemocha paired with Pearsons to provide a premium product that bundled formal language learning methods with social media interaction for a fee. The community remained loyal to its customer base, still providing free courses, which helped it grow its community base to 5 million users by January 2010. Finally, the community engaged accredited teachers on a pay as you go basis, where registered accredited teachers got paid for every interaction they had with a student. Dedicated students were given access to the premier content using their virtual tokens (Gartner 2013).

3.7 Recommendations for Institutions

Institutions willing to consider MOOCs at the current stage have to keep envisioning the possibilities of MOOCs not as a single business model, but as a set of business models centered around the notions of global online access, free or relatively low fee, edification. The use of the term *edification* as opposed to education is used here to connote both engagements in education: (i) those for obtaining formal qualifications for employability purposes, and (ii) those for continuous development through the pursuit of personal interests. With this in mind, interested institutional parties should keep the following in mind during their search for a positioning in the MOOC market.

- Different strands of MOOCs are very likely to develop depending on their utilisation of big data.
- Big data analytics can be utilised as a marketing tool to target potential learners.
- Big data can be utilised as a learning tool to assist help—learning, by profiling students learning patterns and to alert the education institution when human intervention is required to motivate or support student learning.
- Within cMOOCs, big data analytics can be utilised as a tool to source and integrate learning relevant learning material.
- xMOOCs are likely to transform into the MOOC equivalent of vocational education, big data analytics can play a crucial role in matching industry-required employment skills and curriculum development.

3.8 Summary

While MOOCs facilitated the distance learning aspects of formal education institutions, they also introduced an even more fundamental educational change; they opened up participation to education by enabling a peer-to-peer learning. MOOCs open new income streams for traditional institutions by not only relying on state education subsidies and student tuition, but though employment recruiting services, syndication, and sponsoring, as well as by advertising income, selling student information to potential employers or advertisers. Big data analytics can enable the personalization of the online learning process that was missing in previous online instruction methods and facilitate this to happen at a global scale. Used as a pedagogical tool in learning analytics, big data along with educational data mining and teaching analytics can all be seen as three aspects of the same solution to raising the education standards of the youth without necessarily increasing the number of educators required, thus making institutions more cost efficient. Utilizing existing knowledge and education models relating to student effort and success, institutions can use big data technologies to monitor students' interaction with the system, alerting administrators when student engagement patterns change in order to initiate communication with the student, or indeed send a predetermined default email communication. Big data in the form of learning analytics focus on capturing student behavior and correlating it to achieving learning objectives, educational data mining seek to design predictive analytics models for student attainment while teaching analytics helps educator translate such findings into better course design and student support procedures and interventions.

The reality however is quite different, MOOCs platforms do not share some of the basic assumptions about student motivation and institutional norms, expectations, and obligations, so preexisting educational models are not a good fit for their analysis. Moreover, as the Livemocha case suggested, MOOCs could utilize gamification or other learning from online communities and worlds to ensure continuous engagement and commitment.

References

Barabási, A.-L.: Linked: How Everything Is Connected to Everything Else and What It Means for Business, Science, and Everyday Life (2003)

Berger, R.: Why should I take this MOOC anyway?, http://dlmooc.deeper-learning.org/about/why-should-i-take-this-mooc-anyway/ (2014). Accessed 16 Nov 2014

Boyd, D.: Streams of content, limited attention: The flow of Information through social media. Educ. Rev. **45**, 26–36 (2010)

Campbell, B.J.P., Deblois, P.B., Oblinger, D.G.: Academic Analytics A New Tool for A New Era. Educ. Rev. **42**(4), 40–57 (2007)

Charlton, P., Mavrikis, M.: The Potential of Learning Analytics and Big data. Ariadne. (2013)

Coursera, http://www.coursera.org. Accessed 16 Nov 2014

Crosslin, M.: Designing a Dual Layer cMOOC/xMOOC, http://www.edugeekjournal.com/2014/05/04/designing-a-dual-layer-cmoocxmooc/ (2014). Accessed 16 Nov 2014

Crowley, J.: cMOOCs: Putting Collaboration First, http://campustechnology.com/Articles/2013/08/15/cMOOCs-Putting-Collaboration-First.aspx?Page=1, (2013). Accessed 16 Nov 2014

Davidson, C.: Major Players in the MOOC Universe, http://chronicle.com/article/The-Major-Players-in-the-MOOC/138817/. Accessed 16 Nov 2014

Dellarocas, C.: Money Models for MOOCs. Commun. ACM **56**, 25–28 (2013)

edX, http://www.edx.org. Accessed 16 Nov 2014

Executive Office of the President of USA: Big data: Seizing Opportunities., Washington, D.C. (2014)

Fournier, H., Kop, R., Sitlia, H.: The value of learning analytics to networked learning on a personal learning environment. Proceedings of the 1st International Conference on Learning Analytics and Knowledge—LAK'11. p. 104 (2011)

García, O.A., Secades, V.A.: Big data and learning analytics: A potential way to optimize elearning technological tools. Proceedings of the International Conference e-Learning 2013. pp. 313–317 (2013)

Gartner: Business Model Innovation Examples in Education (2013)

Global Industry Analysts: ELearning: A Global Strategic Business Report, http://www.strategyr.com/eLEARNING_Market_Report.asp (2014)

Goldberg, C.: Auditing Classes at M.I.T., on the Web and Free, http://www.nytimes.com/2001/04/04/us/auditing-classes-at-mit-on-the-web-and-free.html (2001). Accessed 16 Nov 2014

Guri-Rosenblit, S.: Digital technologies in higher education: Sweeping expectations and actual effects (2010)

Harvard University: HarvardX, http://harvardx.harvard.edu/. Accessed 16 Nov 2014

Kop, R.: The challenges to connectivist learning on open online networks: Learning experiences during a massive open online course. Int. Rev. Res. Open Distance Learn. Distance Learn. **12**, 19–38 (2011)

Laurillard, D.: Five myths about Moocs, http://www.timeshighereducation.co.uk/comment/opinion/five-myths-about-moocs/2010480.article (2014). Accessed 16 Nov 2014

Livemocha, http://livemocha.com/. Accessed 16 Nov 2014

Liyanagunawardena, T.R., Adams, A.A., Williams, S.A.: MOOCs: A systematic study of the published literature 2008-2012. Int. Rev. Res. Open Distance Learn. **14**, 202–227 (2013)

Marques, J.: A short history of MOOCs and distance learning, http://moocnewsandreviews.com/a-short-history-of-moocs-and-distance-learning/#ixzz36icU7Crp (2013). Accessed 16 Nov 2014

Massachusetts Institute of Technology: OCW is accessed by a broadly international population of educators and learners., http://ocw.mit.edu/about/site-statistics/. Accessed 16 Nov 2014

Miniwatts Marketing Group: Internet Usage Statistics, http://www.internetworldstats.com/stats.htm. Accessed 16 Nov 2014

Morrison, D.: How NOT to Design a MOOC: The Disaster at Coursera and How to Fix it, http://onlinelearninginsights.wordpress.com/2013/02/01/how-not-to-design-a-mooc-the-disaster-at-coursera-and-how-to-fix-it/ (2013). Accessed 16 Nov 2014

Ottmann, T.: MOOCs and/or eLectures; a means of virtualizing university education? Information Technology Based Higher Education and Training (ITHET), 2013. International Conference on. pp. 1–6 (2013)

P2PU, https://p2pu.org/en/. Accessed 16 Nov 2014

Siemens, G.: What are Learning Analytics?, http://www.elearnspace.org/blog/2010/08/25/what-are-learning-analytics/ (2010). Accessed 16 Nov 2014

Summary, E., Findings, I., Among, D., Statistics, D.: HarvardX and MITx : The First Year of Open Online Courses. (2013)

TIME Staff:Livemocha, http://content.time.com/time/specials/packages/article/0,28804,2012721_2012929_2012923,00.html (2010). Accessed 16 Nov 2014

The Economist explains: The backlash against big data, http://www.economist.com/blogs/economist-explains/2014/04/economist-explains-10 (2014). Accessed 16 Nov 2014

Udacity, http://www.udacity.com. Accessed 16 Nov 2014

Udemy, http://www.udemy.com. Accessed 16 Nov 2014

Virtonomics, http://virtonomics.com. Accessed 16 Nov 2014

Watters, A.: Top Ed-Tech Trends of 2013: MOOCs and Anti-MOOCs, http://hackeducation.com/2013/11/29/top-ed-tech-trends-2013-moocs/ (2013). Accessed 16 Nov 2014

Watters, A.: Venture Capital and the Future of Open Education: FWK and MOOCs, https://www.insidehighered.com/blogs/hack-higher-education/venture-capital-and-future-of-open-education-fwk-and-moocs#ixzz36n6Kaqch (2012). Accessed 16 Nov 2014

Wilby, P.: Moocs, and the man leading the UK's charge, http://www.theguardian.com/education/2014/aug/19/moocs-man-leading-uk-foray-simon-nelson-futurelearn (2014). Accessed 16 Nov 2014

Yeager, C., Hurley-Dasgupta, B., Bliss, C.: cMOOCs and global learning: An authentic alternative. J. Asynchronous. Learn. Netw. **17**(2), 133–147 (2013)

Yuan, B.L., Powell, S., Olivier, B.: Beyond MOOCs: Sustainable Online Learning in Institutions Beyond MOOCs : Sustainable Online Learning in Institutions. (2014). Accessed 16 Nov 2014

Yuan, L., Powell, S.: MOOCs and Open Education: Implications for Higher Education. JISC—Cetis (2013)

Big Data Driven Business Models

4

Abstract

This chapter outlines the concept of 'big data driven business model' and utilizes it to describe a set of businesses that rely on big data to achieve their key value proposition and to substantially augment their value proposition to differentiate themselves in order to gain competitive advantage. It describes the impact of big data on each of the elements as identified in the Business model canvas. Also the chapter discusses the potential of big data for mass customization and personalization of product and services, as a value proposition in its own right, on B2B and B2C logistics as well as for customer relationship management and customer service. It also touches upon how big data has facilitated a shift in our conceptions of utility as opposed to resources as the basis for socio-economic value creation. Also, the chapter explores this issue a bit further by understanding the implications of big data on partnerships, monetization, and the opportunities and challenges it raises for accounting, budgeting and performance metrics. In conclusion, the chapter acknowledges the synergistic potential with other emerging technologies such as 3D printing, Robots, Drones, self-driving cars, and the like.

4.1 Introduction

The focus of this chapter merits a more specific definition of the term Business Model. Business models are a natural fit with IT-related business innovations. Although rooted in transaction cost economics, it was really an Information Communication Technology (ICT) related phenomenon. ICT made it feasible and cost effective for businesses to collaborate with value networks in order to compete (Don et al. 2000; Amit and Zott 2001). Bundling of product and services became very popular during the 90s blurring the boundaries between industries.

So, what is a business model? Among the diverse available definitions (Amit and Zott 2001), a business model can be seen as outlining the architectural logic of business elements, such as a business structure, business processes, infrastructure, and systems as well as finance options, i.e. how they all fit together to coordinate value creation. It describes who buys the company's products and services and why, how a company organizes and which resources they utilize in order to finance, produce and deliver their offerings, what they pay for doing so and how they get their money in.

Much like any model (Baden-Fuller and Morgan 2010), business models are abstractions of real life and in this particular case, business models have been used to describe various business phenomena. According to (Osterwalder et al. 2005) people have used the term loosely to describe all real world businesses (e.g. the capitalist model), or particular types of business with common characteristics (e.g. the auction model), or a very particular real world business model (e.g. the Apple model). Furthermore, according to (Osterwalder and Pigneur 2010), business models comprise nine fundamental elements illustrated in Table 4.1.

While in the past, organizations relied on managers intuition to fill in the gaps of scarce incomplete, poor information to make business decisions, the proliferation of data generated every day through social media, cloud computing, and mobile phones and soon the Internet of Things (IoTs) give managers a new headache, more information that what they know what to do about. This combination of digital intensity, connectivity, and big data provides a context of networked abundance (Bharadwaj et al. 2013).

The purpose of this brief introduction of the concept was twofold. First it was necessary in order to clarify how we are going to use the term in this chapter. We are going to use the term 'big data driven business models', describing a set of businesses which rely on big data to achieve their key value proposition and to substantially augment their value proposition to differentiate themselves in order to gain competitive advantage. Second, it would be useful to establish on the outset the scope of this chapter. Most big data driven business models are currently augmentations of existing value propositions (Hagen et al. 2013). Big data driven business models are currently in development. Most businesses have introduced big data in their projects portfolio on the basis of efficiency, which by default means doing the same thing, with less money, and even fewer on effectiveness, i.e. doing things better (Hagen et al. 2013). It will be some time before true visionaries introduce business models whose unique selling point will rely on big data, and

Table 4.1 Nine fundamental elements of business models (Osterwalder and Pigneur 2010)

1	The **customer segments** the company serves
2	The **value propositions** that offer a solution to its customers
3	The **channels** through which the company communicates, distributes, and fulfils its sales
4	The **customer relationships** the company established and maintained with customers
5	The **revenue streams** accruing to the company from its customers
6	**Key resources** or assets required
7	**Key activities**, i.e. the tasks, processes and behaviors required
8	**Key partnerships**, which undertake responsibility for some of the above
9	**Cost structure**, i.e. the cost of maintaining and developing all of the above

4.1 Introduction

very likely such value propositions to be augmented by other innovations also in development in the social, business and technology spheres. So, within this chapter we offer some projections along with descriptions of such scenarios.

Big data will have big implications for various fields (Hagen et al. 2013). Yet, such changes seek to complement today's sectors and business models. It is worth noting that a business sector consists of a number of companies or business units operating effectively under the same or similar business models. Table 4.2 shows some of the indicated changes.

So far, there is a limited impetus for fundamental structural changes that place big data to the core of company value creation as opposed to 'nice-to-have' capabilities. In that sense, the suggested changes seek to enhance existing business models rather than disrupt them. For example, big data has been utilized to improve existing business models as shown in Table 4.3.

Table 4.2 Existing business models currently enhanced by big data

1	Improving customer intimacy through customer profiling and personalized customer service
2	Opening up product/service innovation by explicitly crowdsourcing ideas or analyze social media generated opinions and feedback
3	Improving decision-making by generating business options based on larger amounts of data, triangulated through various sources, filtered down to workable solutions in real time
4	Enabling real-time operations, utilizing smart assets, which can coordinate to carry out a process or shift business processes instantly, while providing real-time tracking feedback

Table 4.3 Industries using big data to transform business models and improve performance in many areas

Retail		Manufacturing	
Customer relationship management	Fraud detection and prevention	Product research	Process and quality analysis
Store location and layout	Supply chain optimization	Engineering analytics	Distribution optimization
	Dynamic pricing	Predictive maintenance	
Financial services		Media and telecommunication	
Algorithmic trading	Fraud detection	Network optimization	Churn prevention
Risk analysis	Portfolio analysis	Customer scoring	Fraud prevention
Advertising and public relations		Energy	
Demand signaling	Sentiment analysis	Smart grid	Operational modeling
Targeted advertising	Customer acquisition	Exploration	Power-line sensors
Government		Healthcare and life sciences	
Market governance	Econometrics	Pharmacogenomic	Pharmaceutical research
Weapon systems and counterterrorism	Health informatics	Bioinformatics	Clinical outcomes research

Adapted from Hagen et al. (2013)

These incremental changes will bring significant value to existing organizations and change our customer expectations, which leave analytics lagging companies behind in the competition game. Then again such models are not fundamentally big-data driven, but big data enabled.

Fundamental changes can be envisioned by combining the analytical power of big data analytics with new production technologies and new concepts about production business value. For example, what business models can evolve by combining the power of big data analytics, with other emerging technologies, such as the ones shown in Table 4.4.

Will social services and primary care become obsolete by smart homes and health tracking devices providing real-time information about the health status of an individual, while artificially intelligent social robotics decide and administer appropriate regular care to the elderly? Will bitcoin become part of the mix of or a substitute for existing finance options? Can we organize centralized farming by utilizing smart assets, drones and swarm robotics to tend to agricultural production. Will the distinction between public and private transport systems disappear by merging to create a new, on demand, door-to-door self-driven transport system? To some of these ideas may seem far fetch, but for others some of these are expected to become mainstream in the next 15–20 years. For example, pod based inner city transport is already a reality in Masdar, Abu Dhabi (Feuilherade et al. 2014).

Real-time, big data analytics can transform production processes. For example, big data analytics is utilized by General Electric as an 'in process' monitoring mechanism to quality control highly sensitive and very expensive industrial 3D printing processes of aerospace components where structural integrity is critical to safety (Gereports 2013). For example, IBM's Deep Thunder program is oriented towards precision agriculture that combines microclimate predictive models with remote drone monitoring to optimize agricultural processes, such as weeding, spraying, watering and harvesting crops.

We continue this chapter by understanding the fundamental implications of big data on each of the nine identified elements comprising a business model.

Table 4.4 Emerging technologies suitable to be combined with big data analytics

1	Home 3D printing
2	Health and fitness monitors
3	Eye and hand tracking device
4	Drones
5	Self-driving cars
6	Bitcoin
7	(Ro)bots
8	Smart homes

4.2 Implications of Big Data for Customer Segmentation

Big data has given the notion of 'mass customization' a new lease of life. Big data can give companies the ability to target each customer individually based on their preferences and purchasing habits, by integrating personal information about website browsing, purchase histories, physical position, response to incentives, as well as demographic information such as work history, group membership and people's views and opinions based on social influence and sentiment data. This data enable ever finer targeting of content, offers, products and services, which can deliver real and substantial returns, by increasing the probability of a final purchase (Offsey 2014).

While mass customization is now enabled by big data, two even more disruptive advancements can be facilities by new technologies. Making customizable products, which can self-customize to suit the preference of their users. As products come with embedded intelligence and machine-to-machine collaboration capabilities, they will be able to undertake responsibility for serving their users. For example, a self-driving car could double up as personal assistant modifying appointment schedules.

While big data is discussed primarily as a business tool, there is no reason why big data cannot be utilized by consumers themselves to search and procure products and services. Cognitive Code for example has invented advanced conversational artificial intelligence that can interact in natural language with human beings while interact in code with machines providing outputs and feedback in natural language (Introducing SILVIA 2014). The perfect personal assistant for the electronic age! It is a pity that companies such as Cognitive Code still orient their business model to companies, such as call centers, as opposed to the public. Yet, I doubt it will take long for consumer electronics giants, such as iPhone to build in such a capability.

4.3 Implications of Big Data as a Value Proposition

There are four big data 'things' that companies can sell for profit: raw big databases, big data analytics services, big data experts, and big data technologies.

According to Forbes et al. (2014), many companies are geared towards selling their customer data as a means to complement company revenues. While this may bare a reputational risk for small companies, large organizations such as mobile companies, banks, and airlines that collect huge amounts of information about our whereabouts and shopping patterns are unfazed by such risks. However, raw data is not of much use unless you analyze for a purpose. Banks are moving away from selling raw data to developing higher value big data analytics services by recruiting big data analytics experts to mine, analyze and synthesize data into consultancy services.

Big data consultancy has become the must have service for Business Intelligence consultancy providers. With big data analytics being harnessed in every aspect of business activity, from strategy development to Human Resources (HR), and with big data analysts being a scarce resource, the opportunity for consultancy work is high. In fact, it would be impossible for a consultancy company to survive, without offering big data consultancy services. Hence, all prestigious consultancy companies as well as smaller boutique ones, offer clients big data analytics services.

Another big data business is related to data scientist recruitment services. Recruiting businesses cannot shy away from the need to recruit and deploy data scientist talent. Yet, big data analysts are currently a scarce resource. So new business models are developing to serve the needs of companies. Kaggle (2014) for example, uses a hackathon type competition model for undertaking predictive modeling to data science projects but also doubles as a learning community for those who want to attain data science expertise.

4.4 Implications of Big Data for Channels

With online shopping taken to new heights, business-to-consumer (B2C) delivery options are open for discussion. A constraint in achieving high operational efficiency in a distribution network occurs at the "last mile", i.e. delivery at a specific destination. Click and collect delivery systems seems to be the hottest trend in B2C logistics, for example, in a town as London in the United Kingdom (Butler 2014). Click and collect seems to work at many levels, people do not need to be somewhere waiting for their parcel, their parcel waits for them at a safe pick-up point, companies don't burden themselves with the cost of unsuccessful deliveries, and citizens do not have to put up with the CO_2 emissions of a fleet making rounds delivering parcels.

Yet, there is scope for applying big data techniques to drive costs down even further, while increase flexibility for customers. One way is to utilize real-time optimization on delivery routing to maximizing the routing schedules of conventional delivery fleet. Another approach would be to utilize combinatorial optimization to deliver product to people on the go. Combinatorial optimization can process, for example, real-time information about recipient's position and direction, thus, deliveries can be schedules dynamically. This involves locating the paths of both recipients and delivery vehicles in order to re-route vehicles on the go to the next best point to meet recipients. Currently, the sequencing of deliveries is carried out manually by drivers following each delivery. A big data driven sequencing software can rapidly process information about deliveries, current traffic conditions, loading bay availability, recipient availability to avoid unsuccessful deliveries, thereby minimizing costs. As, big data have also facilitated a trend towards "crowdsourcing" everything, why not utilize the crowd to deliver packages too?

Even in business-to-business (B2B) logistics, big data predictive modeling can also take just-in-time operational efficiencies to a new level, reducing the space required to store goods while ensuring business continuity. Predictive modeling can now take into account not only customer purchasing patterns and feedback, but also an increasing number of disruptions due to civil unrest, natural disasters, or even sudden economic developments. Big data technology and analytics can keep an eye and keep track of developments in any of the critical risk factors that can compromise the going concern of the organization from a variety of sources (e.g., social media, blogs, weather forecasts, news sites, stock trackers, and the like). It can then alert and instigate risk management scenarios, such are fulfilling an order via another country or route adding to the company's resilience and flexibility.

4.5 The Impact of Big Data on Customer Relationships

Profiling customers utilizing big data capabilities to increase sales have been at the forefront of adopting the new technologies. But how about customer service? With so much information about customers, surely companies can improve customer service to increase customer intimacy and loyalty. One of the key challenges for customer service operators has been the lack of comprehensive customer information at their fingertips. Unavailable data on the front line make customer service representatives unable or slow to respond to customer issues and requests and offer alternative options. Customer Relationship Management (CRM) projects have made big investments towards addressing the matter, yet they have been costly, high maintenance projects. Moreover, standardized siloed supply chain operations made dealing with exception cases an operational nightmare, with such cases falling usually between two stools or requiring expensive dedicated teams to handle them appropriately.

Big data technologies, such as Hadoop, can relate isolated data silos via hyper-fast in-memory analytics platforms, providing representatives with real-time information to assist customers. However, how companies relate this to improve customer service as opposed to sales is not yet clear. Big data customer relationship projects are lagging behind, but this is expected. Customer relationship projects are considered costly compared to their revenue generating potentials and tend to be instigated later in the maturity lifecycle when the market begins to plateau and companies seek to maximize value elicited from business assets.

Banks are likely to be the first to jump into this bandwagon, not only because they have budget to do so, but also because they need to rebuild the trust of the disenchanted public following the global financial crisis. Trends towards rebuilding strong personal relationship can be seen in retail banks' advertising themes. Banorte, a Mexican bank, focuses strongly on its 13 million customer base and capitalizes on new big data technologies to design banking services. Big data enabled marketing automation can help the bank service individual customer needs while keep the costs of marketing, creating a personalized experience at a return on investment. Also, harnessing the power of automated personalized customer service, requires business process reengineering throughout the entire organization and rethinking of the customer journey (Wagle 2014).

Big data will also expand the use of automated call centers using natural language recognition patterns and response, thus, making Artificial Intelligence (AI) becoming increasingly more sociable in terms of responding to customer queries using voice. Hence, companies with large call centers are likely to adopt this next-generation AI enabled and big data informed speech solutions to drive costs down as part of big data oriented business models.

4.6 The Impact of Big Data on Revenue Stream

Social media has enabled peer-to-peer transactions and, in effect, collaborative consumption. Now hotels compete with Airbnb, a peer to peer platform, for holiday makers' cash (Riedy 2014). Airbnb supports the rental of spare bedroom space to private travelers. Established in 2008, Airbnb lists more than 500,000 properties worldwide and has hosted more than 8.5 million people increasing the value of the company at US$2.5 billion (Riedy 2014). The financial crisis has changed social values about re-use, providing impetus for the rise of a sharing economy emerges as a potential threat to established businesses, as consumers are sharing things they already have, then they don't need to buy something new or so often. Blah blah cars (2014), enables car sharing with someone who goes to their point of destination, by match making people with cars with people in need for a ride. big data can make these transactions safer, real-time and efficient. For example, car sharing does not mean you hitching a ride with a complete stranger. Big data technology can advance the safety of car sharing, via car monitoring, passenger and driver health monitoring, and the like, offering precautionary measures and deterrents of common social risks. In transaction cost economics terms, the 'big brother' capability of big data can substitute institutions roles to monitor and 'police' adherence to rules and regulations.

Another disruptive change in the revenue stream is electronic currencies. What will the company of the future be paid with? LeHong, research vice president and Gartner Fellow, also pointed to the cryptocurrency Bitcoin (Nakamoto 2008), as a major disruptive force:

> Typically only national governments could issue currency, but we're seeing people put more trust in a privately funded startup than in most Western governments (Turner 2013).

Of course, the regulatory environment for such currencies is still uncertain and the risks currently not assessed in a systematic way. According to White & Case (Duplat and Vercauteren 2014), the internet environment where virtual money is held and traded is still risky, when trading platform or digital wallet could be hacked, making owners lose their virtual money and systems reliability, particularly with regard to the risk of fraud, actually not properly assessed. In addition, fluctuations in the virtual currency exchange rate can result in substantial financial losses, and there is no legal guarantee that virtual currency can be exchanged at any time for its original value. Finally, virtual currency is not legal tender: no-one is obliged to accept payment with virtual currency. While such fears are currently justified, the future of Bitcoin payments depends on people's acceptance and there are strong proponents for its future.

According to professor Campell Harvey of Duke University (Card 2014), Bitcoin, like all cryptocurrency, bears fewer risks than debit or credit card fraud and hacking, and minimal cost of transacting compared to traditional methods adopted by traditional institutions. Cryptocurrency relies on the power of computers to enable real time exchange of ownership, verification of ownership, as well as the ability to algorithmically design conditional contracts (Card 2014). In addition, cryptocurrency-based transactions require triangulation of data to ensure security, privacy, and trust without using centralized institutions. All of the above issues will require the number crunching and user profiling power of big data analytics, which will have a big role to play in analyzing the huge amounts of data that Bitcoin and cryptocurrency systems will be generating. Companies will be able to issue and guarantee their own currencies, which can then be spent in associated providers. Accordingly, one can only imagine the power of retail suppliers such as Amazon and Google. For example, Google Ventures has put money into Ripple, the open currency exchange called Ripple, which allows users can trade any currency without requiring any broker or third-party to facilitate the trades.

4.7 The Impact of Big Data on Key Resources and Key Activities

Traditionally capital resources are manmade assets organized to generate income. There are certain underlying assumptions in this definition that are likely to be challenged in the future. First, resources presume ownership by the company, and therefore their use and disposal at company will. Second, resources do not give value unless they are used; hence it is utility that provides value, thus, neither resource nor ownership per se. Third, to generate value, the utilization of resources need to be organized into perform key business processes that deliver value, in the form of a product or service desirable to a market. Big data can revolutionize all of the above for business model innovation.

To start with, big data can revolutionize employment relationships, as more and more companies can rely on crowdsourcing, thus, outsourcing a function once performed by employees to an undefined (and generally large) network of people in the form of an open call. This can take the form of peer-production when the job is performed collaboratively. Crowdsourcing growing popularity is due to its cost efficiencies and its global reach potential (Fretty 2014). As organizations rely more and more on crowdsourcing, they will require a strong coordination mechanism, capable to gather and reconcile often diverse information and views. After all, businesses need to be able to judge data quality, find ways to overcome geographical differences and apply to organizational goals (Fretty 2014). Actually, crowdsourcing and big data can revolutionize public service. The United Nations (UN), for example, has started utilizing Mindjet's SpigitEngage, a big data and

Crowdsourcing platform to devise best practice in tackling refugee issues, such as, e.g., learning a new language in order to absorb new culture, finding jobs, and gaining access to information and vital social services. Also, using gamification, SpigitEngage platform allows the grassroots ideas to rise to the top avoiding status quo bureaucratic barriers and gate keeping (Spigitengage 2014).

The above issues have also big implications about management structures and managers. If the end to end decision making process can be coordinated by big data algorithms, and so is the monitoring the implementation processes as well as the dynamic allocation of people and resources, what is the purpose of expensive organizational structures? This may seem farfetched from today's reality where formal organizations are still the dominant work organization structure, but flexing the boundaries has already started and the trend seem irreversible.

Another resource impacted by big data is the capital itself, i.e. the financing of business ventures. Social media and big data have enabled the merging of sales and financing through crowdfunding. A quick study of Kickstarter projects and associated pledges will demonstrate that most people effectively pre-buy the product or service (Jeffries 2013). In that sense, consumers act as financiers of their wanted products, and at the same time as early adopters of it. Take for example, Coolest Cooler (a portable cooler, integrating a cooler, a blender for outdoor party occasion), the most funded Kickstarter project who reached financing heights of more than $13 million. More than 57,000 out of its 62,642 backers were people who wished to pre-purchase the product, creating the market and the revenue for the company way ahead of its production (Grepper 2014).

Finally, big data not only pose enormous challenges and technology investments to access, process, and analyze the massive amounts of data, but requires companies to also make corresponding changes on business processes to capitalise on it. For example, Apple capitalised on market and supply chain data when they improved supply chain management practices to become twice as fast as the average company in the electronics market (Bharadwaj 2013).

4.8 The Impact of Big Data on Key Partnerships

While we already see partnerships in travel and hospitality to scale operation by sharing reservation systems, loyalty programs, and cross-selling opportunities, we will increasingly see the formation of different firms to pull together their strengths, organized through plug-and-play architectures to create competitive advantage (Bharadwaj et al. 2013).

By enabling real-time coordination monitoring and feedback, big data can provide a sense of security to those involved in supply chain collaborations. Previously, supply chain risks were moderated by policies/procedures and contractual agreements that acted as deterrent and provided some security assurances against negligence, deception and deceptive practices. Real-time information analysis of supply chain coordination data could flag issues ahead of time, highlight underlying reasons for delays and offer contingency planning alternatives (Zage and Glass 2013).

Further developments in advanced predictive big data analytics are likely to lead to the development of complex decision making scenarios based on a variety of stress tests, in multiple market conditions, against, numerous key performance indicators (KPIs). Such business simulations, can be used to design and redesign supply chain operations (Groves et al. 2014). For example, by simulating different market and competitor scenarios, big data can assess business agility and resilience of a given supply chain. Price volatility in the commodities and currency fluctuations has made long-term procurement a risky business. For example, organizations buffer themselves from the risks of late delivery and inability to fulfill orders by planning for a minimum safety stock, while price competition on scarce resources and raw material often leads to bidding for more quantities to ensure sufficient orders. Allegedly such risks can be reduced by big data analytics by improving price predictions or bid efficiency. The Internet of Things (IoTs) will also improve the quality of information about the location of physical things in the supply chain. Yan et al. (2014) envision a Cloud of things supply chain solution to facilitate resource sharing and participant collaboration in the whole supply chain life cycle, where supply chain condition perception, heterogeneous network access convergence, and resource "servitization" co-exist.

4.9 The Impact of Big Data on Cost Structures

With crowdfunding, crowdsourcing, and big data-driven supply chain join ventures dismantling the traditional boundaries of organizations, the definition and boundaries of cost economies change dramatically. On the other hand, as data, information and knowledge become the focal point for collaboration at all levels, accounting for intellectual property rights, data, and intangible assets will likely to become a focal point (Viscusi and Batini 2014).

More than 20 % of large companies already class data as an asset on their balance sheets. Data valuation is likely to become a key accounting skill in the future. Valuing data to date have been impossible as intangible assets tend to get hidden in existing reporting and governance systems once developed for the industrial age. Even when visible, data usually gets an arbitrary valuation. Calculating depreciation is difficult, and information velocity makes such calculations even more difficult and unreliable. In addition, like in most assets, the value of data depends on its utilization. To move towards a costing model of data resources, new methodologies need to be developed and agreed amongst accounting and finance professionals that determine key assumptions about what data is of value (Chua 2013).

What matters from an accounting point of view is to assess the monetary value or profit an organization creates out of the internet of everything and big data. To do so, management accountants should combine internal financial data and performance analysis with overall economic performance metrics. They should also be able to compare these to some referent organizational groups within the sector. In addition, these will be affect by political, economic social and technological influences on their industry and on the business. Yet, nowadays all these assumptions are open to negotiation and redefinition. Technology trends redefine industry boundaries, companies' strategic trajectory and capabilities against other organizations. For example, Facebook compete with Google for advertising revenues, even though what they offer to users are completely different value propositions (Dias 2013).

In summary, in the same way defining new markets has been the key driver for tech-driven business models; developments in the area of cost and management accounting will likely follow. Big data driven business models are still in their infancy, hence cost economics are still in embryonic stages.

4.10 Organizational Advantages and Opportunities

The big data era is an open minefield for all who are willing to unlearn their old ways and experiment with new ones. According to McKinsey, some sectors or indeed some players maybe more advantaged over others to making such moves (Gobble 2013). For example, companies those have invested deeply in IT and have large data pools to exploit as well as those in information industries, who have the expertise to perform sophisticated analytic techniques, are likely to be the first to create business value. On the other side of the spectrum, public sector organizations are in need for radical change and can more readily open up their information resources to leverage the value of public services to citizens. They are more likely as well to find large pools of volunteers willing to help with crowdsourcing projects.

Mature sectors characterized by a large number of competing organizations are likely to stay behind, due to ego-driven leadership, strategic myopia, technophobia, and conflicting views about the future of the industry and sector infighting (EY 2014). Are however such sectors that could most benefit from sharing company information, identifying new market opportunities and adopting 'collaborate-to-compete' networking partnerships. The extent to which sector leaders and associations are ready to invest in these opportunities will define the future of their industry.

Companies should be able to reflect on whether and how they can create new business models based on big data. The Internet of Things (IoTs) will intensify information abundance and raise more points for reflection, such as, e.g., how do we convert the data generated or captured by IoTs into knowledge to provide a more convenient environment to people. To be able to devise new business models, companies should open up to new ideas and make sure they can quickly assimilate them wherever these come from, (grassroots initiatives, open innovation competitions). They should also be prepared to modify or fundamentally change their internal structures to deploy new products and services. This requires a 'u-turn' in mentality and culture for most organizations (Tsai et al. 2014). Tsai et al. (2014) identify a number of IoTs applications that will change existing sectors and services. These have been loosely categorized into: (1) smart cities, (2) smart environment, (3) smart water, (4) smart metering, (5) security and emergencies, (6) retail, (7) logistics, (8) industrial control, (10) smart agriculture, (11) smart animal farming, (12) domotic and home automation, and (13) eHealth. IoTs also opens up the possibilities for businesses to think of services that utilize big data analytics to (a) better inform 'human' processes, (b) automate 'human' processes, and to (c) coordinate with other 'things', thus, creating end-to-end automated services.

4.11 Organizational Challenges and Threats

There are a number of challenges with respect to redesigning a big data driven business model. Technology assessment capability, technology maturity levels, evolving legal frameworks around privacy and intellectual property, data analyst talent scarcity, technology investment capability, internal data availability and quality, interoperability, security issues, limited business process understanding and associated metrics, data hoarding and old fashioned hierarchical leadership: these are just few of the barriers to big data driven approaches to business model redesign. These barriers have been referred to also in previous sections and chapters. In this section, it would be appropriate to refer to challenges with respect to adopting a big data driven business model innovation (Osterwalder et al. 2005).

4.11.1 Creativity and Innovation Capability Deficit

The big data innovation era suggest that managers need to think "laterally" outside the box. Many established organizations have promoted to director positions good administrators who can maintain order and efficiency. For many small and medium organizations the top management team is burdened with the day-to-day operation of the business, leaving little time, "headspace" and energy to renew their skills, network and keep up with developments outside their immediate field. Management structures often lack both the personal creativity and innovation skills and the right attitude to foster creativity and innovation required to envision new big-data based business models.

4.11.2 Interrogating Big Data

Big data demands inductive reasoning, a skill much underused in modern society and (Malle 2013) a fundamental element of the big data disruption. Knowledge from big data is produced by "agnostic" statistics, lacking a causal framework to explain it. Induction allows us to generalize a phenomenon, even if it is observed only once. For managers who are used to seek the certainty of reliability, repeatability, standardization, risk assessment, to base business decisions on non-repeatable, inductive observations will be a fundamental paradigmatic change. Inductive reasoning is developed through constant interaction with data examined through various lenses to develop into interpretation patterns (i.e. reasoning heuristics) (Malle 2013).

4.11.3 Plug and Play Architectures

Speed is a core factor for the creation of value through from big data. Big data is going to speed up decision making, requiring operations to leverage to match the rate of change. Can today's established organizations respond with operational agility to such fast-changing, data-driven decisions? Though modularizing the business architecture into Lego-like, component-based, architecture seems ideal, in reality one needs to ponder the feasibility. Consider, for example, human resources. Does the new configuration require staff upskilling? Does it require putting new processes or policies in place? Will people require training? What about the contractual agreements or job descriptions? If a business is using contracting staff or temporary staff, can it source the right people timely? Can the business maintains commitment of getting the job done? In addition, contractual agreements and relationships with suppliers and channels can complicate making changes to operating models (Bürgi et al. 2004).

According to Bürgi et al. (2004) one mitigating strategy is to create a business model portfolio based on market scenarios which organizations can switch as conditions change. While this could be a solution, it does not take into consideration the reality of a turbulent environment, characterised by ambiguity about the factors that will affect the business model. Hence, it is impossible to *foresee them and factor them in* drafting job descriptions or contractual agreements. Perhaps big data will not only change how we develop business models but also our definition of what business models are, what are the elements of their architecture and what is necessary for strategy.

4.12 Summary

This chapter has discussed business models as the architectural logic that identify how business elements (such as a business structure, business processes, infrastructure, and systems) fit together to coordinate value creation (Osterwalder et al. 2005). It then went on to describe the impact of big data on each of the elements as identified in the Business model canvas proposed by Osterwalder and Pigneur (2010). In particular, it has discussed the new impetus that big data and IoTs technologies give to mass customization and personalization of product and services. Furthermore, the chapter has investigated big data as a value proposition in its own right and how an industry may be created around the sales of big data and big data analytics technology, analytics consultancy and data scientist recruitment. The chapter has also touched upon big data solutions for B2B and B2C logistics as well as for customer relationship management and customer service.

Furthermore, the chapter has analyzed the impact of big data on revenues, as it has facilitated new forms of value creation from the emergence of new currencies, in combination with social media and cryptocurrencies. Then, it has been also described how big data has emphasized the value of 'utility from' (as opposed to

4.12 Summary

'ownership of') capital resources. It has also been explained how this shifts the emphasis away from the organization as an entity towards an understanding of the organization as an a dynamic process of value creation. Also, the chapter has explored this a bit further by understanding the implications of key partnerships in the big data era and the spanning of organizational boundaries. It has also discussed the monetization implications; the opportunities and challenges it raises for accounting, budgeting and performance metrics. With these in mind, the chapter has highlighted some of the advantages, opportunities challenges and threats around business model innovation, relating them more to the readiness of organizations to assume such an undertaking, rather than describing the many possible big data driven business models to evolve in the future.

Finally, the chapter concludes acknowledging that while so far big data has been used to improve existing business models, far more futuristic scenarios will emerge in combination with other emerging technologies.

References

Amit, R., Zott, C.: Value creation in E-business. Strateg. Manage. J. **22**, 493–520 (2001)
Baden-Fuller, C., Morgan, M.S.: Business models as models. Long Range Plann. **43**, 156–171 (2010)
Bharadwaj, A., Sawy, OA.El., Pavlou, PA., Venkatraman, N: Digital business strategy: toward a next generation of insights. MIS Q., **37**, 471–482 (2013)
BlaBlaCar: http://www.blablacar.com/ (2014). Accessed 16 Nov 2014
Bürgi, P., Victor, B., Lentz, J.: Modeling how their business really works prepares managers for sudden change. Strateg. Leadersh. **32**, 28–35 (2004)
Butler, S.: Ten things Christmas taught us about the UK retail revolution. http://www.theguardian.com/business/2014/jan/12/10-things-christmas-taught-us-about-uk-retail-revolution (2014). Accessed 16 Nov 2014
Card, J.: Bitcoin: a beginner's guide for entrepreneurs. http://www.theguardian.com/small-business-network/2014/oct/17/-beginners-guide-for-entrepreneurs (2014). Accessed 16 Nov 2014
Chua, F.: Big data: its power and perils. IMA-ACCA. www.accaglobal.com/bigdata (2013). Accessed 16 Nov 2014
Dias, C.: Industry insights: management accountants' role with big data. http://www.cimaglobal.com/Thought-leadership/Newsletters/Regional/The-CIMA-Edge-South-Asia-and-Middle-East/2013/December-2013/Industry-insights-Management-Accountants-Role-in-Internet-of-Everything-and-Big-Data/ (2013). Accessed 16 Nov 2014
Don, T., David T., Alex L.: Digital capital: harnessing the power of business webs (2000)
Duplat, M., Vercauteren, L.: Ban on Distribution of Certain Financial Products in Belgium. White & Case LLP, Belgium (2014)
EY: Big data—changing the way businesses compete and operate. EYGM Limited, UK (2014)
Fakto, S.: Never sell data. http://www.forbes.com/sites/stevefaktor/2014/03/25/never-sell-data/ (2014). Accessed 16 Nov 2014
Feuilherade, P.: Personal systems herald "smart mobility". http://www.iec.ch/etech/2014/etech_0314/ind-1.htm, (2014). Accessed 16 Nov 2014
Fretty, P.: Merging crowdsourcing with big data analytics. http://www.big-dataforum.com/302/merging-crowdsourcing-big-data-analytics#sthash.cby7c3Bk.dpu (2014). Accessed 16 Nov 2014

Gereports: Big data meets 3-D printing: big data to monitor laser-printed jet engine parts. http://www.gereports.com/post/77209216443/big-data-meets-3-d-printing-big-data-to-monitor (2013). Accessed 16 Nov 2014

Gobble, M.M.: Resources: big data: the next big thing in innovation. Res. Manage. **56**, 64–67 (2013)

Grepper, R.: Coolest cooler: 21st century cooler that's actually cooler. https://www.kickstarter.com/projects/ryangrepper/coolest-cooler-21st-century-cooler-thats-actually (2014). Accessed 16 Nov 2014

Groves, W., Collins, J., Gini, M., Ketter, W.: Agent-assisted supply chain management: Analysis and lessons learned. Decis. Support Syst. **57**, 274–284 (2014)

Hagen, C., Ciobo, M., Wall, D., Yadav, A., Khan, K., Miller, J., Evans, H.: Big data and the Creative Destruction of Today's Business Models. AT Kearney Publishing, Chicago 1–18 (2013)

Introducing SILVIA. http://silvia4u.info/silvia/ (2014). Accessed 16 Nov 2014

Jeffries, A.: Kickstarter is not a store, except when it is. http://www.theverge.com/2013/4/17/4230440/kickstarter-is-not-a-store-except-when-it-is (2013). Accessed 16 Nov 2014

Kaggle Inc.: The home of data science. http://www.kaggle.com (2014). Accessed 16 Nov 2014

Malle, J.-P.: Big data: farewell to cartesian thinking? http://www.paristechreview.com/2013/03/15/big-data-cartesian-thinking/ (2013). Accessed 16 Nov 2014

Nakamoto, S.: Bitcoin: a peer-to-peer electronic cash system. bitcoin.org. October 2008. https://bitcoin.org/bitcoin.pdf (2014). Accessed 16 Nov 2014

Offsey, S.: Micro-segmentation in the age of big data. http://marketbuildr.com/blog/segmentation-in-the-age-of-big-data/ (2014). Accessed 16 Nov 2014

Osterwalder, A., Pigneur, Y.: Business Model Generation: A Handbook for Visionaries, Game Changers, and Challengers. Wiley, New Jersey (2010)

Osterwalder, A., Pigneur, Y., Tucci, C.: Clarifying business models: origins, present, and future of the concept. Commun. Assoc. Inf. Syst. **16**, 1–25 (2005)

Riedy, C.: The sharing economy spooking big business. Conversat. Trust. http://theconversation.com/the-sharing-economy-spooking-big-business-19541 (2014). Accessed 16 Nov 2014

Spigitengage. http://www.mindjet.com/spigitengage/ (2014). Accessed 16 Nov 2014

Tsai, C.-W., Lai, C.-F., Chiang, M.-C., Yang, L.T.: Data mining for Internet of things: a survey. IEEE Commun. Surv. Tutor. **16**, 77–97 (2014)

Turner, D.: CIOs must reinvent their businesses on three levels: Hung LeHong. http://www.ibmbigdatahub.com/blog/cios-must-reinvent-their-businesses-three-levels-hung-lehong (2013). Accessed 16 Nov 2014

Viscusi, G., Batini, C.: Digital information asset evaluation: characteristics and dimensions. In: Caporarello, L., Di Martino, B., Martinez M. (eds.) Smart Organizations and Smart Artifacts SE—9, vol. 7, pp. 77–86. Springer International Publishing (2014). doi:10.1007/978-3-319-07040-7_9

Wagle, L.: How big data helps banks personalize customer service. http://www.forbes.com/sites/ibm/2014/06/16/how-big-data-helps-banks-personalize-customer-service/ (2014). Accessed 16 Nov 2014

Yan, J., Xin, S., Liu, Q., Xu, W., Yang, L.: Intelligent supply chain integration and management based on cloud of things. Int. J. Distrib. Sens. Netw. **624839**, 1–15 (2014) doi: http://dx.doi.org/10.1155/2014/624839

Zage, D., Glass, K., Colbaugh, R.: Improving supply chain security using Big data. In: 2013 IEEE International Conference on Intelligence and Security Informatics. IEEE, pp. 254–259 (2013)

Part II
Organization

Big Data Governance 5

Abstract

The aim of this chapter is to help readers gain an overview of the topic of 'Big Data Governance' to find easily the information it offers. Over the past few years, many organizations have begun their adventure with big data. While many are only experimenting with new technologies and innovations to improve their competitive advantage, few are truly thinking ahead for long-term success and even fewer will truly succeed in gaining such competitive advantage. The reason is simple: you cannot compete on analytics alone. After all, what do analytics analyze? Information needs to be trusted in order to be acted upon, but how that could be accomplished? That is the traditional role of data and information governance, which also the case of big data has to create trusted high quality information to make big data analytics more effective, which brings us to the subject of this chapter. Thus, this chapter reviews the common definitions of big data governance and its core components. Then the chapter focuses on common big data maturation models. The next section is the organizational benefits and challenges of governing big data, followed by three case studies to establishing a business case for big data governance.

5.1 Introduction to Big Data Governance

'Big Data' is less about size and more about quality. Indeed, data comes from a variety of sources such as RFID tags, social media, GPS signals, traffic flow sensors, satellite imagery, broadcast audio streams, banking transactions, digital pictures, the content of web pages, online videos, telemetry from automobiles, financial market data, the list goes on. From organizational perspectives, as organizations have grown, the data associated with them also grew exponentially and today there are many complexities related to their data resulting in a great challenge; to give them a single consistent view of their data.

Most of the big organizations have data in multiple applications and in different formats. The mobile revolution, which business firms are experimenting nowadays, has completely changed how they capture the data and build intelligent systems. Big data tends to be operational in nature and are characterized by '3 Vs'—large volumes, high velocity and a variety of formats such as structured, unstructured and semi-structured (Bertot and Choi 2013; Kruger and Foster 2013; Michael and Miller 2013; Sathi 2012; Steele and Nash 2012; Zicari 2012). Figure 5.1 shows big data's three dimensions. These three dimensions and related characteristics are a useful lens through which we can understand the nature of data and how it can be interpreted. Also, Table 5.1 illustrates the measures of scale of data.

Big data challenges are therefore multifaceted and characterized by a combination of the so-called '3 Vs' (shown in Fig. 5.1 and also mentioned in the Preface), that make it difficult to extract information and business insight. Furthermore and in addition to those three characteristics, when big data is processed and stored, other dimensions such as governance, ethics, security, and policies come into play (Cline 2014; Franks 2012; Hurwitz et al. 2013; Jee and Kim 2013; Michael and Miller 2013; Raghupathi and Raghupathi 2014; Russom 2008; Warden 2011; Webb 2006). Considering governance, there are currently various definitions available for data and information governance. For example, Data Governance Institute (DGI) (2014) defines *Data Governance* as

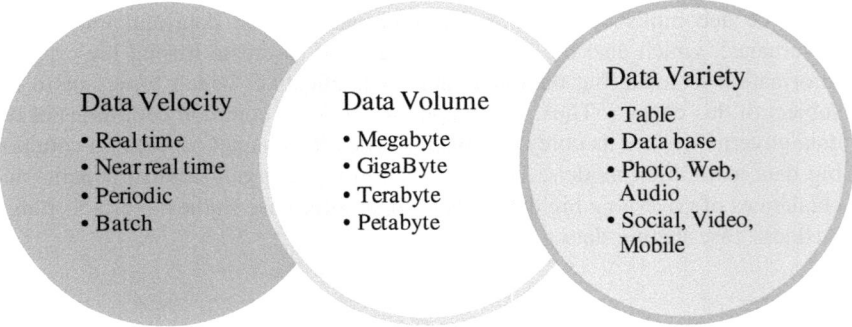

Fig. 5.1 Big data's growths dimensions and related characteristics

Table 5.1 Measuring big data

Measuring big data
1,000 Gigabytes = 1 Terabyte (TB)
1,000 Terabytes = 1 Petabyte (PB)
1,000 Petabytes = 1 Exabyte (EB)
1,000 Exabytes = 1 Zettabyte (ZB)
1,000 Zettabytes = 1 Yottabyte (YB)
Adapted from Mohanty et al. (2013)

5.1 Introduction to Big Data Governance

a system of decision rights and accountabilities for information-related processes, executed according to agreed-upon models which describe who can take what actions with what information, and when, under what circumstances, using what methods.

Furthermore, Debra Logan Vice President of Gartner defines *Information governance* as

the specification of decision rights and an accountability framework to encourage desirable behavior in the valuation, creation, storage, use, archival and deletion of information. It includes the processes, roles, standards and metrics that ensure the effective and efficient use of information in enabling an organization to achieve its goals (Debra Logan 2010).

As for big data governance, Soares (2013) defines it in a clear and comprehensive manner as follows (p. 4):

Big data governance is part of a broader information governance program that formulates policy relating to the optimization, privacy, and monetization of big data by aligning the objectives of multiple functions (Soares 2013)

He then explains the main parts of the definition in greater detail to illustrate different aspects of 'big data governance' as described in Table 5.2. Also, summary of the main parts of big data governance is shown in Fig. 5.2, where the role of information governance is highlighted, likewise.

After explaining the key aspects of big data governance, we are now moving to the big data framework. Effectively managing big data requires skill sets and technologies different from those used to manage "regular" data. It may also require a change in business processes.

Companies need to start with a big data governance program to ensure there is clarity on data access, integration, usage, management and ownership of big data. Therefore, it is important for organizations to expand the scope of their existing data governance program to include big data or, if one does not exist, to establish a data governance program to support your existing enterprise data and your big data. A high-level framework for big data governance adapted from Soares (2012, 2013) is shown in Fig. 5.3. This high-level framework includes three key dimensions: *big data types*, *information governance disciplines*, and *industries and functions*, which will be discussed in what follows.

5.1.1 Big Data Types

As data volumes and complexities continue to grow and as organizations continue to acquire big data, this massive amount of data will be overwhelming without strong data governance frameworks. Big data can be classified into five distinct types: web and social media, machine-to-machine, big transaction data, biometrics, and human generated (Soares 2012, 2013). In this classification, web and social media includes clickstream and social media data such as Facebook, Twitter, LinkedIn, and blogs. Machine-to-machine data (or M2M) refers to technologies that allow wireless, wired or hybrid systems to communicate with other devices such as

Table 5.2 Definition of the key components of big data governance

Components	Description
Big data is part of a broader domain of information governance	Organizations should extend the current scope of information governance to include big data, using power users of big data such as data scientists as well as supporting big data with other associated disciplines such as metadata, privacy and master data
Big data governance is about policymaking	A data governance policy should obey the organization's legal and regulatory requirements. A big data governance policy might state that an organization will not integrate a customer's online social account into his or her master data record without the customer's informed consent
Big data must be optimized	Organizations need to optimize and improve the quality of their big data in the following areas: • Metadata: to build information about inventories of big data • Data quality management: to cleanse big data just as companies conduct preventive maintenance on physical assets • Information lifecycle management: to archive and retire big data when it no longer makes sense to retain these massive volumes
Privacy and confidentiality of big data is essential	Organizations also need to create and follow appropriate policies and procedures to prevent the misuse of big data, considering regulatory, and legal risks when handling social media, geolocation, biometric, and other forms of personally identifiable information
Big data must be profitable and monetized	Monetization is the process of converting an asset such as data into money by selling it to third parties or by using it to develop new services
Big data represents natural tensions across multiple functions	Big data governance needs to make a balance between competing objectives across multiple functions, but how can it be achieved? In this situation, big data governance needs to bring all the parties together to determine whether the potential revenue from the new services outweighs the associated reputational and regulatory risks

Adapted from Soares (2012, 2013)

utility smart meter readings, RFID readings and GPS signals. Biometric data refers to the automatic identification of a person based on his or her anatomical or behavioral characteristics or traits such as fingerprint, a face, an outline of a hand, an ear shape, a voice pattern, DNA or even body odor. Big transaction data can be referred to as healthcare claims, telecommunications call detail records, and utility billing records. Finally, human generated data can be considered as call center agents' notes, voice recordings, email, paper documents, surveys, and electronic medical records.

5.1 Introduction to Big Data Governance

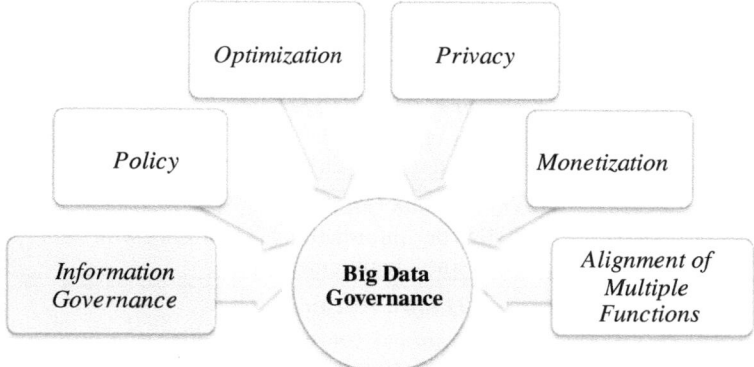

Fig. 5.2 Summary of the key components of big data governance. Adapted from Soares (2013)

Fig. 5.3 A high-level framework for big data governance. Adapted from Soares (2012, 2013)

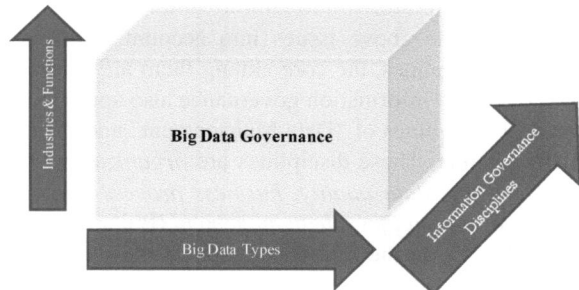

5.1.2 Information Governance Disciplines

It can be said that information governance is the glue that drives value and moderates risk for big data exploitation in organizations. It enables an organization to leverage information as a competitive asset.

Information governance, in essence, is the set of principles, policies and processes by which an organization ensures that information is protected and aligned with its needs and objectives (Bonenfant et al. 2012; Eisenhauer and Young 2012; Newman and Logan 2008; Santovena 2013; Steele and Nash 2012; Tsai et al. 2011; Big Data Now 2012; Oracle 2011). Information is an organizational asset that includes both data and the context by which that data has meaning (Soares 2013).

Eisenhauer, the chair of Data Governance Society (DGS) and Rick Young the managing director of 3Sage consulting company consider the information governance framework as a pyramid with corporate strategy at the top and IT infrastructure (i.e. data capture and storage) such as enterprise platforms (CRM, ERP, Portal), data base management and network systems at the bottom (Fig. 5.4).

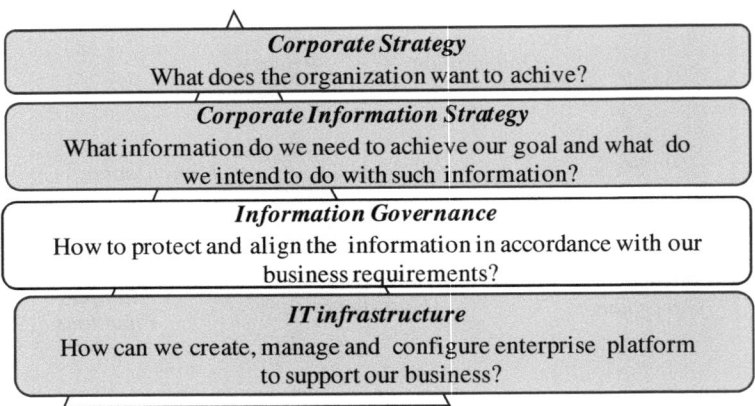

Fig. 5.4 Information governance. Adapted from Eisenhauer (2012)

Taking the above issues into account, information governance encompasses several disciplines, the core among them are illustrated in Fig. 5.5. The traditional disciplines of information governance also apply to big data governance and require several disciplines of "Data Management" and their respective solutions in order to deliver value. These disciplines are *organization, metadata management, security and privacy, data quality, business process integration, master data integration,* and *information lifecycle management* (Ballard et al. 2014; Santovena 2013; Soares 2012, 2013). In the following, each of these areas will be explained briefly.

Fig. 5.5 Core disciplines of information governance

Organization The information governance organization needs to consider adding big data to its overall framework such as organization structure, roles and responsibilities. In doing so, the information governance council might seek new members who can provide a unique viewpoint on big data such as data scientists. It might also decide to appoint stewards for social media or add additional responsibilities to the job description of existing stewards.

Metadata management The big data governance program needs to integrate big data with the enterprise metadata repository for example by adding big data terms within the business glossary. In this respect Ballard et al. (2014) explains: "providing context around content through tagging, using the wealth of available metadata, and implementing governance processes can rapidly accelerate progress in this area" (p. 17).

Security and privacy Enhancing security and maintaining privacy is an emerging concern for the majority of, if not all, big data projects. There are many discussions as to how big data affects security- and privacy-related matters such as legal, moral, safety, and political aspects in organizational settings. In many of these areas, the consequences are only beginning to emerge. Big data governance needs to identify sensitive data and establish policies about its acceptable use. Although organizations must comply with security and privacy regulations, nevertheless, there are few regulations governing the protection of new data categories, such as geolocation.

Data quality Data quality management is a discipline that includes the methods to measure, improve, and certify the quality and integrity of an organization's data (Batini and Scannapieco 2006; Huang et al. 1999). Indeed, quality is relative to the business requirement, which is drawing from governance principals to provide data that is fit to purpose of the organization.

Business process integration The program, initially, needs to identify key business processes that require big data and then needs to define key policies to support governance of big data (Soares 2012). For example, drilling and production are key business processes within the oil and gas industry. The governance program must establish policies around the retention period for sensor data such as temperature flow, pressure, and salinity on an oilrig.

Master data integration Master data is the high-value information that is used to support critical business processes across the enterprise such as information about products, materials, employees, partners, and accounts to name a few. Many organizations imagine that they want to analyze social media to find out customers' expectations, likes and dislikes, but do they know who their customers are? Do they know their best customers? (Ballard et al. 2014). Therefore, the big data governance program needs to identify and design policies with regard to the integration of big data into the master data management environment (Ballard et al. 2014; Bonenfant et al. 2012; Dyche 2012; Mohanty et al. 2013; Morabito 2014c; Sathi 2012; Soares 2012, 2013).

Information lifecycle management The increase in big data volumes make the situation challenging for organizations to understand the regulatory and business requirement that determine what data to retain in operational and analytical systems,

Table 5.3 The description of supporting disciplines in information governance

Supporting disciplines	Description
Classification and metadata	Since big data rely heavily upon large volumes of unstructured data, it is assumed that data classification takes on a lesser role. The reality however is quite different. The users of the information rely upon segmentation to create order out of chaos and to enhance the insight that the data provides. As a result, this situation requires improved capability to separate the unstructured content, then rearrange and compare them in a new and meaningful manner
Audit information logging and reporting	Sadly, most organizations consider the importance of this capability when the situation becomes problematic; when they realize they are unable to trace back to the root cause of the corrupted data. Often, there are issues with no audit information logging for the data, or the time stamps are not captured and retained at all. As a result, the slowly changing nature of data cannot be tracked and reviewed
Data architecture	Some of the factors that affect the design of your architecture include integration of big data sources, consideration of suitable data governing functions such as information security and privacy, information quality validations as well as storage and separation of big data to enhance its consequent use

Adapted from Ballard et al. (2014)

what data to archive and what data to delete. With IT budgets continuing to be under pressure, over managing information is a gross waste of capital resources. Consequently, the program needs to expand the retention schedule to include big data based on regulations and business requirements (Morabito 2014a). Therefore, the big data governance program needs to influence compression and archiving policies, tools and best practices to reduce storage costs and to improve performance.

However, while Soares (2012) considers all the above areas as core disciplines of information governance, Ballard et al. (2014) divides the key areas into two categories of '*Core Disciplines*' and '*Supporting Disciplines*'. In this classification, the core disciplines include areas such as: *information security and privacy*, *information lifecycle Management* and *data quality management*, which highly overlaps with Soares's definition of these key aspects. The supporting disciplines (shown in Table 5.3), however, include domains such as *classification and metadata*, *audit information logging and reporting*, and *data architecture*.

5.1.3 Industries and Functions

Considering now big data analytics, they are determined by use cases that are specific to a given industry or function. Such industries can be customer service, insurance, retail, healthcare, marketing, risk management, information security, information technology, and human resources.

Healthcare Industry

- *Solution*: Sentiment analysis
- *Big data type*: Web and social media
- *Related disciplines*: Privacy
- If someone posts a complaint on Twitter, the health plan might want to first post a limited response and then move the conversation offline.

Telecommunications Industry

- *Solution*: Location-based services
- *Big data type*: M2M data
- *Related disciplines*: Privacy
- The marketing team wants to sell geo-location data to third parties to offer coupons to subscribers. However, the privacy department is concerned about the regulatory risks associated with sharing such data.

Fig. 5.6 Different business use cases of big data analytics. Adapted from Soares (2012)

Figure 5.6 illustrates two different use cases in the areas of healthcare and telecommunication. The figure shows how big data analytics differ from one industry to another.

5.2 Big Data Maturity Models

Many data governance maturity models are in use, but they all share one key characteristic (Krishnan 2013; NASCIO 2009; Newman and Logan 2008; Sathi 2012; Oracle 2011): the organization's climb to the top level is challenging, and sustaining that level will be even more challenging in the case of big data. This section focuses on some of these models in order to introduce the reader with some of the key concepts underlying the big data evolution topic. Reviewing and evaluating maturity models should occur early in the process in order to form an understanding of the end state. Furthermore, it must be noted that the delivery process is an ongoing enterprise operating discipline, which fits under the greater umbrella of enterprise architecture (Hurwitz et al. 2013; Russom 2008, 2013).

5.2.1 TDWI Maturity Model

The first maturity model is The Data Warehousing Institute (TDWI) maturity model. TDWI explains that the many goals and tasks related to data governance can be refined down to four main imperatives or requirements, which in turn group into a pair of organizational imperatives and a pair of technical ones, namely (Mohanty et al. 2013; Russom 2008), as shown in Fig. 5.7.

Data governance imperatives in this classification have two key characteristics. First, each data governance imperative has lifecycle stages, which unfold over time, and progression through them means a form of development. Second, the imperatives as a group imply a time sequence. For instance, it is apparent that imperative 1 must create a cross-functional team before imperative 2 can actually harmonize team goals with business initiatives.

As to the imperatives 3 and 4 Russom (2013) explains: "less obvious, however, is that imperative 3 should be governing IT systems before imperative 4 starts using IT systems to automate governance processes. Although dependencies like these determine an order for commencing the imperatives, the imperatives must eventually coexist and interact" (p. 3). Taking these issues into account. The TDWI Maturity Model is illustrated in Fig. 5.8 and described in Table 5.4.

The idea behind the TDWI Maturity Model is to show a course of development/ evolution for organizations that need to know where to start and where to go with a particular type of initiative. The Gulf and Chasm stages represent the difficulties and challenges that early- and later-stage programs encounter during their BI journey, respectively. Organizations in the Gulf struggle with sponsorship, funding,

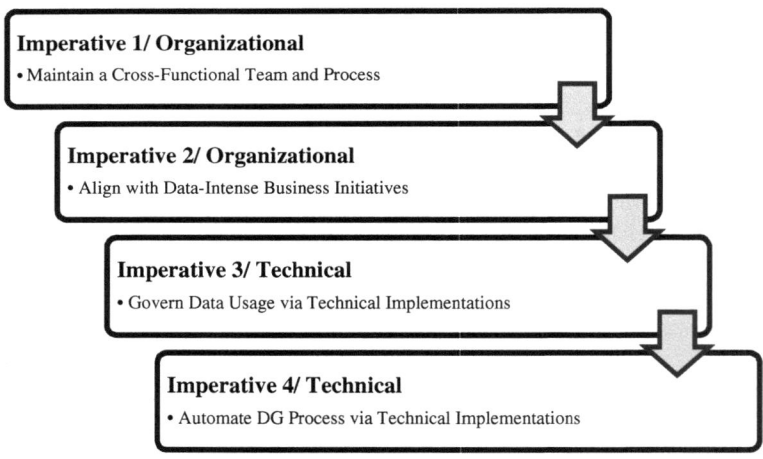

Fig. 5.7 Four imperatives of data governance. Adapted from Russom (2008, 2013)

Fig. 5.8 TDWI maturity model. Adapted from Russom (2013)

Table 5.4 Description of stages in TDWI maturity model

Stages of maturity	Description
Prenatal and infant stages	In this phase, organizations rely heavily on manual means applied in an ad hoc manner as a low-end solution to their business or technological concerns. By moving towards the infant stage and over time, a study of requirements has led the organization to a specific technology or practice
The Gulf	Jumping this obstacle depends on the organization institutionalizing the solution concepts it has already verified in the previous step
Child and teenager stages	At this stage, the organization expands its technological initiatives or practices it recently committed to. However, growth could emerge in a limited context, such as a handful of divisions. As a result, growth slows down in the teenager stage
The Chasm	Crossing the chasm successfully requires dramatic global changes, like enterprise adoption or solution re-architecture
Adult and sage stages	In the adult stage best practices and technology implementation details established and developed in the teenager stage continue to mature. The silo deployments of the child stage are gone, replaced in the sage stage by centralized organizational control and technology integration

Adapted from Russom (2013)

data quality and project scope (TDWI Blog Contributors 2014). Companies in the Chasm, on the other hand, struggle with the politics, logistics, and dynamics of delivering an enterprise BI environment (TDWI Blog Contributors 2014). Although each organization must customize it according to its own situation and needs, the maturity model can ultimately help with preparation and provides an objective yardstick for evaluating the current state of an initiative.

5.2.2 Analytics Business Maturity Model

Sathi (2012), by taking a different approach with regard to the TDWI one, introduces the analytics business maturity model (with five levels of maturity) and explains that this model allows organizations to specify current and target levels of maturity and what can be achieved in each phase. The stages are as follows: ad hoc, foundational, competitive, differentiating and breakaway (Fig. 5.9).

At the ad hoc *stage* the company is generally falling behind other companies in the corresponding sector information. This stage is an initial phase in which the company starts to develop the capability to gather consistent information from its key functional areas. Beyond basic reporting is not available or possible and time-consuming, manual efforts are generally required to gather the information needed for day-to-day business decisions.

Considering the *foundational stage*, the company is still unable to gather key information and falling behind the majority of its competitors. Indeed, information

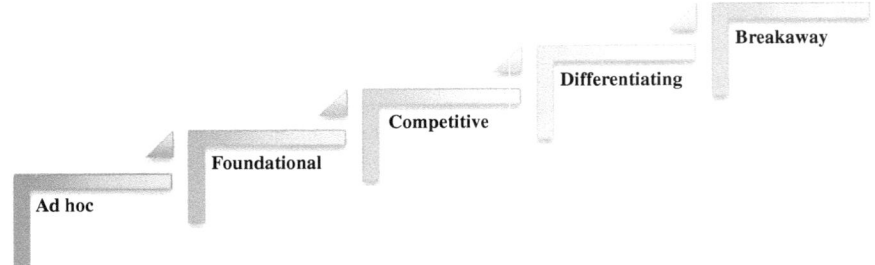

Fig. 5.9 Analytics business maturity model. Adapted from Sathi (2012)

is not consistently available or utilized to make enterprise-wide business decisions and a degree of manual efforts to gather information is still required. On the contrary, *competitive stage* represents companies whose capabilities in gathering key information generally are in line with the majority of similar companies. This maturity level is also the starting point to establish some consistency in key business metrics across the enterprise.

Once at a *differentiating stage*, a company whose execution of key business strategies through utilization of information is considered as better than most other companies in its sector. Management has the ability to adapt to business changes to a degree and business leaders as well as users have visibility to key information and metrics for effective decision-making.

Finally, when at the *breakaway stage*, a company is generally considered to be the best in the class in its execution of key business strategies, where information is utilized enterprise-wide for multidimensional decision making and key predictive performance indicators are used in modeling for outcomes.

5.2.3 DataFlux Data Governance Maturity Model

DataFlux is another comprehensive framework for data governance maturity models. According to this model, as the organization moves through the sequence from stage one to stage four, the value harvested increases and simultaneously the risk associated with "bad data" decreases (Table 5.5). Tony Fisher, President and General Manager of DataFlux explains that the term 'data governance' can get gray in different conversations such as in big data governance, data management, knowledge management, data assets and information assets (Data et al. 2013; Morabito 2014c; NASCIO 2009; Soares 2012, 2013; Tallon 2013). DataFlux has improved its maturity model to highlight a business perspective that drives the need for managing data as an enterprise asset and to achieve the necessary levels of data quality.

5.2 Big Data Maturity Models

Table 5.5 DataFlux data governance maturity model

Level of maturity	Characteristics
Undisciplined (Stage 1)	There is redundant and duplicate data, divergent sources and records at this stage. The main problem is that bad data and information will lead to bad decisions, and lost opportunities
Reactive (Stage 2)	This is the beginning of data governance. Improvements are experienced at the department level
Proactive (Stage 3)	The enterprise recognizes the value of a unified view of information and therefore begins thinking about Master Data Management (MDM). IT and business groups collaborate at this stage. At this phase the culture is also preparing to change
Governed (Stage 4)	Information is unified across the enterprise. Business needs drive IT projects. The enterprise has a sophisticated data strategy and framework. Employees have realized that information is a key enterprise asset

Adapted from NASCIO (2009)

5.2.4 Gartner Maturity Model

Gartner maturity model (Fig. 5.10) makes the point that enterprise information management (EIM) is not a single project per se. Rather, it is a long-term program that evolves over time. Gartner developed the maturity model to give insight and provide guidance to organizations that are serious about managing information as a strategic asset (NASCIO 2009; Newman and Logan 2008).

While this maturity model shows the steps in the maturity process and application of big data governance, it also presents action items for each level of maturity (Table 5.6). Gartner's EIM concept presents an integrated approach to managing information assets and has five major goals including: unified content, integrated master data domains, seamless information flows, metadata management and semantic reconciliation, and data integration across the IT portfolio.

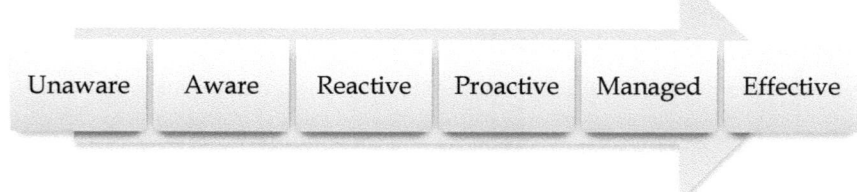

Fig. 5.10 Gartner maturity model. Adapted from Morabito (2014c) and NASCIO (2008, 2009)

Table 5.6 Action items related to each stage of maturity in Gartner maturity model

Level of maturity	Features (Action items)
Unaware	• Strategic choices are made without adequate information • Lack of information architecture, principles, rules and procedures for sharing information • Lack of information governance, privacy, security and accountability
Aware	• Recognizing the value of information • Starting to realize the risks associated with not accurately managing information and information sharing
Reactive	• Business understands the value of information as an organizational asset • Information is shared on cross-functional projects • Taking steps towards cross-departmental data sharing
Proactive	• Governance roles and structure becomes formalized • Data governance is incorporated with systems development methodology
Managed	• Policies are developed for achieving consistency and accepted throughout the organization • Governance organization is in place to address concerns related to cross-functional information management and sharing
Effective	• Top management sees competitive advantage to be gained by properly exploiting information assets • EIM strategies link to risk management and productivity targets

Adapted from NASCIO (2009)

5.2.5 IBM Data Governance Maturity Model

Data governance has gained such importance that IBM has formed a Data Governance Council to define and issue master data quality policies (Mohanty et al. 2013). One of the initiatives from this council is the 'data governance maturity model' based on the Software Engineering Institute (SEI)) Capability Maturity Model (CMM) (Fig. 5.11).

IBM data governance council explains that there are currently eleven data governance domains, which reside within four major categories: *Outcomes*, *Enablers*, *Core Disciplines*, and *Supporting Disciplines* (Table 5.7 (NASCIO 2009)).

Accordingly, business outcomes require enablers and enablers that are supported through core and supporting disciplines (see also the above discussion on information governance core disciplines).

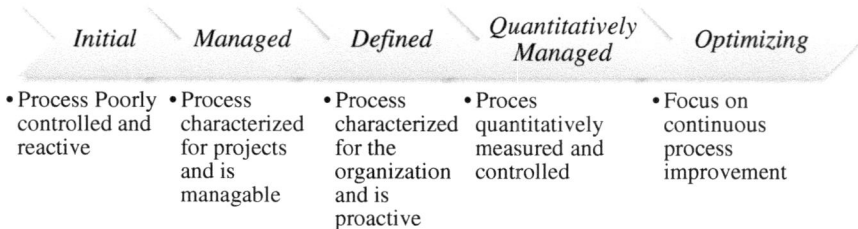

Fig. 5.11 IBM Data Governance Council maturity model. Adapted from NASCIO (2008, 2009)

Table 5.7 The four major groups in IBM data governance council maturity model

Outcomes	Core disciplines
• Data risk management and compliance	• Data quality management
• Value creation	• Information life-cycle management
	• Information security and privacy
Enablers	Supporting disciplines
• Organizational structures and awareness	• Data architecture
• Policy	• Classification and metadata
• Stewardship	• Audit information logging and reporting

Adapted from NASCIO (2009)

As described earlier, maturity models and frameworks are necessary tools for the data governance program. The maturity models describe the relevant milestones in the process of big data governance. While such frameworks present concepts and the relationships among the concepts, a methodology is needed by which organizations can move from one level to another and travel up the maturity model. Having introduced some of these models here, it should be said that there are several other maturity models such MDM Institute Data Governance Maturity Levels, Oracle Data Governance Maturity Model (NASCIO 2008, 2009) and so on that can also be looked at. This subsection attempted to introduce the readers with some of the key concepts of maturity models in the area of big data/ information governance. Maturity models provide a measure for enterprises to measure their success in managing data and recognizing information as an enterprise asset. As for these issues, in what follows, a discussion is provided on the organizational challenges and benefit related to big data governance.

5.3 Organizational Challenges Inherent with Governing Big Data

While big data can yield exceptionally useful and valuable information, they also present new challenges with regard to how much data to store, how much this will cost, whether the data will be secure, and how long it must be maintained (Ballard et al. 2014; Michael and Miller 2013; Russom 2013; Santovena 2013; Soares 2013; Zicari 2012). For example, inaccurate, incomplete or fraudulently manipulated data pose increasing risk as enterprises become more dependent on the data to drive decision-making and assess results (Craig 2011; Fischer 2013; Hurwitz et al. 2013; Jee and Kim 2013). Whether it is a SAP ERP system or a big data database, top management must think about how bad data can and will get into their system. Richard Neale who is a business intelligence industry veteran points to the importance of attention to data quality and explains (Interview: The Need For Big Data Governance 2014):

> There's no silver bullet, no shortcut to fantastic business insight just because you're using a new technology. It may sound boring, but you have to pay attention to data quality, and cut bad data off at the source using a "data quality firewall" approach to your big data repository. (Interview: The Need For Big Data Governance 2014)

He then refers to the newer, less-structured data such as social media feeds that complicate the notion of "data quality". Other commonly cited barriers organizations must overcome to implement data governance policies and procedures (NASCIO 2008) are as follows:

- Defining *requirements* and interpreting and understanding the strategies and procedures concerning data sources
- To encourage *agreement* of all parties regarding appropriate rules and policies
- Developing new *tools* to help governing big data
- The cost of implementing *policies* for sustainable data governance
- Incompatible *systems and IT infrastructures*
- Divergent and opposing *priorities* within the organization
- Getting *management* to understand what is necessary

Data quality (see dimensions in Table 5.8) is just one of the key components of the information governance program. Data quality is about how good is the data? How broad is the coverage? How fine is the sampling resolution? How well understood are the sampling biases? A good process will, naturally, make bad decisions if based upon bad data.

Another issue is compliance and security, as also noted in the previous sections. Big data governance helps organizations to protect their sensitive and strategic information such as intellectual property, business plans and product designs, key performance indicators, sales figures, financial metrics and production metrics used to make critical decisions. The following list was also presented in SearchDataManagement.com as the key reasons that data governance projects fail (NASCIO 2008; Oklahoma 2013):

- Cultural barriers
- Lack of top management support
- Underestimating the amount of work involved in data governance projects
- Lack of understanding that business definitions vary
- Trying to move too fast from no-data governance to enterprise-wide data-governance

Table 5.8 Definition of data quality dimensions

Dimensions	Characteristics
Accuracy	Data precisely reflects the object or transaction it describes
Reliability	Data is consistent across multiple transactions
Credibility	The degree to which decision makers trust both the accuracy and reliability of data
Timeliness	Data is available to the information consumer when it is needed
Appropriateness	The degree to which the data itself is relevant to the needs of an organization
Completeness	All of the relevant or required data is readily available for use when required

Adapted from NASCIO (2008)

Data governance in essence can be viewed as a formal orchestration of people, process, and technology to enable an organization to leverage data as an enterprise asset. Without a proper data governance process, big data projects can lead to a lot of trouble such as misleading data and unexpected costs (Jee and Kim 2013; Morabito 2014c; Mouthaan 2012; Steele and Nash 2012; Warden 2011). By controlling how information is created, shared, cleansed, consolidated, protected, maintained, retired and integrated within your enterprise, information integration and governance strategies turn uncertain data into trusted and insightful information (Bonenfant et al. 2012; Dyche 2012; NASCIO 2008; Sathi 2012; Soares 2012, 2013; Best Practice Guidelines 2013). Analytic and operational applications can overcome the dual challenge of rising uncertainty in data combined with overwhelming growth in the volume and variety of information. Data governance programs provide a framework for setting data-usage rules as well as implementing controls designed to ensure that information remains accurate consistent and accessible (Fischer 2013; Santovena 2013; Soares 2013; Zicari 2012).

5.4 Organizational Benefits of Governing Big Data

Why do data governance? Basically, organizations do data governance for three main reasons (Kruger and Foster 2013):

(1) to increase their revenue and/or value by improving the quality of data,
(2) to manage data complexity by addressing data integration issues, reducing data redundancy and reducing organizational and/or systems complexity, and
(3) to ensure survival through attention to risks by supporting privacy, formalizing internal checks-and-balances and avoiding data disasters.

Based on 2,583 responses from 461 respondents with respect to 'big data management', Russom (2013) reports that the vast majority of them consider big data management (BDM) an opportunity (89 %). Conventional wisdom today says that big data enable data exploration and predictive analytics to discover new facts about customers, markets, partners, costs, and operations (Russom 2013). A tiny minority of the respondents to the survey reported by Russom, however, consider BDM a problem (11 %). Undoubtedly, big data offers technical challenges due to their size, speed, and diversity. According to the survey, for example, data volume alone is a showstopper for a few organizations. To determine the most compelling reasons for big data management the survey asked respondents: "If your organization were to successfully manage and leverage big data, which business and technology tasks would improve?". At the top of the list, survey respondents selected data analytics (61 %) more than any other answer. According to survey respondents, common analytic applications can benefit from BDM, including fraud detection (21 %) and risk quantification (16 %). Respondents also mentioned that BDM delivers value to the business. This is borne out in the ranking of survey responses, which place near the top of the list business value from big data (33 %)

and numerous and accurate business insights (34 %). Similar benefits of BDM include business optimization (28 %), addressing new business requirements (22 %), and understanding business change (22 %).

According to the survey reported by Russom (2013), big data's large data samples and diverse range of data sources can lead to broader data sourcing for analytics (32 %), more data for data warehousing (24 %), and improved data staging for data warehousing (23 %). Finally, according to the survey sales and marketing activities improve with BDM. These include the recognition of sales and market opportunities (28 %), definitions of churn and other customer behaviors (18 %), better targeted social influencer marketing (16 %), and understanding consumer behavior via clickstreams (16 %), as well as related analytic applications such as customer-base segmentation (27 %) and sentiment analytics and trending (24 %) (Russom 2013).

5.5 Case Studies

This section discusses three sample examples to establishing a business case for big data governance: (1) quantify the financial impact of big data governance on patients' privacy, (2) the value of big data quality, and (3) the impact of data quality and master data on big data initiatives (Soares 2012).

Case 1: Quantify the financial impact of big data governance on patients' privacy
A major health insurer had over 50 unencrypted hard drives stolen from a call centre facility, which had been closed. The stolen drives contained big transaction data including sensitive information such as patient names, social security numbers, date of births and diagnosis codes.

> **Point of Attention:** One advantage that a big data governance program gives is that of adhering to the privacy, security, financial standards and legal requirements.

The insurer reached a settlement for $1.5 million with the United States Department of Health and Human Services. Furthermore, the insurer spent more than $17 million to notify the more than one million members who were affected. In order to prevent recurrent of a similar event the health insurer implemented data encryption on all types of big and small data, including 1,000 servers, 6,000 workstations and 136,000 volumes of backup tapes (Soares 2013).

Case 2: The value of big data quality
The big data governance program needs to establish an operational control to ensure the accuracy of big data to underpin and support analyses. For example, geospatial data are critical to exploration and production companies in the oil and gas industry. These data might be about land-based drilling and offshore drilling as well as wells

Table 5.9 The business benefits from using sentiment analysis and sound product master data

A. New product line value at list price	$10,000,000
B. Discount at the end of the season	70 %
C. Start of the season discount	30 %
D. Difference in discounting levels (B − C)	40 %
E. Gross profit benefit as a result of better market trends analytics A × D	$4,000,000

Adapted from Soares (2013)

that might be abandoned. There are several examples of poor geospatial data governance that have had an intense business impact. An oil company used incorrect geospatial coordinates to drill a well at the exact location of an abandoned well. Because of this inaccuracy, the crew had to reposition the rig and start work all over again which resulted in losses of millions of euros.

> **Point of Attention:** Big data governance is essential for maintaining the quality of big data analysis, allowing managers to make decisions and take action with confidence.

In another instance, the Exploration and Production (E&P) teams used incorrect navigational coordinates to drill a hole in an adjacent field that belonged to another company.

Case 3: the impact of data quality and master data on big data initiatives
A popular global retailer was experiencing reduction in product profit margins due to increased promotional activity (Soares 2013). To address this business concern, the retailer decided to collect and analyze product feedback from customers in social media websites such as, e.g., twitter to determine the pricing strategy for new products.

If the sentiment analysis (Morabito 2014b) was not very promising during the product launch, the retailer would decide to update its pricing in the master product catalog and offer discount of 30 %.

This would replace its usual strategy of selling merchandise at the end of season at the discount of 70 %. As a result, the retailer was able to improve its profit margin (see Table 5.9).

5.6 Recommendations for Organizations

Organizations need to establish a big data governance program to ensure clarity on various aspects of data access, integration, usage, management and ownership of big data management (Ballard et al. 2014; Craig 2011; Fischer 2013; Michael and Miller 2013; Mohanty et al. 2013; Morabito 2014c; Mouthaan 2012; Santovena 2013; Soares 2012; Big Data Now 2012). Maturity models, as mentioned earlier, are one of the widespread areas in the field of improving organizational performance as well as process management capabilities.

As with many other organizational initiatives, successful implementation of big data governance requires an enterprise perspective (NASCIO 2008, 2009). A systemic perspective on information governance is therefore needed to fully exploit the benefits coming from big data, in order to assure that organizations can answer these key questions (Big Data Governance 2014):

- What are the data sources?
- Which are the most valuable among the data sources?
- What are the requirements by line of business or division?
- What is the purpose, definition as well as usage of each data attribute?
- Do you need data stewards? What can they do for the organization?
- Is it possible to integrate big data into existing infrastructure?
- How accurate does the data need to be?
- What rules, policies and strategies are required for managing, monitoring, stewardship, privacy and security?
- What are the permissions for sharing data?

Other key questions could be: How do we verify the authenticity of the information? Can we verify how the information will be used? What options do we have as for the decisions to be taken? What is the context for each decision? How will organizations protect all of their sources, processes, and decisions from theft and corruption? Without a clear framework for big data governance and use, none of the above questions can be properly answered. Furthermore, businesses run the risk of becoming paralyzed under a chaotic mixture of data, much of which has become obsolete and past its expiration date. Indeed, big data governance helps the business to get a clear understanding of what the organization wishes to achieve from its data sources. Data governance frameworks helps organizations govern appropriate use of and access to critical information such as customer information, financial details and unstructured content, measuring and reporting information quality and risk to enhance value and mitigate exposures. Without data governance, it becomes difficult for organizations to maintain their competitive edge. The implemented technology may function exactly as designed, but the information deriving from the technology may be suspect.

5.7 Summary

This chapter attempted to introduce the readers with several guiding principles for data governance in a big data environment. Indeed, organizations need to take the right step in time to get the best out of enterprise data and big data. Without data governance, the data will be inconsistent, unreliable and unrepeatable. Data governance helps ensure that metrics are defined consistently within the organization. Clearly documented standards and definitions mean everybody can understand precisely what everybody else is talking about. Data governance provides confidence in key decisions, limit organizational costs and prevent analysis and reporting issues. Data governance encourages the measurement of successes and failures.

Furthermore, maturity models provide a framework for organizations to measure their success in managing data and information as an enterprise asset. Thus, data governance maturity models can be used and looked at as references in communication, awareness building, and the marketing of data governance. Big data governance is more than standards, reporting, and prioritization of projects; it is a business function providing structure for maintaining high data standards and securing against the risks of data theft or loss. Within 'Big Data' projects, privacy and regulatory controls play a pivotal role.

Finally, big data governance is not static; it must evolve over time to meet the changing objectives of the organization. Indeed, with the inclusion of big data, e.g., in decision-making or operations, changes may be bigger and, hence, governance has to be more comprehensive.

References

Ballard, C., Compert, C., Jesionowski, T., Milman, I., Plants, B., Rosen, B., Smith, H.: Information Governance Principles and Practices for a Big Data Landscape. IBM (2014)

Batini, C., Scannapieco, M.: Data Quality: Concepts, Methodologies and Techniques. Springer, Heidelberg (2006)

Bertot, J.C., Choi, H.: Big data and e-government: issues, policies, and recommendations. In: The Proceedings of the 14th Annual International Conference on Digital Government Research, pp. 1–10 (2013)

Best Practice Guideline: Big Data. A guide to maximising customer engagement opportunities through the development of responsible big data strategies (2013)

Big Data Governance is Key to Harnessing Insight from Big Data. http://www.firstsanfranciscopartners.com/practices/big-data/big-data-governance/ (2014). Accessed 16 Nov 2014

Big Data Now: 2012 Edition. O'Reilly (2012)

Bonenfant, M., Ménard, M., Mondoux, A., Ouellet, M.: Big data and governance. Research Group on Information and Surveillance in Daily Life, GRICIS Research Centre of the University of Québec, Montréal (2012)

Cline, J.S.: The promise of data-driven care. N. C. Med. J. **75**(3), 178–182 (2014)

Craig, F.C.T., Ludloff, M.: Privacy and Big Data. O'Reilly Media, Sebastopol, CA (2011)

Data, B., et al.: Australian Public Service Better Practice Guide for Big Data and Big Data Analytics (2013)

Data Governance Institute (DGI). http://www.datagovernance.com/adg_data_governance_definition/ (2014). Accessed 16 Nov 2014

Debra Logan: What is information governance? And why is it so hard? http://blogs.gartner.com/debra_logan/2010/01/11/what-is-information-governance-and-why-is-it-so-hard/, (2010). Accessed 16 Nov 2014

Dyche, J.: The Intersection of Big Data, Data Governance and MDM (2012)

Eisenhauer, J.A., Young, R.: Big Data. 3Sage Consulting Company, Atlanta (2012)

Fischer, U.: Big Data: Impact, Benefits, Risk and Governance. Fischer IT GRC Consulting & Training Group, Wettingen, CH (2013)

Franks, B.: Taming The Big Data Tidal Wave: Finding Opportunities in Huge Data Streams with Advanced Analytics. Wiley and SAS Business Series. Wiley, Hoboken, New Jersey (2012)

Huang, K., Lee, Y., Wang, R.Y.T.: Quality, Information and Knowledge. Prentice-Hall, Inc., Upper Saddle River (1999)
Hurwitz, J., et al.: Big Data for Dummies. Wiley, Hoboken (2013)
Interview: The Need For Big Data Governance. http://timoelliott.com/blog/2014/01/interview-the-need-for-big-data-governance.html, (2014). Accessed 16 Nov 2014
Jee, K., Kim, G.-H.: Potentiality of big data in the medical sector: focus on how to reshape the healthcare system. Healthc. Inform. Res. **19**(2), 79–85 (2013)
Krishnan, K.: Data Warehousing in the Age of Big Data. Elsevier, Amsterdam (2013)
Kruger, K., Foster, J.: Big Data Governance. ISACA SA 2013 Annual Conference, Johannesburg, SA (2013)
Michael, K., Miller, K.W.: Big data: new opportunities and new challenges. Computer **46**(6), 22–24 (2013)
Mohanty, S., Jagadeesh, M., Srivatsa, H.: Big Data Imperative: Enterprise 'Big Data' Warehouse, 'BI' Implementations and Analytics. Apress, New York (2013)
Morabito, V.: Big Data. Trends and Challenges in Digital Business Innovation, pp. 3–21. Springer, Heidelberg (2014a)
Morabito, V.: Social Listening. Trends and Challenges in Digital Business Innovation SE, pp. 67–87. Springer International Publishing, Heidelberg (2014b)
Morabito, V.: Trends and Challenges in Digital Business Innovation. Springer International Publishing, Heidelberg (2014c)
Mouthaan, N.: Effects of big data analytics on organizations' value creation. University of Amsterdam (2012)
NASCIO: Data Governance: Managing Information as an Enterprise Asset Part I—An Introduction, 859 (2008)
NASCIO: Data Governance Part II: Maturity Models—A Path to Progress, USA (2009)
Newman, D., Logan, D.: Gartner Introduces the EIM Maturity Model (2008)
Oklahoma Office of Management and Enterprise Services: Oklahoma Interoperability Grant Data Roadmap (2013)
Oracle: Enterprise information Management: Best Practices in Data Governance, Oracle Inc. (2011)
Raghupathi, W., Raghupathi, V.: Big data analytics in healthcare: promise and potential. Health Inf. Sci. Syst. **2**, 1, 3 (2014)
Russom, P.: The Four Imperatives of Data Governance Maturity. TDWI Monograph (2008)
Russom, P.: Managing big data. TDWI Research. TDWI Best Practices Report (2013)
Santovena, A.Z.: Big data: evolution, components, challenges and opportunities. http://hdl.handle.net/1721.1/80667, (2013). Accessed 16 Nov 2014
Sathi, A.: Big Data Analytics: Disruptive Technologies for Changing the Game. MC Press, Boise, ID, USA (2012)
Soares, S.: Big Data Governance. Information Asset, LLC (2012)
Soares, S.: A Platform for Big Data Governance and Process Data Governance. MC Press Online, LLC, Boise, ID, USA (2013)
Steele, J., Nash, C.: Ethics of Big Data. O'Reilly, Sebastopol, CA (2012)
Tallon, P.P.: Corporate governance of big data: perspectives on value, risk, and cost. Computer **46**(6):32–38 (2013)
TDWI Blog Contributors, Crossing The Chasm Part 1: Delivering Strategic Value. http://tdwi.org/blogs/wayne-eckerson/2009/10/chasm-1.aspx (2014). Accessed 16 Nov 2014
Tsai, J.Y. et al.: The effect of online privacy information on purchasing behavior: an experimental study. Inf. Syst. Res. **22**(2), 254–268 (2011)
Warden, P.: Big Data Glossary. O'Reilly Media Inc., Sebastopol (2011)
Webb, P., et al.: Attempting to define IT governance: wisdom or folly? In: HICSS'06, pp. 1–10 (2006)
Zicari, R.V: Big Data: Challenges and Opportunities. This is Big Data (2012)

Big Data and Digital Business Evaluation 6

Abstract

The advances in data and processing technology has radically changed the way today's digital business operates. Big data technology provides analytics tools that allow digital businesses to identify useful insights about their customers and create products to meet their customer's requirements. However, digital businesses working with big data technology face various challenges including the data acquisition, the storage space and the evaluation of the data as well as the right choices of the big data applications and the infrastructures. This review will explore digital business evaluation using big data and the advantages as well as the challenges of big data technology in digital business.

6.1 Introduction

Innovations in technology and greater affordability of digital devices have allowed digital business to collect a vast amount of data in digital form. These big data are often generated from social networking interactions, videos, emails, images, audios, logs, mobile phones, apps postings and many other sources (Sagiroglu and Sinanc 2013). Several research in the big data topic have proved that, in years to come the concept of big data in digital businesses will be intensified and diversified as the amount of data produced increases (Zhang 2013; Zheng et al. 2013; Katal and Wazid 2013). For example in 2003, 5 exabytes of data information were created around the world but today this number of data is created in just 2 days (Sagiroglu and Sinanc 2013). Only in 2012, the digital data produced was extended to 2.72 zettabytes, this made 10^{21} bytes, which is expected to double every 2 years, making approximately 8 zettabytes in 2015.

Results from recent studies indicated that, mobile phones have become one of the main generators of big data, with 6 billion of mobile subscriptions worldwide generating alone around 10 billion of text messages every day. Digital services such as, e.g., Google controls around 7.2 billion pages per day, processes approximately 20 petabytes of data every day, and it has over one millions servers globally (Sagiroglu and

Sinanc 2013; Muhtaroglu et al. 2013). Facebook with 1.3 billion active accounts, every month received about 140 billion photos with 125 billion friend connections in 70 languages (Wikipedia 2014). Twitter with 271 million monthly active users processes around 500 million tweets every day (Wikipedia 2014).

These digital businesses have radically changed the way data are used in a digital world. Over the past years we have seen a great increase in the number of digital business, around 571 new websites are deployed every minute. However, a big question remains on how digital businesses use bid data to evaluate and enhance their productivity. To understand this problem, we will briefly explore the concept of digital business evaluation using big data. The advantages and challenges of big data technology in digital business and finally we will provide some case studies and recommendations for institutions.

6.2 Digital Business Evaluation Using Big Data

Some of the challenges in today digital services are the economic uncertainty, and the increase on innovation in services or products and new business models. Most digital business, regardless of the market type, begins with some elements of research including customer acquisition, products and services development, partnerships and merging. In current big data driven competitive market, it is critical to proactively restructure the business model to push revenue by evaluating all the key structures of the digital business (Rajpurohit 2013).

Most efficient digital businesses have technology and research procedures in place that use big data analytics to evaluate their business models by identifying the best opportunities and excluding the wrong ones easily and quickly. Nevertheless, to achieve this type of intelligent business innovative technique, it is necessary to develop a research process that uses concept based factors to allow big data analysis find opportunities that are relevant to the business's priorities. For example, a digital business may want to develop a new service that will target a set of customers in the market. With real time big data, researchers are capable of identifying patterns that can estimate whether or not a new service or product are financially viable, which will make the decision-making efficient and effective (Rajpurohit 2013; Gopalkrishnan and Steier 2012).

Taking the above issues into account, the analytics searches to identify opportunities and drive revenue are often iterative and interactive as shown in Fig. 6.1. This process generally includes six steps (Rajpurohit 2013), that are known and applied in traditional intelligence activities, but require different application policies and protocols due to the characteristics of big data:

- *Analytics goals*: identifying key priorities is a very important step to understand the business context and efficiently set up analytics goals. For example some digital businesses may look for new insights, while others are evaluating their businesses models against competitors.

6.2 Digital Business Evaluation Using Big Data

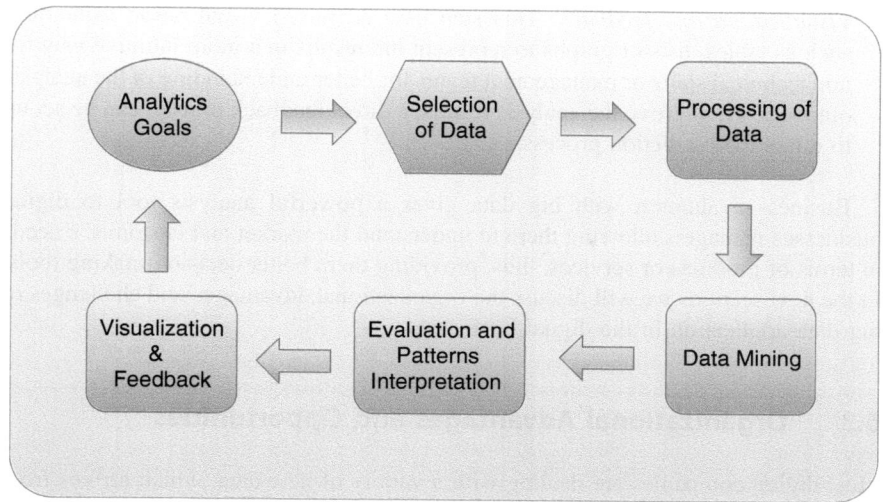

Fig. 6.1 Big data analytics process. Adapted from Rajpurohit (2013)

- *Selection of data*: After defining the goals, it is very important to select the right data required for the analysis. Since big data are made up of references to a variety of information, selecting the relevant data allow the analytics processes to be focused and efficient.
- *Processing data*: this step is designed to enhance data reliability by defining missing data, identifying and removing no relevant data or outliers. Since big data come from many different sources, this step also include the data transformation, which compiles all the data to one consistent format that can be easily analyzed by later steps. The complexity of this step often depends on the size and the variety of the data and the nature of the research. Thus, a good processing step will simplify later processes of the analysis.
- *Data Mining*: at this stage, the data is processed to extract meaningful signals based on the goals of the analysis. Consequently, the complexity of this step depends on the nature of the business and the goals of the analysis. Most data mining operations include computational algorithms such as classification, clustering or regression, to mention a few, which are capable of extracting patterns that would otherwise remain undiscovered using traditional assessment methods. A suitable data mining method is the selection based on the business goals. The performance of the data mining methods generally improves as they process more data.
- *Evaluation and patters interpretation*: this consists of evaluating the results of the analysis. Depending on the goals originated at the first step, the resulting patterns are evaluated to extract meaningful insights that can enhance the business performance.

- *Visualization and feedback*: This step uses advanced visualization techniques such as tables, lists or graphs to represent the results in a more intuitive way for non technical staffs or management teams for better understanding of the analysis outcome. To improve the analysis results, a direct feedback process can be set up to refine the prediction process.

Business evaluation with big data gives a powerful analysis tool to digital businesses managers allowing them to understand the market and customer's needs in terms of products or services, thus, providing them better decision-making tools. In the next sections we will discuss the organizational advantages and challenges of big data application in the digital businesses.

6.3 Organizational Advantages and Opportunities

Most digital companies are dealing with a variety of new data, which arrives from many different sources (see Fig. 6.2). Companies, which can adapt the big data technology into their day to day operations have significant advantages over those without any big data technology capability (Muhtaroglu et al. 2013). Big data resources present a great opportunity for digital business models, as we have seen with Google, eBay, Amazon, Facebook and Netflix, Borders and many other

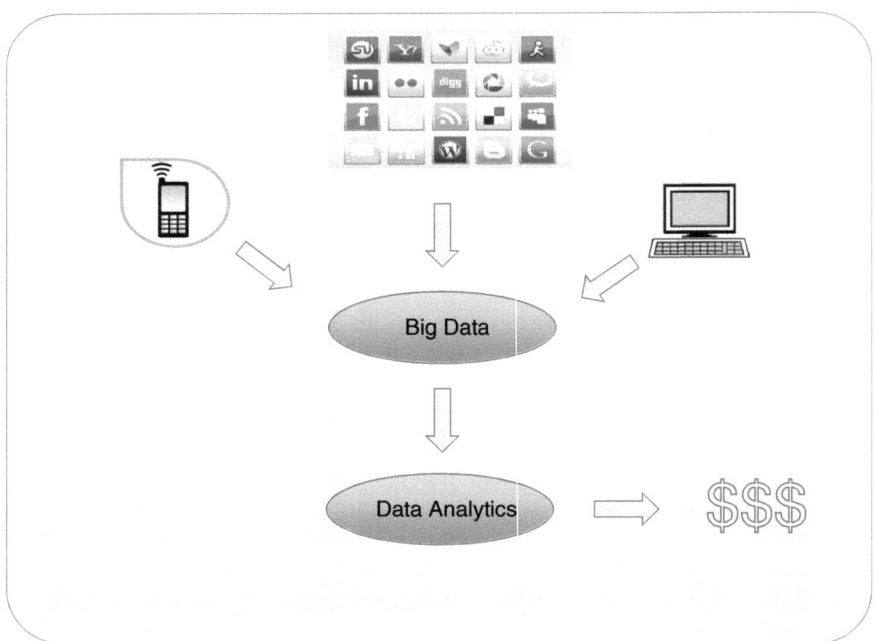

Fig. 6.2 Big data and analytics configuration for business value (Mithas and Lucas 2010)

businesses (Mithas and Lucas 2010). Therefore, the big data technology is often used in digital business for two main reasons, as follows:

(1) The first reason for big data technology is to provide analytics tools (as seen in Sect. 6.2) that allow a company to gain useful insights about their business and guide the management in high-level decision making process.
(2) The second purpose of this technology is to provide tools for customer's satisfaction. Big data allow the development of different application platforms and real-time services and products that leverage a variety of data in order to satisfy consumer needs and provided value to the business such as efficient, intelligent service and many others.

The aforementioned argument can be supported by looking at the way organizations invest on Big data. Over the past years global spending on digital business IT resources (big data) have exceeded 3 trillion US dollar per year (Mithas and Lucas 2010). However the main questions remain: what is the return from all this investments? How does big data technology provide tools in order to gain completive advantages in digital business? To address these questions, it is vital to highlight and analyze the digital business models in terms of fundamental concepts such as customer value of proposition, consumer segmentation and key revenue channels (Muhtaroglu et al. 2013; Osterwalder et al. 2010; Morabito 2014).

6.3.1 Customer Value Proposition

The customer value proposition focuses on how products and services offered by a company satisfy customer's needs with regard to competitors' offering. With the application of big data technology in digital business, a variety of innovative products and services can be delivered to add more value or solve customer's challenging problems. Recently many innovative applications have been built off the back of smart use of big data to fulfill customer's needs, replacing the use of traditional data models. Examples of those applications are the price comparison applications, which enable customers to view pricing information on products from different sources. Many studies have shown that, with these applications customers can save around 10 % on every shopping they made on digital market (Manyika et al. 2011). RedLaser is one of the applications that give customers the power to shop around by scanning the bar code of a product with their smart phone devices and receive price comparisons for the products and other related products. Other customer value proposition applications are provided by digital businesses including eBay and Amazon. They provide tools that allow customers to search a product from a large number of sellers. These services provide transparency, producing "buy" or "sale" opportunities for customers and businesses (Manyika et al. 2011). The application also offers more information about the products including customer's reviews and quality of the products.

Also, the big data technology has added great value to digital entertainments companies such as, e.g., Netflix, whose digital business model is to provide films, TV entertainment. To establish itself in the digital market, Netflix was able to design an application that offers consumers searchable films from a large set of movies and TV series. The service also provided more information about the films including customer's reviews and suggestion on related films. The big data applications have, thus, helped Netflix to provide innovative and efficient services to its clients and increased its revenue to 4.3 billion US dollars with more than 50 million subscribers in 2014 (Wikipedia 2014). Considering all these applications of the big data technology, the customer value propositions of digital business are expected to improve further in near future.

6.3.2 Customer Segmentation

Delivering the right products or services to the right customer groups can significantly increase the profitability. Equally, delivering products or services to wrong customer groups will turn them away from an organization to its competitors.

With the success of modern technology, the Internet usage has dramatically increased; digital market is becoming more demanding and sophisticated. In this complex market customers are demanding more from their services providers and with an excessive competition, digital businesses that are unable to fulfill theses expectations are swiftly left behind by the competition. Understanding your customers, products and services have never been more important in digital business. Customer segmentation based on big data applications allows digital businesses understand key characteristics and behaviors of their customers, enabling them to design and deliver products and services, which are more likely to be relevant to a target customer segments. Complete relevance can lead to greater conversion rates, which eventually will lead to more profitability (Experian Hitwise 2010).

In a large group of customers there are different type of customers and each type can have many characteristics that define them. Using segmentation based on the big data information analytics allows a digital service to group these individuals by similar characteristics. Simple examples of this are dividing your customer group into female and male customers or young and old customers; or more complex such as developing a search engine to locate a group of individuals who have express some interests in your new products. With the customer segmentation tools based on big data technology, digital businesses can have a greater flexibility in developing products or services depending on a specific demand of the target segment or the most profitable customers groups.

The big data applications in customer segmentation are very wide and depending on how niche a digital business want each segment to be. However, there are four main types of data in the big data including demographics, lifestyle, behavior and value, that can be used to perform the customer segmentation (Experian Hitwise 2010).

- *Demographics*: customer segmentation according to demography is mainly based on characteristics such age, gender, ethnicity, race. These characteristics cannot depend on an individual willingness or action.
- *Lifestyle*: consists of characteristics that can be influenced by an individual. These range from household income, locations, entertainments, attitudes, beliefs and so on.
- *Behavior*: defines the decision making processes of customers, it also help to understand how emotions affect customer's buying behavior as well as their usage rate and response with regard to a given product. For examples, how often a customer visits websites or social networks to look for the products or brands she or he like.
- *Value*: this process uses past transactional information of a customer to identify how profitable a customer is to the company. The process defines the buying power of a customer.

In general the segmentation process help digital business to target groups of customers who are likely to respond to given products or services offerings. These groups must have similar attributes and each group should have a characteristic that makes it different from others. Each group must be large enough to generate significant additional value to the business.

6.3.3 Channels

Channels constitute different ways on how a digital business gets in contact with its clienteles and provides them value propositions. The big data driven applications of digital businesses collect information and reach customers through many different channels. These channels can be used as mediums to deliver products as well as collecting information from customers. Furthermore, the applications are generally delivered through two main channels, web based applications and/or mobile applications. The web based applications for desktop and notebook users can be delivered through the product website such as, e.g., eBay and Amazon, which offer services that allow customers to search products from a large number of merchants and provide customers reviews for more transparency. Whereas the mobile applications can be delivered using stores like Google play (2014) and Apple Store (2014). The increase in mobile applications will allow more innovations and efficient delivering of big data driven applications through marketing channels (Manyika et al. 2011).

6.3.4 Customer Relationship

The customer relationship is defined as the relationship a digital business builds and preserves with its clienteles (Manyika et al. 2011). With the growth of competitions and technology such as Internet and mobile applications, a digital business lives or dies based on how it build relationship with the customers. In the past, digital business often relied on broadcast mediums to build and maintain relationship with customers, while today's technology allows customers to connect and interact with each other around the world, which has dramatically changed the customer's relationship in digital market. To succeed in today digital market, companies need network systems beyond traditional marketing and sales advertising messages.

The big data applications provide a network tools that take advantage of the customers interaction with the technology to create and manage relationships with customers or clients that goes beyond simple marketing and sales promotional offers. As discussed above, these applications may include automated systems that can recognize some characteristics of a group of customers and provide information associated to transactions. For example, a tool in an online retail business may recommend or suggest products an individual customer may be looking for based on information of the customer's previous purchases (Manyika et al. 2011).

These applications may also offer products information and customer's feedback on individual products, which enable businesses to become a part of their customer's conversations (Rogers 2011). Figure 6.3 shows a summary of few advantages of big data in digital business.

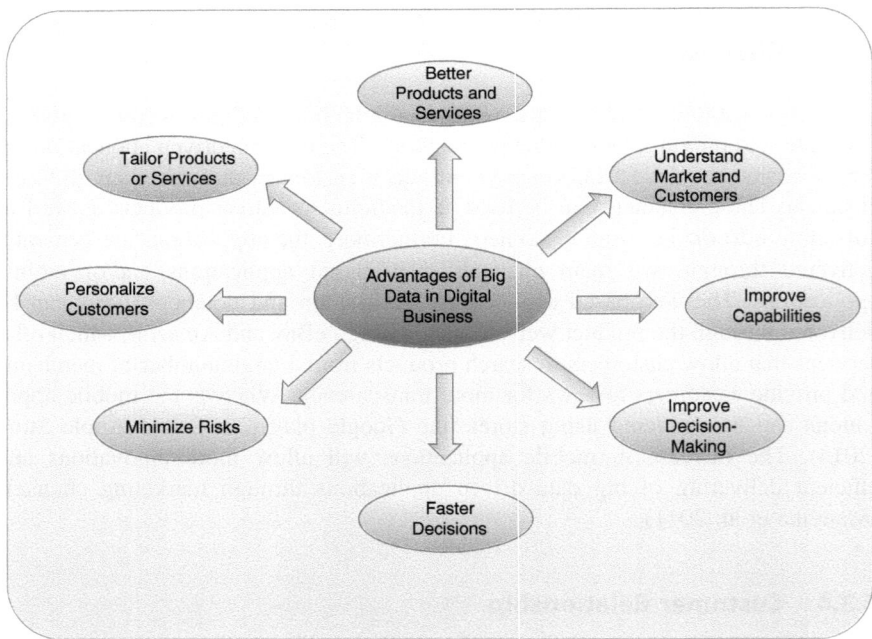

Fig. 6.3 Big data advantages. Adapted from Rogers (2011)

6.4 Organizational Challenges

The increased diffusion and adoption of smart phones technology and social networks have changed the way digital businesses operate. To be a major player in the digital market, many digital businesses have adopted big data technologies. Indeed, taking advantage of the customer's interaction with the technology and with each other on a global scale, digital businesses have managed to target customers with the right products and services. This has provided them with a better understanding of their customers, products, hence made them more efficient and increased their profitability (Experian Hitwise 2010; Rogers 2011).

However, digital businesses working with big data technology face various challenges, including the acquisition of the data, the storage space, the right choices of the big data applications and the infrastructures. Businesses using big data technology need to understand both the needs of the technology and customer's, because choosing a big data application without knowing its advantages may result in a waste of resources (Rogers 2011). Digital businesses need to understand their clienteles and identify their businesses goals before adopting any big data applications. Whether you are an online retails or provide digital technology, having knowledge about your customer's behavior and coming up with new ways to add values in your products or services are the key drivers to succeed in today's digital market (Rogers 2011).

Addressing challenges presented by big data technology will be difficult considering the volume of the ever-increasing data and its variety. Currently available big data tools, analysis methods, technology architecture and management are not fully capable in dealing with the complexity of the big data (Katal and Wazid 2013). In what follows, some of the main challenges in the big data application in digital business are briefly discussed.

6.4.1 Key Resources

Key resources refer to data, infrastructures, analytics and skilled people a digital business needs in order to provide value to its clienteles through big data applications (Morabito 2014). The data access and management can be a great obstacle for many digital businesses. Due to the high volume of data and privacy laws, a majority of digital businesses do not have the right platforms for data collection and management across the enterprise. Moreover, the success of big data technology relies on its capability of assessing data in a timely manner. However, designing tools for storing and managing real time data is very complex and require time and money. Therefore, digital companies might need to develop partnerships with other companies to share the costs associated with data acquisition. This form of data collection, however, may threaten the culture of competitiveness and secrecy (Katal and Wazid 2013). Other strategies to mitigate costs related to the increase in volume of data, is to use cloud technology. However, uploading terabytes of data in real time will require a large amount of time (Katal and Wazid 2013). Accordingly, storing and accessing large data in timely manner as well as reducing the processing time remain some of the biggest challenges in big data technology (see again Fig. 6.1, showing the processing involved in big data analysis).

Furthermore, a company might also face challenges in identifying the right data and defining advantages the data have to offer. Because data related business models are often different to the traditional business revenue models, as discussed above. This type of analysis will require more sophisticated analytics tools and highly skilled people with statistics and computing knowledge and capabilities, which in turn, is one of the biggest challenges of big data projects. There is a shortage of qualified skilled people capable of understanding and interpreting raw data using technology to find some meaningful business insights (Davenport and Patil 2012).

The big data applications also require a more sophisticated technology landscape due the growing nature of different data sources (Morabito 2014). Therefore, leveraging big data requires strong collaboration with more innovative technology services that can help to develop the right IT infrastructures capable of adapting in efficient manner to the changes occurring in the technology landscape. Consequently, many digital businesses actually require assistance from companies offering platforms and infrastructures solutions. Because big data technology needs continuous maintenance and development of different infrastructures and platforms, especially when the number of customer's increases and the volumes of the data get even bigger. In addition to companies offering platforms and infrastructures, several middle class servers have developed and employed together with existing computing platforms like Hadoop (Katal and Wazid 2013), an open source project by Apache Software Foundation. The aim of this project is to provide a reliable and efficient share storage capacities with robust analytics systems. This will significantly improve the processing of data, which is considered to be one of the big issues in big data analysis (Katal and Wazid 2013).

6.4.2 Privacy and Security

Privacy and security have become some of the biggest challenges in the big data technology (Morabito 2014). Digital businesses dealing with big data applications are required by the law to protect the privacy and the security of its customer's data as well as setting clear boundaries of some personal information. With the increased in the data volume and the consequent risk of cyber attacks, it is becoming progressively difficult for digital businesses to protect data privacy (Katal and Wazid 2013). For example the United States (US) based digital company eBay, which has 128 million active customers had its customers database hacked between late February and March 2014 (Kelion 2014). The database included users name, email address, date of birth and phone number. This personal information can be used to steal customer's identities and even access other systems. Thus privacy and security are major concerns when dealing with sensitive information.

6.4.3 Cost Structure

The cost structure aims to define to the costs of all the projects incurred by a digital business, including the investment in customer value propositions, and other business activities such as marketing, infrastructures and building partnerships with others companies (Muhtaroglu et al. 2013). The biggest cost of the big data technology comes from the infrastructure and data management tools. Companies such as Microsoft, Oracle, IBM have spent over $15 billion on software companies specializing in data analytics and management (Cukier 2010). In 2010, big data analytics and management firms were reported to be worth more than $100 billion and this value is estimated to grow by 10 % every year due to the increased demand of more efficient data management and analytics tools (Cukier 2010).

The availability of the cloud based infrastructures and application stores have significantly decreased the financial resources requirement to enter the big data technology (Muhtaroglu et al. 2013; Morabito 2014). Some businesses, like, e.g., eBay and Amazon, may develop in-house infrastructures and applications. These applications need be developed with real time processing features. With these applications and infrastructures, the businesses may also need to continually invest and improve their big data services with innovations to create new solutions to customers growing problems and maintain their place in the vast and competitive

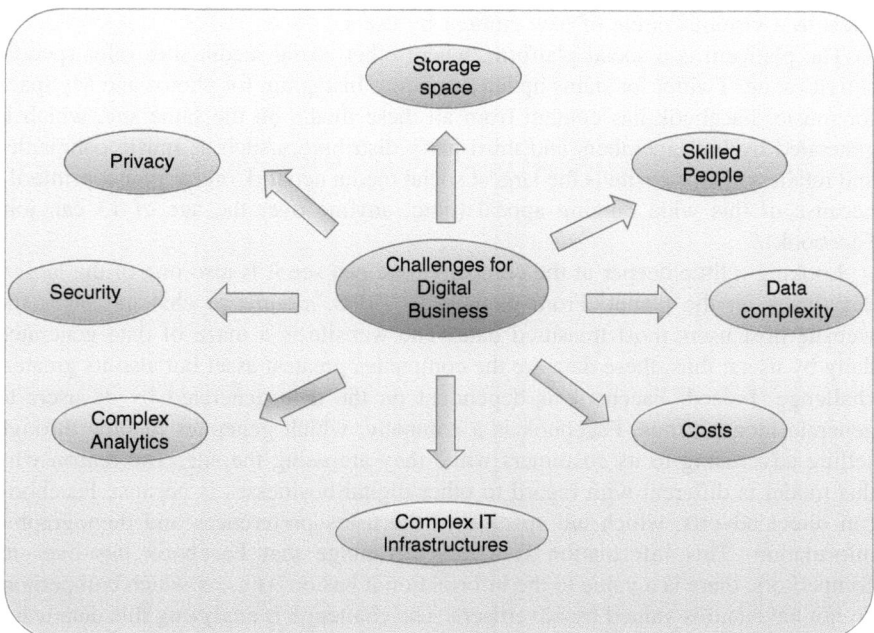

Fig. 6.4 Big data challenges in digital business. Adapted from Muhtaroglu et al. (2013), Morabito (2014)

market. Figure 6.4 summarizes some challenges of the big data application in digital business explored in previous sections.

To illustrate how big data are being used in industry, two examples of digital businesses using big data are discussed in the following sections. The examples aim at highlighting the key challenges facing the organizations and to discuss the way they are using big data solutions to overcome these challenges. The two organizations considered within the case studies are Facebook and Netflix, both highly successful digital businesses and both facing complex data challenges.

6.5 Cases Studies

This section will analyze two organizations that are pioneers in the digital business domain: Facebook and Netflix. Particular attention will be paid to the way they use big data technologies to evaluate business performance and adjust their strategies accordingly.

Facebook is one the most relevant and diffused social media platform, which allows users to connect to friends and family using a webpage called a profile. The majority of the content on Facebook is user generated, from user comments, likes, photos and videos. The profile acts as a medium from which to interact with other members' profiles. New content is generated and members further add to this new content with comments likes and other interactions. For Facebook this in effect leads to a virtuous circle of new content by users.

The platform is a social platform, where other social media sites offer specific activities, i.e. Twitter for status updates or news, Instagram for photos and MySpace for music. Facebook has content from all these media on the same site, which is generated by both members and third party distributors such as music companies and retailers. The website is the largest social media network on the planet primarily because of this wide ranging appeal (note: anyone over the age of 13 can join Facebook).

Looking a little deeper at the company, one can see it is also one of the largest data hosts on the planet. From pictures to video, albums to chat messages the website host users most treasured data. The website is a maze of data generated daily by users; thus, these data are the companies greatest asset but also its greatest challenge. Indeed, Facebook is dependent on the data generated by its users to generate income; thus, Facebook is a company, which generates income through selling advertising to its customers while they are using the site. The reason why this model is different with regard to other digital businesses is because Facebook can direct adverts, which are specific to the users preferences and demographic information. This information is a key advantage that Facebook has over its competitors, there is a value to the information it has on its users which competitors do not have and is valued by advertisers. The challenge is analyzing this data using big data methods to effectively target users and provide them with relevant advertising.

Facebook has 1.3 billion monthly users worldwide, some 830 million of them using the site on a daily bases. Also, the users generate 4.5 billion activities including updating photos, video and sharing comments and messages.

In recent estimates Facebook has been shown to produce over 4.5 billion pieces of content and over 750 Terabytes each day. This large volume of data makes the process of analysis very cumbersome. Further Facebook has indicated its users use 7 petabytes of photo storage on its website each month with data centers that have a capacity of 100 petabytes. This excess capacity is a necessity as content on the site is always increasing.

> **Point of Attention:** The problem with having big data is that the vast majority of data never gets used. A recent article surveying big data issues noted that only about 0.5 % of all data is ever analyzed (Barrenchea et al. 2013). Thus, the vast majority or 99.5 % of data is not used as part of the analytics processing. This means storage space is allocated for this data but may not be required for viewing by the users or as part of customer analytics.

As there is a vast amount of information, which the company process each day, Facebook has developed tools to manage how the data are processed and analyzed to bring users more relevant information. These tools also provide users with more relevant social media content, including articles and statuses; for example, the algorithms implemented provide users with targeted advertising content.

Thus, Facebook uses big data analytics to direct advertising most relevant to its user base. The advertising is based on geo locations as well as age, sex and other demographic factors. This means that there is a unique set of adverts presented to each user of the Facebook system. The advertising on Facebook helped the company bring in $7.8 billion in revenue during 2013 (Wikipedia 2014). Furthermore, Facebook tweaks its algorithms on an on-going basis and one example is the tweak of its advertising delivery formula. This has allowed it to move from generating only a small proportion of its income from mobile advertising in 2012 to now generating over 60 % of its revenue from mobile devices. As the site grows, predictions say that more and more content will be generated from mobile devices. Thus, mobile devices have helped increase revenue growth at Facebook but this was only after changing the advertising algorithms and making content more location specific, this in turn allowed Facebook to charge more for the advertising.

Considering now the infrastructure, Facebook opened a Prineville data center, which is 62 k square feet in size. It houses over 500 cold storage racks, which can hold 2 Terabyte of data. The standard data storage rack in the data center facility uses about 8 kW of power. Facebook also has more than 100 petabytes data capacity in this facility. However, Facebook has also admitted that it only uses about 7 petabytes for storage photo in its facilities each month. This means there is a lot of redundancy built for future growth. To empower this capacity, Facebook switched on more secure offline storage facilities (cold storage) at its Prineville data center, for storing pictures and other user media on hard disks. As well as using existing data storage technologies Facebook has also worked with vendors to create cheap storage vaults that keeps files on Blu-ray discs. Each vault contains about 10,000 discs with each containing around 100 Gigabyte storage space, a single one of these cabinets has room for one petabyte, which is 1,000 Terabyte of data. Though this technology is still in development it has the potential to change how data is stored and further reduce storage costs.

Facebook has data in two forms. Flash data are stored on flash drives and are quickly accessible (for example the login data for user or the most recently uploaded articles). These data are easier to analyze because the upload times for performing analytics is relatively quick. The second type of data is long standing 'cold' data which are rarely accessed (for example a photo album from a few year earlier which has not been access since upload). The majority of data will fall into the 'cold' form meaning that whilst they are valuable customer data, they may not be accessed, but need to be retained in the likelihood the customer attempts to access them in the future.

Finally, Facebook has a number of analytics tools to analyze and manage data. Facebook manages its server data using the hadoop 2.0 platform and it has developed a Hive tool which is a software fork sits on top of the Apach Hadoop infrastructure to support the processing of data. Figure 6.5 shows a sample diagram illustrating how the Facebook hive platform fits within the Hadoop software stack.

Hive provides an SQL-like interface to query data stored on Apache hadoop platform. The Apache Hive is considered the standard for SQL queries over a petabyte. It is a comprehensive and compliant engine that offers a powerful set of tools for analysts and developers to access Hadoop data. Facebook initially developed the Hive platform but other vendors now use it and have further developed the tool. For example, Amazon web services maintains a software fork of Hive that is included in Amazon MapReduce on Amazons Web Services, which in turn are used by amazons web services and cloud client (including Netflix, whose case is discussed in what follows).

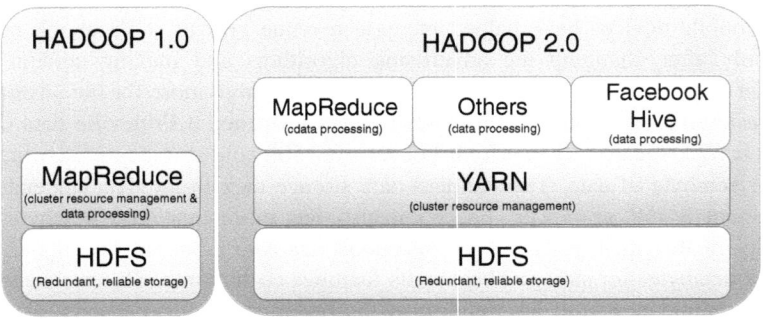

Fig. 6.5 Big data Hadoop structure. Adapted from Mayer (2013)

6.5 Cases Studies

> **Point of Attention:** The selection of hardware and software infrastructure to support Big data analytics is a key factor that can help to evaluate the novelty of a digital business.

The second case study of this Section considers Netflix one of the largest streaming sites on the planet, working in 40 countries, and providing a streaming service for movies, TV shows and factual content. The service offers access to premium content based on a monthly subscription fee (Wikipedia 2014).

Netflix faces similar big data issues to the ones seen above for the case of Facebook; however, the company has adopted slightly different approaches to how it deals with these challenges. The volumes of data and complexity of analytics are both equally challenging but the main difference is that Netflix data are not user generated but rather videos licensed by the digital rights owners. Netflix then provides a service in which allows users to stream the videos in exchange for a monthly fee. The Netflix business model is based upon customers using the service and paying the monthly subscription fee for a continued use of the service.

> **Point of Attention:** Big data and analytics driven business models require a careful attention to sourcing, computing, and data storage strategies for their effective implementation and valuation in digital business competitive environment.

The primary motivation for Netflix is to ensure customer have access to content which would ensure they continue to be customers of Netflix. It has often been compared to a pay per view TV station; however, unlike, television stations Netflix customers are a part of a continuous loop of feedback with users using their membership fees, actual viewing as well as content ratings to provide feedback to Netflix. This instantaneous feedback allows the organization to always be in step with its customer's needs and demands. Big data analytics have helped in this analysis process and supported the creation of new content such as the "House of Cards" and "Orange is the new black" drama television series, content which is only available on Netflix, which in turn has got more people using the service. Furthermore, Netflix estimates that 75 % of viewers are from recommendations from its customer recommendation engine (Vanderbilt 2013). The recommendation engine is pivotal to how Netflix retains customers. As the business model is based on customer continuing to use the service and continuing to pay the monthly subscription fees. The recommendation engine has been created with using a number of mathematical techniques to improve the performance of the recommendation system. The goal is to primarily increase the likelihood someone watches content provided by the recommendation engine.

Thus, the key data problem for Netflix is twofold: first, using the customers viewing information and rating to provide users with appropriate recommendations for viewing; then, ensuring the quality of the customer experience when the customer is viewing content. In order to meet the requirements for streaming such a large data capacity Netflix had two options to stream content to customers:

1. Build out the own data center to service clients streaming needs or
2. Use a cloud service from a third party to meet client requirements.

Netflix chose to meet client requirements using a cloud service provided by Amazon web services. Using this service has allowed for Netflix to have on demand access to hosting services from the providers. Reducing costs when demand is lower but this cost would be increased costs when demand was higher as the extra capacity is charged at a premium. Therefore, the hardware for Netflix data is cloud data center run by Amazon's web service. Storing data in a cloud environment can be much cheaper than hosting it locally. While using the cloud solves the problem of data cost and has the benefits of scalability. The problem with cloud computing is the geographic proximity of data across potentially multiple location. Netflix has a number of server centers it uses across the globe under the Amazon web service. This allows for it to have geographical presence of its content in multiple regions

Box 1

- ***Data Size***: There are 80 clusters with over 2,500 nodes (May 2014).
- ***Challenge***: To maintain service and high quality of videos and customer data, while also creating agility for development of new tools for Netflix's technology teams.
- ***Solution***: An open source Apache data platform called Cassandra, this allows Netflix to create and manage large data and minimize the chance of failures and outages to customers.

without having employees in that region. An example is the Amazon web service server Netflix had planned to use in Brazil for its South American and Central American customers. Indeed, Netflix found there was no performance advantage to using servers in Brazil. One advantage of the cloud service is that it could be switched off relatively quickly and moved to a new location. And this is exactly what happened in the case of Brazil. Because there was not advantage in using the server in Brazil to serve those customers, Netflix reverted to serving them from the United States (US) East Coast as the traffic would have been via Miami in any case. For its European customer Netflix began serving them through Ireland, in the Amazon web service server centers in Dublin. There were slightly higher costs to perform this operation in Dublin as compared to the east coast US but the company chose this approach as it reduced latency for streaming because of geographic proximity. Another key component in cloud computing is disaster recovery in the event a server is knocked out but act of nature. Having multiple data centers aids to have contingency plans in the event a single data center is knocked out.

Furthermore, as the cloud brings a number of challenges to managing data in a geographically distributed environment Netflix has developed new tools to manage this highly complex environment. In particular, Netflix uses a tool called Cassandra, which is an open source SQL database; this tool was initially created by Facebook and now is under the open source Apache license. It scales across multiple data centers all over the world. This tool is optimized for random write/reads, which makes real-time queries efficient. The example in the box 1 shows how Netflix manages the large data and it holds how the analytic tools help they have developed help to manage complex challenges inherent in big data.

6.6 Recommendations for Organizations

Big data and big data analytics require not a single methodology or approach for their use in digital business evaluation. What seen in both the above case studies is the way in which the approaches change to meet the needs of each company. In particular, there is no perfect fit in terms of the hardware or software. The challenge is identifying the most appropriate technique for the organization and this would vary from one organization to another. In what follows recommendations are provided for these issues.

6.6.1 Hardware

When we speak about big data, the first suggestion for holding this vast influx of data is cloud computing. Though in the case study this is not necessarily the right approach for companies such as Facebook whose intrinsic value comes from having direct access to user data. The two options open to digital businesses is to decide on whether to use the traditional data center model in which the organization owns and runs data centers or to use cloud based services. The choice for organizations is usually determined by the organizational strategy and cost.

Another challenge when dealing with big data is finding the right balance between processing power and data storage. Getting the right balance is important as it ensures the right mix of hardware components can be identified and acquired. Key to this process is benchmarking the activities that would be commonly expected from the data center.

6.6.2 Software

The main framework used for data management is currently Hadoop. This is an Apache software infrastructure used by Facebook, Amazon, Netflix and many other digital businesses. The key advantage of this tool is that many of its components are open source. Key Hadoop users such as Facebook (Hive) and Netflix (Cassandra) have developed add-ons to Hadoop framework, which adds further value to Hadoop ecosystem.

Key to the evaluation of how digital businesses should use big data is understanding how its customers utilize the data and then creating solutions, which fit these specific requirements. In the case studies we see how hardware and software vary though the data are seemingly similar. This is because key to the big data agenda is flexibility in how digital businesses organize and utilize their data for maximum business gain. This gain is only possible when companies understand their data and implement strategies to effectively monetize it without alienating customers. In conclusion data can be used to create information and information to create knowledge, and knowledge for a digital business is money.

6.7 Summary

This chapter discussed how big data and analytics can be used to evaluate business performance. It described six steps that summarize this process: Goals, Selection of Data, Processing Data, Data Mining, Evaluation and Visualization & Feedback. It then presented an analysis of the advantages and opportunities of using big data and analytics, identifying customer value proposition, customer segmentation, channel diversity, and better customer relationship as the most important ones. On the other hand, it also analyzed the challenges that organizations are facing when they want to adopt these technologies and create organizational advantage and highlights the importance of having skilled people in this area that is relatively new and thus the talent supply is scarce. Privacy and Security and the relatively high costs were also identified as challenges. Finally, this chapter closes with the analysis of two case studies: Facebook and Netflix, to demonstrate how these organizations have used big data and analytics to evaluate and shape their business models.

References

Apple Store. http://store.apple.com. Accessed 16 Nov 2014

Barrenchea, M.: Big data: big hype? http://www.forbes.com/sites/ciocentral/2013/02/04/big-data-big-hype/. Accessed 16 Nov 2014

Cukier, K.: A special report on managing information: data, data everywhere. http://www.economist.com/node/15557443 (2010). Accessed 16 Nov 2014

Davenport, T.H., Patil, D.J.: Data scientist: the sexiest job of the 21st century. Harvard Bus. Rev. **90**, 70–76 (2012)

References

Experian Hitwise. Getting to grips with social media—An Experian Insight Report, Experian Limited (2010)

Google Play. http://play.google.com/store. Accessed 16 Nov 2014

Gopalkrishnan, V., Steier, D.: Big data, big business: bridging the gap. In: BigMine '12: Proceedings of the 1st International Workshop on Big Data, Streams and heterogeneous Source mining, pp. 7–11 (2012)

Katal, A., Wazid, M., Goudar, R.H.: Big data: issues, challenges, tools and good practices. In: 2013 6th International Conference on Contemporary Computing (IC3 2013), pp. 404–409 (2013)

Kelion, L.: eBay makes users change their passwords after hack. http://www.bbc.co.uk/news/technology-27503290. Accessed 16 Nov 2014

Manyika, J., Chui, M., Brown, B., Bughin, J., Dobbs, R., Roxburgh, C., Byers, A.H.: Big data: the next frontier for innovation, competition, and productivity. McKinsey Global Institute, San Francisco (2011)

Mayer, C.: Hortonworks show YARN future Hadoop with HDP 2.0 preview. http://jaxenter.com/hortonworks-show-yarn-future-hadoop-with-hdp-2-0-preview-106254.html (2013). Accessed 16 Nov 2014

Mithas, S., Lucas, H.C.: What is your digital business strategy? IEEE IT Prof. **12**, 4–6 (2010)

Morabito, V.: Trends and challenges in digital business innovation. Springer International Publishing, New York (2014)

Muhtaroglu, F.C.P., Demir, S., Obali, M., Girgin, C.: Business model canvas perspective on big data applications. In: Proceedings—2013 IEEE International Conference on Big Data, Big Data 2013, pp. 32–37 (2013)

Osterwalder, A., Pigneur, Y., Smith, A., Movement, T.: Business model generation: a handbook for visionaries, game changers, and challengers. Wiley, New York (2010)

Rajpurohit, A.: Big data for business managers—bridging the gap between potential and value. In: Proceedings—2013 IEEE International Conference on Big Data, Big Data 2013, pp. 29–31 (2013)

Rogers, D.: The network is your customer: 5 strategies do thrive in a digital age. Yale University Press, UK (2011)

Sagiroglu, S., Sinanc, D.: Big data: a review. In: International Conference on Collaboration Technologies and Systems (CTS), pp. 42–47. IEEE, San Diego, CA (2013)

Vanderbilt, T.: The science behind the Netflix algorithms that decide what you'll watch next. http://www.wired.com/2013/08/qq_netflix-algorithm/ (2013). Accessed 16 Nov 2014

Wikipedia: Facebook. http://en.wikipedia.org/wiki/Facebook?uselang=ja?iframe=true&width=90%&height=90%. Accessed 16 Nov 2014

Wikipedia: Netflix. http://en.wikipedia.org/wiki/Netflix. Accessed 16 Nov 2014

Wikipedia: Twitter. http://en.wikipedia.org/wiki/Twitter. Accessed 16 Nov 2014

Zhang, D.: Inconsistencies in big data. In: Proceedings of the 12th IEEE International Conference on Cognitive Informatics and Cognitive Computing (ICCI*CC), pp. 61–67 (2013)

Zheng, Z., Zhu, J., Lyu, M.R.: Service-generated big data and big data-as-a-service: an overview. In: IEEE (ed.) IEEE International Congress on Big Data, pp. 403–410. IEEE, Santa Clara, CA (2013)

Managing Change for Big Data Driven Innovation

Abstract Big data is now becoming a key organizational asset, which represents a strategic basis for business competition. This development is making organizations to consider new innovative techniques on maximizing the potentials of big data as well as the challenges it creates. Yet, the success of many organizations demands new skills as well as new perspectives on how the epoch of big data could advance the speed of business processes. With the growth of big data, new analytics tools have evolved together with new progressive business models. In this chapter, we explore the innovative capabilities of the growing big data phenomenon by discussing issues concerning its methodologies, its impact on organizations business models, novel tools for analytics including challenges encountered by many business organizations. Our findings are substantiated by describing the real-life cases of Adobe and Hewlett Packard organizations.

7.1 Introduction: Big Data—The Innovation Driver

Numerous organizations are hunting down better approaches to always innovate and optimize their practices, products, and services in today's competitive business environment (Piatetsky-Shapiro 2013). Traditionally, innovation is seen as a factor of consistent research and improvement processes using manual conventional procedures (Gobble 2013). Due to the rise of big data, organizations are gradually depending on accumulated computerized data acquired from different sources such as their suppliers, customers and shareholders for recognizing innovative products and service systems (Sagiroglu and Sinanc 2013). Although access to information for many business organizations seems like a 'walk in the park', there exist enormous challenges of identifying valuable information, analyzing, adapting, or applying it for the development of productive business performance (Yan 2013).

Today, numerous organizations are progressively investing their resources on big data as a business asset including mechanisms for its analytics as one of their core profitable capabilities (Louridas and Ebert 2013). However, big data also encompass organized in-house commercial data produced from daily trade transactions, such as sales, suppliers, customers, and inventories. Moreover, unstructured peripheral and non-transactional data are also in the fore, which includes online behaviors of customers', interactions on social media and ecommerce dealings indexed by big data giants e.g. Google and Facebook. Nevertheless, many experts share similar opinion about the innovative strategies of big data, although, a few admit that the innovative capabilities of big data are still relatively unclear and unexploited. Some have offered useful suggestions and guidelines for business organizations to generate innovative services and products from big data applicable to various fields (Groves et al. 2013; Wielki 2013). In the next section, we present some well-researched guidelines for deriving innovation from this huge asset called 'big data'. Remarkably, some technology business giants are already implementing some of these innovative guidelines for improving their products and services (Davenport and Dyché 2013).

7.2 Big Data—The Key Innovative Techniques

The big data age has produced innovative principles for business management. In previous eras of technological innovation, business pioneers learnt that the smallest well-organized scale was a crucial factor of competitive success (Cui et al. 2014). Similarly, competitive profits are possible to be accumulated by organization's collecting more and enhanced data but also utilize such data at an efficient scale (Bjelland and Wood 2008).

Be it as it may, in what follows we critically reflect on the five techniques shown in Fig. 7.1 (i.e., integration of data platforms, testing through experimentation, real-time customization, generating data-driven models, and algorithmic and

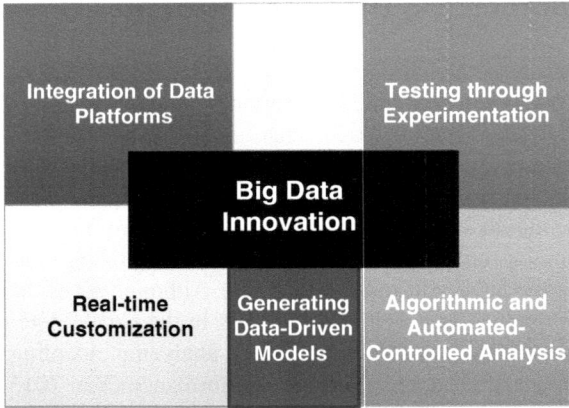

Fig. 7.1 The big data innovation techniques. Adapted from Davenport and Dyché (2013)

automated-controlled analysis), in order to identify how big data may further assist business organizations in developing innovative strategies, which are adaptable to the rapidly changing models occurring in today's highly extrinsic technological era.

7.2.1 Integration of Data Platforms

One of the biggest challenges encountered by many business organizations is accrual of datasets lurked departmentally, e.g. sales, marketing, service operations etc. (Dandawate 2013). Unfortunately, this business model impedes the timely utilization of the datasets for complex synthesized analytics (Dean and Ghemawat 2008). In addition, the amassing of information within business units brings a huge challenge for innovation. For example, numerous financial organizations stay limited from the failure to share their huge data between assorted business areas, such as money management, lending and financial markets (Economics 2013). Consequently, business organizations are being prevented from developing a coherent outlook of understanding inter-relationships amongst financial markets as well as individual customers (Davenport and Dyché 2013).

Due to the growth of technological devices, information is now readily available to almost anyone (Mithas et al. 2013; Russom 2013; EY 2014). This development poses a threat to the innovative potentials of organizations solely depending on exclusiveness of their data as the core resource of their competitive advantage (Davenport and Dyché 2013). Considering the real-estate sector, which relies on trades of asymmetric information such as, e.g., access to transaction data and awareness of the 'bid and ask' behavioral pattern of purchasers. Such information entails a momentous financial cost as well as energy. Conversely, real-estate online experts in big data and analytics are now bypassing agents; thus creating online forums to allow purchasers and sellers to share their views on the value of properties as well as generating parallel bases for real-estate data (Dandawate 2013).

A further put-down at exclusive or proprietary data is the assemblage of freely available satellite imagery that, when processed and analyzed, comprises indications about physical amenities of an organization's competitors (Stonebraker et al. 2013). These satellite detectives collect insights into business checks as exposed by the capacity of the physical amenities e.g. goods movements etc.

In order to develop innovative products from big data, organizations are now attempting to uncover their departmental reserves of exclusive data: the integration of datasets from multiple systems and the search of external suppliers' and customers information to create new products is now a crucial determinant of their manufacturing costs. Extra integrated data platforms now permit organizations and their suppliers to pool insightful resources during the design phase (Cui et al. 2014).

7.2.2 Testing Through Experimentation

With the advent of big data, there arise a novel potential for a different sort of decision making using controlled experiments. Currently, organizations are testing hypotheses and analyzing results to inform their business operational processes. Testing through experimentation are helping administrators differentiate causality from correlation, therefore decreasing the inconsistency of results and improving product performance (Mithas et al. 2013).

For example, many online business organizations are continuous testers; by apportioning a quota of their web page views to undertake experiments that identifies the elements that motivates the active engagement of end-users (Cui et al. 2014; Davenport and Dyché 2013; Parmar et al. 2014). In addition, businesses marketing their products physically also make use of experiments in order to influence their marketing strategies. For example, fast food merchants McDonalds, has equipped some of their outlets with devices that collect data about customer interactions, ordering patterns as well as in-store consumer traffic. The importance of these huge datasets is that experts are able to model the effect of variations on restaurant designs, menus sales and productivity (Kelly et al. 2014; Qubole 2014).

7.2.3 Real-Time Customization

In this section, we describe how organizations are innovatively using big data by making real-time customization conceivable. Organizations are now able to monitor the behavior of customers from click streams on the Internet, modify their inclinations, and most importantly model their possible actions in real time. Furthermore, they are learning to ascertain when customers are close to making a buying decision and then pre-empt the transaction process to a finishing point by bundling desired products combined with a reward offer. Real-time custom analysis can also increase procurements of products by the most valuable customers of a business organization (Drake et al. 2014).

As an innovative driver, big data real-time customization is relatively obvious in retail sectors due to the size and value of data available from online procurements, interactions on online social networks (OSNs) and more lately, location-specific smart phone communications. Nevertheless, other sectors can also gain from this novel system of Big-Data application, owing to the growth of sophisticated analytical tools for distributing customers into more insightful micro-segments (De Fortuny et al. 2013).

7.2.4 Generating Data-Driven Models

The growth of big data has enhanced the creation of innovative groups of businesses that have accepted data-driven business models. Several of these businesses perform inter-dependent roles in value chains generating valuable consumable data formed by business transactions (Economics 2013; Eisenhardt and Martin 2000; Fan and Bifet 2012). For example, a transport business organization recognized that during their daily business operations, enormous volumes of information on product deliveries are being collected. In order to maximize this opportunity, the organization created a division that trades the data to complement business and economic predictions (Kelly et al. 2014).

Another good example of the development of new models is an organization that got so many insights from analyzing data as part of a manufacturing improvement, which prompted a decision to build a business to do similar work for other organizations (Hartmann et al. 2014). Currently the business combines supply-chain data for many manufacturing customers and sells software tools to improve their performance. Outstandingly, the newly developed service business now overtakes the income generated by the organizations parent manufacturing business (Provost and Fawcett 2013).

7.2.5 Algorithmic and Automated-Controlled Analysis

As also discussed in previous chapters (see, e.g., Chap. 6), big data increase the development and implementation for algorithmic and automated-controlled analysis. In some manufacturing organizations, algorithms are used to analyze sensor data from lines of production, in this manner, the wastage of raw materials are limited, production outcomes are increased and then costly human involvements are avoided (Mithas et al. 2013). This type of data is usually analyzed by groups of computers to enhance production and diminish downtimes through the process of imputing their results to real-time tasks. Products such as photocopying machines used to aircrafts can now create streams of data capable of tracking their usage. In some situations, manufacturers are able to analyze the inward data and then automatically repair software malfunctions. Besides, computer hardware merchants are collecting and analyzing such data to plan pre-emptive maintenance before customers' operations are interrupted by system failures. As a means of innovation, such automatic-controlled data is also utilized to make necessary changes in product design (Elmqvist and Irani 2013).

The key point is value-added performance, improved risk assessment, as well as the capability to uncover useful insights that would otherwise remain unknown. Recently, more business organizations are participating in this decision-making industrial revolution due to the massive reduction in price of sensors, communications devices and analytic software (Özcan et al. 2014).

7.3 Big Data: Influence on C-Level Innovative Decision Process

A lot has been stated about the emergent significance of big data as a tool for business innovation. But how are these types of data utilized to drive innovation? How does it affect the in-house tactical initiatives of business managers and executives? Is big data beginning to influence C-Level decisions?

As earlier mentioned, big data offer enormous benefits to senior executives of a business organization. Big data have the capacity to improve insights into customers buying patterns, forecasts as well as increasing productivity and efficiency for a sales executive (Taylor and Labarre 2006).

Furthermore, big data through analytics can assist a Chief Marketing Officer (CMO) in developing a vibrant marketing strategy, social media analysis and customer subdivision. They can also be utilized to understand impending design needs to make logical business decisions. For Chief Information Officers (CIOs), big data can establish the link between IT and business goals during board meetings with the Chief Executive Officer (CEO) (Lohr 2012; Piatetsky-Shapiro 2013; Taylor and Labarre 2006).

7.3.1 Stimulating Competitive Edge

In order to be a source of business advantage, big data systems need to build new types of processing to data-sets targeted at stirring innovative impact through the formation of ground-breaking business models, goods or services (see, e.g., the discussion in Chap. 4).

As of the time of putting this book together, big data driving income generation, optimization and business benefit which is getting the attention of C-Level executives. It covers many areas from direct advertising, to scam detection as well as transaction optimization. For example, in the financial sector, banks emphasize on performing analyses on in-house and customer transactions aimed at detecting scams; likewise retail outlets are modifying their inventories based on previously aggregated insights made possible by big data. A key strategy in getting measurable value from big data is actually analytics; this usually attracts the curiosity of C-Level executives who seek to drive a competitive edge in the global economy (Economics 2013).

In a survey lead by a technology research organization, Economist Intelligence Unit discovered that senior executives require big data for their workforces due to the perceived belief that the use of analytics tools will enhancement productivity within the organization (Manyika et al. 2013). Thus, business organization CIOs are now playing the role of software evangelists for big data analytics solutions. They are also making sure that the CEOs and other C-Level executives realize that insights derived from big data can be the key edge to drive a competitive advantage which results to the targeting of innovative markets, fraud reduction, better-informed business decisions etc. (Lohr 2012; Taylor and Labarre 2006).

7.3.2 Predictive Analytics: Data Used to Drive Innovation

The explosion of big data implies that predictive analytics is gaining wider acceptance for operational use. For example, SAP's vice-president of product marketing analytics, James Fisher, predicts that advanced analytics market will be worth about $3bn by the year 2016. He highlighted that many SAP customers make use of the organization's predictive analytics platform—Hana, to improve profit and reduce expenses (Bell 2013; Fan and Bifet 2012). Although in the environment of customer relationship management (CRM), predictive analytics is at an experimental phase which explains the reason organizations whose business model are technologically driven, are in the forefront with applying predictive analytics to CRM (Huo et al. 2014). In what follows examples of businesses using big data analytics are discussed.

Bigpoint, a games development organization, are utilizing predictive analytics to monetize players and upsurge their revenue by an estimated 10 and 30 % a year (Bell 2013). The predictive model of the organization allows them to make clever real-time decisions about a player's actions. For instance, it acts as trigger for the predictive system to analyze prior gaming behavior when a player's 'ship' is damaged. If applicable, a custom-made context-related note offers the player a new 'ship' for a minimal fee (Yan 2013).

Her Majesty's Revenue and Customs (HMRC) has framed a predictive analytics platform called 'Adept' keeping in mind the end goal to build debt collection and risk estimation. Adept incorporates analytics into the debt administration process with a specific end goal to development debt gathering interruptions for deferred tax payments on a yearly premise. HMRC's systems are integrated with 'Adept' utilizing predictive modelling techniques to inform a comprehensive risk and behavior-driven collection tactics. Remarkably the technology also recognizes diverse types of debtor categories and then targets its communications to these categories through particular attributes. By March 2015, it is estimated that HMRC will have the capacity to collect an extra £3bn of debt (HM Revenue and Customs 2013).

In the financial services sector, predictive analytics is used to improve the methods of debt collection. Various organizations are attempting to identify that a certain type of customers responds undesirably to payment prompts, while some will make timely payments without reminders; others tend delay payment when prompted. By means of recognizing these behavioral tendencies, business organizations are able to enhance their processes as well as effective customer relations.

In the retail segment, Tesco is building on its reputation for new technologies to enhance CRM. Tesco has started a scheme, which offers suggestions to customers about products related to their purchases in real time. A 'loyalty card' is injected into a device attached to a shopping trolley, through which personalized suggestions are presented to the customer during the final buying process. For instance, a customer may place an electronic shaving clipper in the shopping trolley: as a result he receives a 2-for-1 offer related to the item, such as batteries for clippers. With the availability of data related to the customer's identity as well as their purchases, Tesco is making an effort to forecast their next actions and then provide intervention mechanisms showing related offers.

7.4 The Impact of Big Data on Organizational Change

In order to fully explore the existent and prospective capabilities of the big data boom, business organizations need to enforce certain modifications to their in-house operational procedures by considering the three kinds of stakes described in what follows (see also what discussed in Chap. 6).

- *Data*: Business organizations need systems to collect large magnitudes of information in specific industrial formats allowing for stress-free accessibility and analysis. However, due to the enormous proliferation of online social networks and allied technologies, most large organizations now have this—in fact; they normally have more than they are able to utilize (Bughin et al. 2010; Groves et al. 2013).
- *Analytical tools*: The second stake required is cutting-edge analytical tools, such as, e.g., NoSQL and Hadoop (see also the Preface and Chap. 6 in this book). NoSQL and Hadoop are proprietary open-source tools and platforms which are universally accessible (Morabito 2014); but the biggest challenge is getting the right people proficient enough to make good use of them (Kelly et al. 2014; Olson 2010).
- *Expertise*: This is usually the most challenging category of the stakes: advanced analytics necessitates a workforce with high-tech skills in data science to global privacy laws, as well as a proficient knowledge of the business including relevant sources of value (Lohr 2012).

Nevertheless, the mere acquisition of the aforementioned stakes is insufficient in helping organizations because big data is not a standalone additional technology initiative. Frankly, big data is not a technology initiative at all; it is actually a business system that needs technical savvy. Therefore, the sheer addition of capability and expertise alone cannot enable the information technology functions to start engendering database insights. The big leaders of analytics have discovered that to succeed with big data, organizations need to practice the consistent process of deeply embedding big data into their business models (Manyika et al. 2013). This is the most efficient technique to guarantee that derived insights are pooled and shared across all units within the organization. It also guarantees that the entire organization identifies the combined effects and scale benefits that well-conceived analytics proficiency can deliver (Ji et al. 2012). Taking the above issues into account, big data analytics can be relevant to organizations in four areas listed below:

- Refining current products and services
- Refining in-house processes
- Developing innovative product offerings
- Changing business models.

To get a clearer meaning of the concepts mentioned above, the following sections presents a guideline for business organizations to follow if they are keen on modifying their operational procedures in order to develop innovative products from the insights derived from big data's analytics.

Firstly, however, let us consider a basic aspect of starting any business organization: *goals*. This is the best place for organizations to start the big data embedding process; clarifying out their goals. Examples of some useful goal-oriented statements are; "we will integrate cutting-edge analytics and insights as the critical component of all major decisions" or "we will adopt big data systems as a new-fangled way of undertaking our marketing strategies". A well-defined goal by C-Level executives is a vital prerequisite for the kind of organizational change big data offers. Additionally, C-Level executives also need to answer these sorts of questions e.g., "How far are we ready to go"? "How will our business performance improve through big data"? "What do we need to focus on"?

7.4.1 An Incentivized Approach

Many organizations are possess opportunities for complex analytics, still, very little of them have the capabilities to further improve their trajectory by accurately defining priorities and selecting the right angle of entry. With the organization's goals well defined, executives can work on developing a horizontal analytics capability. They learn how to overcome internal struggle and create the skill to utilize big data throughout the organization (Yan 2013).

Organizations do not easily change and the value of analytics may not be obvious to everybody. Therefore, a continuous work in helping employees and customers change their daily behaviors as well as continuing in the new innovative path without lapsing is necessary. Business organizations need to clearly define the owners and sponsors for analytics initiatives. By providing adequate inducements for behaviors that are analytics-driven, they will ensure that big data is integrated into processes for making key decisions (Russom 2013).

A good example of an incentivized approach for adopting analytics is Nordstrom; Nordstrom, a leader in the retail space when it comes to enhancing the online shopping experience raised the obligation for analytics to an upper managerial level in its organization in order to make analytical tools and insights extensively accessible including integrated analytics-driven goals into its vital tactical initiatives.

7.4.2 Creating a Centralized Organizational 'Home'

Leaders of big data need to create an organizational 'home' for their progressive analytics proficiency, which can be supervised by a principal analytics officer. The process of creating an organizational 'home' embroils some important design choices (Demchenko 2013). An organization has to define its approach for the deployment of big data. Furthermore, the collection and ownership of data across corporate functions has to be assigned and a well-structured plan to generate insights must be implemented (Yan 2013). The technological infrastructure, privacy policy and access rights must be hosted and maintained by the organization. However these tasks seem quite burdensome to achieve, hence we present four models organizations need to adopt in order to comply with the needed changes for big data optimization.

- *Organizational division*: If each business organization's division have their distinct data sets they become capable of making their specific big data decisions with reduced supervision or monitoring. An example of organizations that uses this business model are AT&T and Zynga (Pearson and Wegener 2013).
- *Organizational division with central support*: This is when organizational divisions decide their own choices then co-operate to work on designated initiatives. An example of organizations that uses this business model are Google and Progressive Insurance. Progressive, Insurance depends on it to capture driving behaviors and define customer risk profiles (Bain Insights 2013; Pearson and Wegener 2013).
- *Center of Excellence* (*CoE*): In this model, a self-governing center supervises the organization's big data. Various organizational divisions follow initiatives guided and coordinated by CoE. Also, Amazon and LinkedIn are examples of organization's that depend on this model (Demchenko 2013).
- *Fully centralized*: In this model, the corporate center is responsible for prioritizing business creativities. Netflix is an example of a business organization that adopts this approach (see also Chap. 6). The business goals and operating model of an organization greatly affects the type of model they adopt for big data change (EMC 2013). An organization with in-depth analytics capabilities as well as a focus on experimentation, testing and innovation, such as, e.g., Google, normally depends on a decentralized method (Couchbase 2010). However, CoE is found to be the mostly adopted model due to its enormous advantages and the fewer restrictions. An operational CoE allows cross-business-division access and data sharing capabilities. In addition, CoE assists in providing organizations adequate analytics strategies thereby setting the roadmap for the maintenance of privacy policies (Pearson and Wegener 2013). For example, a foremost European telecommunications organization, is attempting to change its internal procedures by deploying big data to analyze customer data in order deliver improved services and offers as well as utilizing network traffic data to enhance network supervision and investments. These capabilities will all be coordinated by a CoE.

7.4.3 Implementing the Changes—First Steps

As business organizations are already delving into the world of big data, the complexities we have discussed necessitate the need for analytics capabilities to be anchored in the organization in order to create substantial insights (Meeker and Hong 2014). Currently, many organizations executives are carting beyond competitors, while others are making intense efforts to keep up with pace. Nevertheless, the first step needed is the benchmarking of the organization and determination of the organization's present situation in big data analytics, compared with that of rivals. This process will further assist the organization in deciding the essential investment needed to advance their relative position. In circumstances were an organization is considerably behind the rivalry, a rapid innovative platform is often compulsory to create and withstand change. This begins by testing hypotheses in order to study where and how cutting-edge analytics is most expected to benefit the organization (Computer Research Association 2011).

7.5 Methodologies for Big Data Innovation

7.5.1 Extending Products to Generate Data

Data generated by products can stimulate the development of better business models, product innovations and business work effectiveness (Bughin et al. 2013). Extending products to generate data is highly influential in conditions where data can stimulate enhancement in the characteristics of products. Moreover, another benefit of this methodology is supporting product manufacturers to maintain interaction with the products regardless of their physical locations. Connectivity can offer the platform for developing existing connections or forming completely novel types of consumer connections (McAfee and Brynjolfsson 2012). For example, the Engine Health Management (EHM) proficiency of Rolls-Royce uses embedded sensors to observe and store parameters of aircraft engines such as temperature, pressure, altitude, and vibration.

7.5.2 Digitizing Assets

The ability to produce a physical illustration of a digital design using a 3 Dimensional (3D) printer external to old-fashioned supply chains has the prospective to be totally disruptive. Recently, business organizations are considering the vast business opportunities of these types of technologies. This methodology will also facilitate the expansion of measurement capabilities and additional backup capacity for other systems of value enhancement. Peking University People's Hospital are digitizing healthcare records as well as integrating telemedicine that leverages real-time alerts and mobile communications. The goal however, is to observe the vital signs of patients in real time for the sustenance of individualization and responsiveness (Groves et al. 2013). In Korea, HomePlus, a retail chain business, has made computer-generated stores in physical surroundings such as subway stations. Today, consumers can scan items on supermarket shelves with their smartphones and then get the products brought to their homes within a short period of time (Lavalle et al. 2011).

7.5.3 Trading Data

Data as a business asset has the capacity of motivating new business models through commerce, distributing acquired knowledge and engendering creativeness (Wielki 2013). Through this means, the process of trading data can encourage bigger union between businesses. The Marine Institute of Ireland is an example of an organization making accessible data it collects on ecological situations, contamination levels and marine life open to external bodies. Their collected data is utilized to advance the safety of the public and increase economic activity by refining the accuracy of flood forecast as well as allowing well-organized seafood and shipping procedures (Bollier and Firestone 2010; Chen et al. 2012). Likewise, a huge community-based traffic and navigation application called Waze facilitates traffic and information about maps to be swapped among linked users to develop their daily commute in real-time (Obeng-Odoom 2009). The volume of data rises proportionately to the participation of its users, hence, refining the quality of data as users outwit traffic and boost routes.

7.5.4 Forming a Distinctive Service Capability

The internal data within business organizations can be converted into self-standing businesses themselves (Computer Research Association 2011; Ji et al. 2012; Meeker and Hong 2014). Transforming such capabilities into distinct novel businesses can be fruitful when the capabilities of the particular data can be explored across various market situations, especially where new developing economic environments are evolving to exploit new prospects. For example, IBM computerized its in-house transportation booking system and expenditure reporting methods, which reduced their managerial budgets up to 75 %. With this success, they further advanced the system into a distinct internal business known as the Global Expense Reporting Solutions for IBM customers (Parmar et al. 2014). Citigroup did a comparable demonstration as they created models to reveal market inadequacies that stalled their customers' ability to make the best utilization of payment systems. It refined and extended its models into a set of particular customer benefits under the standard of Citidirect BeMobile (Parmar et al. 2014).

7.6 New Big Data Tools to Drive Innovation

As earlier discussed in previous chapters, the growth of technological platforms such as online social media (OSNs) has resulted in the massive growth of big data. More recently, every time users attempt to monitor the distance covered in the course of driving a car, surfing the Web and interacting with their smart phone applications to find the closest café, data are being created at an alarming volume, velocity and variety. However, retrieving the right information in time to answer quick inquiries remains a huge test for people, as well as for organizations.

Having the right devices or tools to execute a relatively accurate analytics is highly significant and can lead to the most creative business systems. In the era of big data, tools such as Hadoop, 1010data, Actian etc. are all extremely useful in analyzing and gaining insights from data architectures by applying hybrid data modeling concepts (Jinbao and Wang 2012). In this section, we extend the discussion in Chap. 6, briefly describing the Hadoop big data robust platform as well as four top tools, which can be integrated with it in helping business organizations maximize the opportunity provided by big data for their productivity.

7.6.1 The Hadoop Platform

Hadoop is an open source software platform that facilitates the distributed processing of huge datasets through collections of product servers. The platform is developed with scalable capabilities from a sole server to thousands of machines. Hadoop platform has an extraordinary level of fault tolerance and its resiliency stems from the software's ability to detect and deal with failures at the application layer rather than depending on high-end hardware systems (Yan 2013).

7.6.2 1010DATA Cloud Analytics

1010data's database provides support for parallel processing with its own query language that supports a subsection of SQL functions comprising graph and time-series analyses. 1010data also possesses the capabilities to deal with semi-structured data and machine data. Additionally, the platform owners offers a whole stack which comprises of data-visualization tools, data integration, monitoring and reporting and many other innovative analytic functions e.g. machine learning and statistical analysis (Saleem 2014).

The private-cloud method of 1010data helps their customers in managing and scaling infrastructure easily. Other features include the capability for a central data management and application programming interfaces (APIs) which are integrated with back-end systems access controls. As a custom services provider 1010data creates private-cloud applications aimed at meeting customer needs, which is highly in contrast to cloud provider—Amazon, which conveys low-cost services to tens of thousands of customers (Batty 2013; Bughin et al. 2010).

7.6.3 Actian Analytics

Actian analytics is an open-source transactional database with a high-speed analytical database management system (DBMS). In April 2013, Actian analytics acquired another big data analytics company, ParAccel, which introduced a better move into big data analytics with an enormously parallel processing database system currently referred to as Actian Matrix (Bughin and Chui 2010; Groves et al. 2013; Russom 2011).

Actian analytics depends on the synthesis of cloud services, data-integration and analytical DBMS options in which Hadoop is a fixture of the architecture of data management. SQL ETL (ETL which means Extract, Transform and Load, is a technique used to collect data from various sources, transform the data depending on business needs and load the data into a destination database) is included in Actian dataflow and data cleansing on Hadoop alternatives that work with distributions from Cloudera, Apache and others.

7.6.4 Cloudera

The big data tool—Cloudera, provides support for Hadoop in order to ensure enterprise-grade performance, data-access control, security and reliability. In addition, Cloudera offers exclusive software components such as Cloudera Navigator, Cloudera Manager as well as mechanisms for backup and recovery (Batty 2013; Groves et al. 2013; Russom 2011). This tool is massively rich with open-source components such as, Cloudera Search, best controlled by Cloudera Manager to deliver and monitor workloads. Another software component, Cloudera Navigator enables the provision of access control and auditing. Cloudera big data software is gradually growing to become a "heavy weight" for data analytics. (Wanderman-milne and Li 2014). Furthermore, it provides reference hardware configurations for leading Hadoop software distributors. It is also a hugely parallel processing columnar analytical database management system aimed for swift analysis of large structured datasets. HP Vertica Analytics competes with the similar tools such as IBM PureData and Pivotal Greenplum; it is designed to match legacy enterprise data warehouse settings such as Teradata (Özcan et al. 2014). Accompanied with the development and release of the Vertica 7, HP integrated "FlexZone" intended allow their users search data in huge datasets beforehand and then the database scheme is defined with related analyses.

Based on the above highlighted new tools of big data, we can state that the progression of big data is relatively proportionate to the innovative development of the tools required for its analysis. The growth rate of big data is at an alarming rate which motivates business organizations to start innovating how to collect, store, organize, and analyze it. For a rapid progressive change to occur within the business processes of organizations, innovation must be at the fore. Frankly, there can be no innovation without adequate information (big data), combined with the right analytical tools and accurate interpretation from analyzed datasets.

7.7 Models of Big Data Change

As the size and velocity of data grows from gigabytes to terabytes and petabytes, the sorts of data generated by various software applications (Web and Mobile Based) becomes more dynamic to deal with than traditional data structures. Therefore, traditional database structures are now faced with the challenge to gather, store, explore, share, analyze, and visualize data. As a result many business organizations are now adopting new data models to manage big data challenges such as NoSQL (Not Only SQL) database, e.g. Cassandra, HBase (Couchbase 2013; Morabito 2014). In addition, they employ a distributed computing infrastructure such as Hadoop. NoSQL databases are referred as key-value stores that are distributed, highly scalable and most importantly non-relational.

In this section, we present rational descriptions of the data models of collecting and storing big data from a technological perspective. Thereafter, we focus on explaining how business organization models are changing due to the technological advances in the data models of big data (Jinbao and Wang 2012).

7.7.1 Big Data Business Model

In this section we continue and extend the discussion in Chap. 4, examining the model that guides business organizations in adopting and utilizing the innovative data processing model of big data as well as innovative analytics to build a sustainable competitive edge. Although within the context of the big data business models, many business organizations are changing their processes quite carefully due to few uncertainties about the starting process. In addition, some concerns are also about the multitude of new technological innovations needed to be deployed in order start a successful journey with big data (Parmar et al. 2014).

Conversely, other organizations are innovatively changing their processes at a more rapid pace for the integration of big data analytical systems into their current business models with the sole aim of improving their decision-making competences.

In order to get a good grasp at big data business model, the next sections describes what is popularly known as the "Big Data Business Model Maturity" (see Fig. 7.2) (El-Darwicheet al. 2014; Schmarzo 2012). This model provides a clear insight on how business organizations can take advantage of the changing data storage model in order to push the big data opportunity in a global business ecosystem (EY 2014).

7.7.2 The Maturity Phases of Big Data Business Model

1. Business Monitoring: In the business-monitoring phase organizations are positioning Business Intelligence (BI) systems to keep track of their continuing market performance. Business monitoring utilizes fundamental analytics to

Fig. 7.2 The maturity phases of big data business model. Adapted from El-Darwiche et al. (2014) and Schmarzo (2012)

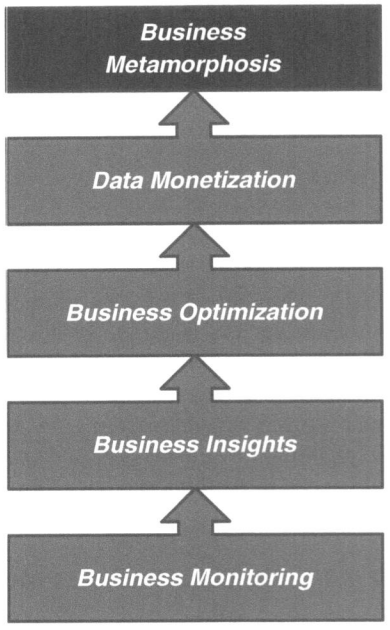

highlight market performance areas and sends automated alerts with relevant information to concerned entities. One of the benefits of the business monitoring phase is the leveraging of benchmarks retrieved from the innovative big data storage model, which also includes indices such as *product performance* and *customer satisfaction* for the accurate identification of less and more-performing market areas or segments (Drake et al. 2014; De Fortuny et al. 2013; Serenko et al. 2014).

2. Business Insights: In the business insights phase, the storage model of big data) is fully utilized. This is executed by way of making logical meaning of the "schemalessly" gathered data using statistics, predictive analytics and data mining in order to discover substantial and executable market insights (Fayyad and Uthurusamy 2002). Consequently, the results of the insights analyzed are then integrated into their existing business processes. This situation is quite similar to the concept of an "intelligent" dashboard such as Facebook's insights and Google Analytics but in this case, instead of only displaying tables and graphs of data, materials and relevant insights are uncovered. Additionally, the insights provide specific and executable recommendations. At the later part of this chapter, a real life case study on the utilization of big data is presented which demonstrates how the Business Model of big data has brought innovative changes to business organization with the aid of business insights. Nevertheless, below are some few instances of the impact of the business insight phase on businesses:

- In *marketing*, the business insights could help in identifying, e.g., that certain in-flight promotion activities are more effective than others, combined with detailed recommendations on how much is expended on marketing in order to shift to the more efficient activities (Eisenhardt and Martin 2000).
- In *manufacturing*, the business or market insights could, e.g., also help in finding observations that some machines used for manufacturing are operating beyond the bounds of their control coupled with a well-selected maintenance timetable which may include part replacement for each problematic machine (Economics 2013).
- In the area of *customer sales support* the business insights phase has the capabilities, e.g., of detecting observations that select "Special Card holders" procurement activities have reduced below a particular threshold of regular activity and then an automated alert can be sent to customers through the monitoring phase with email information about a reduction coupon.

Thus, the business insights phase is arguably the core of big data's business model due to its direct connection with the data itself combined with its extensible integration capabilities with other phases (Miluzzo 2014).

3. Business Optimization: In the business optimization phase, organizations normally utilize embedded analytics systems in order to improve various components of their business processes in an automated manner. For most organizations involved with big data modeling, this is the phase where some components of business operations can experience a massive turn-over (Gobble 2013).

Some good examples of business optimization includes:

- Expenditure budgets built upon in-promotion performance.
- Scheduling of resources founded upon customer purchase logs, and buying behaviors.
- Inventory optimization using existing and forecasted buying patterns, alongside local demographic and events data.
- Product valuing founded on existing buying patterns and brand interest insights collected from social media sites.

4. Data Monetization: This phase involves the process where business organizations attempt to package their data with analytics insights for sales transactions with other organizations. They achieve this by integrating analytics directly into their products in order to produce "smart" products to upscale their customer relationships and radically re-develop customer satisfaction (Kelly et al. 2014).

An example of this phase is a smartphone application whereby insights about product performance, customer purchasing behaviors and trends of markets are sold to marketers and promoters. For instance, the application "MapMyRun" (see Fig. 7.3) could collate data from their smartphone application with users and product insights in order to sell to sports wears manufacturers, retailers of sporting goods, healthcare providers and insurance organizations.

Fig. 7.3 The "MapMyRun" application source: captured by the author

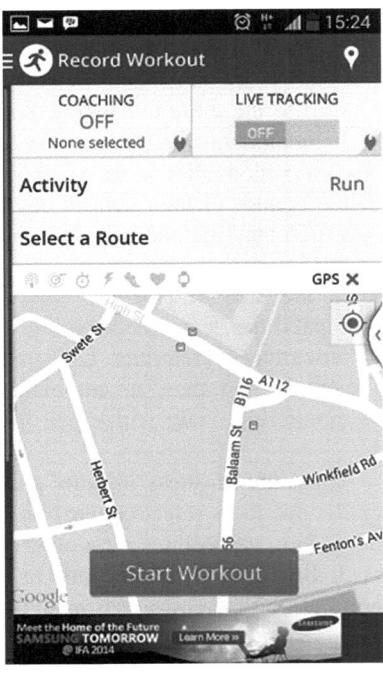

5. **Business Metamorphosis**: In the business metamorphosis phase, the critical objective for business organizations is to leverage the captured insights about their customers' behavior patterns, product performance and general market trends in order change their business models into innovative services in novel markets. In the sections below, we present three unique examples of business organizations operating in the business-changing phases of big data business model.

7.7.3 Examples of the Business Metamorphosis Phase

Globally, many energy organizations are migrating into the "Home Energy Optimization" business by providing recommendations on replacing appliances using predictive maintenance data gathered from accurate insights (Lavalle et al. 2011; Morabito 2014). In addition, they recommend the particular brands to buy through decisions centered on the performance of dissimilar appliances as compared to consumer usage patterns, weather data and ecological circumstances e.g. energy costs and situations of local water supply.

Secondly, retailers are also migrating into the "Shopping Optimization" occupation by endorsing some particular products given a customer's existing purchasing patterns as compared with other customers alike (Manyika et al. 2013).

Thirdly, major airlines migrating their business processes into the "Travel Delight" business which exceeds the offering of rebates on air travel based on the travelling behaviors, frequencies and preferences of customers; but also re-searching on economically viable deals on rental cars, hotels, local tourist sites, shows, and shopping in the areas of interest.

7.8 Big Data Change Key Issues

We suggest there are three fundamental issue areas that need to be addressed in dealing with big data: *storage issues*, *management issues*, and *processing issues*. It is worth noting that each of these represents a large set of technical research challenges in its own right, likewise.

7.8.1 Storage Issues

The amount of information has blasted each time a new storage medium that has been invented. What is different the most recent explosion—mainly because of online social networking—is that current storage medium is not suitable to face it. Besides, information is continuously made by everybody and everything (e.g., gadgets, and so on.), and not just, as to this point, by experts, for example, researcher, columnists, scholars, etc. (Wielki 2013).

Current disk technology cut-off points are around 4 TB for every disk. In this way, 1 EB would oblige 25,000 disks. Regardless of the possibility that an Exabyte of information could be transformed on a single computer system, it would be not able to directly attach the vital number of disks. Access to that information would overpower current communication networks. Expecting that a 1 GB for every second system has a compelling feasible exchange rate of 80 %, the acceptable data transmission is around 100 MB (Russom 2013). Thus, exchanging an Exabyte would take around 2,800 h, in the event that we accept that a maintained exchange could be maintained. It would take more time to transmit the information from an accumulation or capacity point to a processing point than it would to transform it. Two results show themselves in this situation. First and foremost, process the information "set up" and transmit just the resultant data. Consequently, "bring the code to the information", in contrast to the conventional technique for "bring the information to the code" (Kaisler et al. 2013). Secondly, perform triage on the information and transmit just that information which is critical to downstream analysis. Notwithstanding, integrity and source metadata ought to be transmitted alongside the actual data (Computer Research Association 2011). Also, with the growing challenges of transmitting and storing the massive volume of data, the reliability of results derived from downstream analysis needs to undergo effective validation processes in order to produce accurate insights.

7.8.2 Management Issues

Management is the most challenging issue in dealing with big data. This issue initially surfaced 10 years prior in the UK eScience activities where data was circulated geologically by numerous elements. Determining issues of access, metadata, usage, overhauling, and influence have ended up being significant hindrances. Dissimilar to the accumulation of data by manual systems, where thorough conventions are regularly followed with a specific end goal to guarantee correctness and validity, computerized data gathering is significantly looser. The wealth of advanced data representation precludes a tailored technique for data gathering (Kwon et al. 2014).

Data capability frequently centers more on missing data than attempting to validate every item. Information is regularly fine-grained, for example, clickstream or metering information. Given the volume, it is unrealistic to accept each data item: new methodologies to data validation are required. The wellsprings of this data vary—both transiently and spatially, by organization, as well as system for accumulation. People help advanced data in mediums convenient to them: such as reports, drawings, pictures, sound and multimedia recordings, models, programming practices, client interface outlines, and so on—with or without sufficient metadata depicting what, when, where, who, why and how it was gathered and its provenance. Still, these categories of data are promptly accessible for assessment and analysis (Kwon et al. 2014).

7.8.3 Processing and Analytics Issues

The effective processing of Exabyte's of data necessitates wide-ranging parallel processing and novel analytics algorithms for the purpose of well-timed and

Table 7.1 Summary of differences between big data analytics and traditional data analytics (Dandawate 2013; Yan 2013)

	Big data analytics	Traditional data analytics
Data structures	An ecosystem appropriate for semi-structured and un-structured data	An ecosystem appropriate for structured data only
	The volume unit is usually in terabyte or petabyte	The volume unit is usually in megabyte/gigabyte
Population used for analysis	Data analysis of unknown population samples	Data analysis of known population samples
Technologies adopted	NoSQL approach to data	Relational database models
	Uses Hadoop framework	SQL approach
	Parallel data processing	Batch processing of static data
Research and development	Collaborative working ecosystem	Individuals can work independently

Traditional data are normally collected in a structured manner while big data takes an unstructured form actionable information (Kaisler et al. 2013). Traditional data processing systems are unfit for absorbing the vast volumes of big data and cannot be executed in seconds or a couple of minutes (see Table 7.1 for a comparison between big data analytics and Traditional Data Analytics). There are relatively few available guidelines to achieve expansive amounts of insights from semi- or unstructured data (Jacobs 2009). Unfortunately, this issue cannot be tackled by dimensional modeling and online analytical processing (OLAP). To enhance a faster processing time, some technical considerations which are calculated into the systems design, e.g. the degree of the ratio of the speed of sequential disk reads to the speed of random memory access. However, we aim to elucidate more on this issue in the following section as we delve into the organizational challenges and opportunities of big data.

7.9 Organizational Challenges

Big Data comes from various data generating sources such as, e.g., scientific experiments and simulations, which are capable of producing petabytes of data on a daily basis. A huge volume of these data are relatively irrelevant and therefore can be filtered by orders of scale. These challenges requires urgent research in the science of data reduction that can logically process raw data into a size that users can deal with without losing useful insights. Likewise, online analysis methods capable of processing such streaming data at real time are also needed to solve these challenges. The organizational challenges discussed are concerning data acquisition, information extraction, Data Integration, Aggregation, and Representation.

7.9.1 Data Acquisition

One of the major organizational challenges is associated with the process of data collection and processing. For instance, if a sensor analysis results vary considerably from others: it is probably because the sensor is damaged, nevertheless there is also an uncertainty if the artifact that deserves attention (Madden 2012). Additionally, the data collected by these sensors are mostly spatially and temporally correlated (El Abbadi 2011).

Another enormous challenge is to automatically create the appropriate metadata to portray the type of data recorded as well as how it is recorded and measured. For instance, in experimental analysis, extensive insight in regards to particular exploratory conditions and methods may be required to have the capacity to translate the results accurately, and it is vital that such metadata be recorded with observational data (Hampton et al. 2013). Metadata procurement frameworks can minimize the human load in recording metadata. An alternate imperative issue here is information provenance. Recording data about the information at its introduction to the world is not valuable unless this data might be deciphered and helped along through the data analysis pipeline. For example, a processing blunder at one stage can render ensuing analysis futile; with suitable provenance, we can undoubtedly distinguish all subsequent data processing that relies on this stage. Hence, research is needed into producing suitable metadata and into data frameworks that convey the provenance of data and its metadata through data analysis systems.

7.9.2 Information Extraction

Recurrently, the data collected exists in a format, which may be unready for analysis. Let us consider the gathering of health records electronically, which involves transcribed notations from numerous doctors, organized data from sensors and measurements and image data such as X-rays. Such data cannot be left in this form and efficiently analyzed. Reasonably, a data extraction process is needed to draw out the essential information from the underlying sources and then present it appropriate for analysis (Sagiroglu and Sinanc 2013).

The process of achieving this goal is an on-going technical challenge. The myth that "Big data is always accurate" is essentially far from the truth. For instance, hospital patients may decide to protect unsafe behavior and then medical personnel may occasionally misdiagnose an illness. In addition, patients may also incorrectly remember the name of a drug which could lead to misplaced information about their medical records (Yan 2013). Current work on data cleaning accepts well-recognized restrictions on well-understood error models; for many evolving big data fields these do not exist (Blohm 2011; Williams et al. 2014).

7.9.3 Data Integration, Aggregation, and Representation

With the surge of big data, capturing and tossing it into an archive is insufficient. Let us consider for instance the data acquired from a scope of scientific investigations. In the event that we simply have a bundle of data sets in a storehouse, it is unlikely that anyone will ever have the capacity to discover, let alone reuse the data. For many organizations, the availability of satisfactory metadata offers hope on better analytics, although, a few reliability challenges may be faced due to inconsistencies with results derived from repeated analytics (Russom 2013; Wielki 2013).

Moreover, the process of data analysis is significantly challenging, considering that the greater part of data integration, aggregation and representation needs to occur in a totally automated way in order to enable an efficient and extensive scale analysis. This process requires variations in the structure of data and semantics to be communicated in structures that are machine justifiable, and afterward mechanically resolvable. In this regard, an extra research work is needed to accomplish a computerized-fault free uniqueness determination in data structuring (Dandawate 2013).

7.10 Case Studies

In this section we discuss fact-sheets of case studies, which illustrate at a glance how the issues presented in previous sections have been addressed by real businesses.

The first case study considers Adobe, the multinational computer software company headquartered in San Jose, California, United States, focused upon the creation of multimedia and creativity software products. However, the business model of Adobe has profoundly improved over the last few years. Alongside the sales of software manually, Adobe has integrated cloud-based subscriptions to its business model (Cui et al. 2014). Consequently, products now quickly released and upgrades are incessant as compared to their previous business model of providing upgrades every 18 months (Mullich 2014). A significant part of this innovation is the customer interactions, which are now incessant and happening through multiple channels, e.g. social media, e-mail, the call center, direct sales and display ads. Also, there has been a radical transformation on the types of customer, transactions and product data now accessible by Adobe. Although before the evolution of concept of big data, the Adobe customer data were restricted to name, location and billing details. The explosion of big data has pushed Adobe into collecting information on how customers are using their products. With these sorts of data, they are able to gain better understanding about the purchasing behavior of customers and probably meet their future expectations (Davenport and Dyché 2013). Though customer insights were provided through their multiple interactive channels, Adobe encountered the problem of fractured and channel-specific views. The organization desired to advance an all-inclusive assessment of customers to convey an extremely custom-made, appealing user-experience. In addition to this challenge, the organization needed a real-time data on business performance information to enable employees find the precise data they desired rather than sorting through dumps of data.

Adobe implemented a cross-functional cooperation, integrating large sets of data, providing a single form of performance metrics, reacting to customer indications in milliseconds and enabling data-driven exploits in order to solve the challenges highlighted. One of the huge breakthroughs of Adobe regarding big data is the provision of analytics and other promotion tools by offering Creative Cloud to enable access to Adobe applications. Even though the organization was able to monitor how customers reacted to a definite marketing inventiveness the combination of such information with customers e-mail messages and posts on social media was quite cumbersome (Cui et al. 2014).

Point of Attention: The creation of a comprehensive strategy driven by analytics is a core factor for managing effectively change for big data driven innovation, due to its direct connection with the data itself combined with its extensible integration capabilities with other business processes.

To solve the data correlational issues, Adobe executed a comprehensive data strategy called the Adobe Dash (Mullich 2014). Adobe Dash is a commercial intelligence platform that performs real time connections of data across numerous sources. In-memory computing was also adopted due to the weakness of traditional databases in aggregating data at a proportionate speed. Therefore, with the ability to rapidly aggregate data from various channels through in-memory computing, Adobe now provides more tailored customer interactions and a reliable user-experience. For example, once customers click on online classified ads, Adobe provides them a matching identity and a custom-made message built on that information. Such personalized marketing often conforms to the preferences of their customers.

The second case study analyses Hewlett-Packard (HP) as a leading advocate of big data. As at the time of putting this book together, HP had an intensive supply chain which delivers 120 PCs, 100 printers, 1,200 inks and toner cartridges, seven network devices, seven terabytes of storage and five servers every 60 s (Prophet 2013). The greatest factor that has ensured the successes of their shipments is the result of limitless actions and timely decisions made during the course of the worldwide supply chain. One of the biggest challenges technology giants like HP encounters is the means of coordinating their decisions to enhance pricing, decrease out-of-stocks and move manufacturing to support the ever-increasing demands of their customers. Similar to Adobe, HP has adopted in-memory computing, which allows real-time resolutions through rapid analysis of big data. With In-memory computing, HP is able to take speedy actions based on insights into its financial scheduling, inventory processes and Enterprise Resource Planning (ERP).

Point of Attention: The impact of Storage and Processing hugely affects the reliability of insights derived from big data, consequently impacting on real time decisions made by business organizations. Therefore, organizations have to improve the storage and processing capacity of their systems to prevent making flawed critical business decisions.

Using the testing and experimentation big data innovative technique previously discussed, the data query speeds of HP has been enhanced from a 2 h average with traditional relational databases to only 88.23 s using in-memory computing (De Fortuny et al. 2013; Jain 2011; Prophet 2013). The implication of these outstanding results is that the employees of HP will never encounter the normal fluctuations in processing times, which differs depending on the storage location of the data. This has a positive effect on employee satisfaction as well as motivation towards meeting market demands and customers' varying desires. Employees' motivation to fulfill market demands could be related to the efficient performance of the system enabling them to meet various organizational goals are targets. Furthermore, data can now be processed and accessible automatically due to in-built analytics, dashboards and reporting tools, empowering employees to rapidly take remedial actions and grab prospects. By means of improved insights into economic, inventory and supply-chain data, HP is now able to respond to technical and business concerns more swiftly while effectively managing risk and predicting future customer demands just like Adobe. In today's era of big data, the goal for an insightful-driven analytics is to develop transforming data processes and enabling novel capabilities for business innovation (Prophet 2013).

7.11 Recommendation for Business Organizations

As earlier mentioned, organizations are now integrating the dataset of each in-house business units in order to pool resources that provides useful insights from large data-sets. Some of the innovative techniques we mentioned such as, integration of data, testing through experimentation, real-time customization, algorithmic and automated-controlled analysis and generating data-driven models need to work a relatively inter-connected fashion for a revolutionary innovation to occur. Nevertheless, there are gaps for improvement especially in the extraction and interpretation process of big data. A more efficient method of accurate big data analytics needs to be developed because major decisions are now being made from this process.

Consequently, managing effectively change for big data driven innovation, C-Level employees are now being influenced by insights gathered from big data. This was not the case before; Big Data is now making non-technical employees becoming relatively technical (Davenport and Patil 2012). In addition to these discoveries, we have learnt that the distinctive advantage of big data as compared to many other technological advances is the predictive analytical insights it offers. With the right tools and skilled persons, the impact of big data is far-reaching beyond what we can ever imagine. However, business organizations have a lot of technical and non-technical modifications to make on their existing models if they are keen to optimizing the gains of big data. Thus, adopting an incentivized approach which will ensure that employees are encouraged to integrate big data to their daily operations is a strategic change absolutely imperative.

From this we can understand, that the adaptation to big data and analytics must be a culture for every employee and not only the ones that are technically savvy. Moving along, we identified certain methodologies, which existing business organizations are using to actively introduce new products and services. From the examples provided on IBM, a startling discovery on how a unique business system can be developed from the key business process of an organization was identified. This means that a business organization has the capability of reducing its in-house managerial budgets if the innovative methodologies discussed are implemented. The actual and potential benefits provided by big data and analytics come with severe challenges for a business. We explained the complex issues surrounding data acquisition, information extraction and data aggregation as well as possible remediation techniques. So far the capabilities of big data by far outweigh the obvious challenges encountered by many organizations. The world of business is now experiencing a radical change not only with scale but most importantly speed. Therefore, we highly recommend that on-going research work and action at organizational level in this field should focus on novel approaches for reducing errors during big data extraction and analytics processes. This would increase the reliability of gathered insights and then lessen the risks associated with devastating decisions made due to a faulted computerized data structuring system.

7.12 Summary

This chapter has discussed how big data has become a key organizational asset, which represents a strategic basis for business competition. The radical development illustrated in previous sections is now influencing business organizations to consider new innovative techniques on maximizing the potentials of big data. We highlighted that the success of many organizations demands new skills as well as new perspectives on how the epoch of big data could advance the speed of business processes. One important factor of this technological process is the new analytics tools that have evolved together with new progressive business models. In this chapter, we explored the innovative capabilities of the growing big data phenomenon and addressed various issues concerning its methodologies for changes. Our findings are substantiated by describing the real-life cases of Adobe and Hewlett Packard organizations, which are globally considered as one of the biggest drivers of big data analytics.

We have addressed various issues concerning big data's innovation techniques and modeling strategies adopted by many large business organizations. Without a doubt, it is clearly seen that big data is now integrated into the business processes of most organizations not because of the buzz it attracts but for its innovative capabilities to completely transform any business landscape. Although there the innovative techniques of big data are ever evolving, we were able to cover five significant ones, which are paving way for the development of new products and services for many organizations. We gave illustrations on Adobe and HP organizations that have increased the velocity of their decision making processes as well as improving consumer-buying behaviors through the integrated dashboard processing analytics capabilities of big data.

References

Bain Insights: The big data boom is your company ready. http://www.forbes.com/sites/baininsights/2013/10/30/the-big-data-boom-is-your-company-ready/ (2013)
Batty, M.: Big data, smart cities and city planning. Dialog. Hum. Geogr. 3(3), 274–279 (2013)
Bell, S.: Data-driven innovation. http://www.computerweekly.com/feature/Data-driven-innovation (2013). Accessed 18 Nov 2014
Bjelland, O.M., Wood, R.C.: An inside view of IBM' s "innovation jam". MIT Sloan Manage. Rev. 50101 (2008)

Blohm, S.: Large-Scale Pattern-Based Information Extraction from the World Wide Web. KIT Scientific Publishing (2011)

Bollier, D., Firestone, C.M.: The Promise and Peril of Big Data. The Aspen Institute (2010)

Bughin, J., Chui, M., Manyika, J.: Clouds, big data, and smart assets: ten tech-enabled business trends to watch. McKinsey Q. **56**, 1–14 (2010)

Bughin, J., Chui, M., Manyika, J.: Ten IT-enabled business trends for the decade ahead. McKinsey Q. (2013)

Chen, H., Chiang, R.H.L, Storey, V.C: Business intelligence and analytics: from big data to big impact. MIS Q. **36**(4), 1165–1188 (2012)

Computer Research Association: Challenges and opportunities with big data. Community white paper. http://cra.org/ccc/docs/init/ (2011). Accessed 18 Nov 2014

Couchbase: Making the shift from relational to NoSQL. Couchbase (2010)

Couchbase: Why NoSQL? Couchbase (2013)

Cui, B., et al.: Big data: the driver for innovation in databases. Natl. Sci. Rev. **1**(1), 27–30 (2014)

Dandawate, Y. (ed.): Big data: challenges and opportunities—big data: countering tomorrow's challenges. Infosys Labs Brief. **11**(1) (2013)

Davenport, T.H., Dyché, J.: Big data in big companies. Int. Inst. Anal. (2013)

Davenport, T.H., Patil, D.J.: Data scientist: the sexiest job of the 21st century. Harv. Bus. Rev. **90**, 70–76 (2012)

De Fortuny, E.J., Martens, D., Provost, F.: Predictive modeling with big data: is bigger really better? Big Data **1**(4), 215–226 (2013)

Dean, J., Ghemawat, S.: MapReduce: simplified data processing on large clusters. Commun. ACM **51**(1), 1–13 (2008)

Demchenko, Y.: Defining the Big Data Architecture Framework (BDAF). SNE Group, University of Amsterdam, Amsterdam (2013)

Drake, J.L., et al. (eds.): New Trends in Earth-Science Outreach and Engagement. Springer International Publishing, Cham (2014)

Economics, P.: Big data, big brother, big money. Q. J. Econ. **11**, 85–89 (2013)

Eisenhardt, K.M., Martin, J.A.: Dynamic capabilities: what are they? Strateg. Manag. J. **21**(10–11), 1105–1121 (2000)

El Abbadi, A: Big data and cloud computing: current state and future opportunities. In: Proceedings of the 14th International Conference on Extending Database Technology. ACM, pp. 530–533 (2011)

El-Darwiche, B., Koch, V., Meer, D., Shehadi, R.T., Tohme, W.: Big data maturity: an action plan for policymakers and executives. In: Bilbao-Osorio, B., Dutta, S., Lanvin, B. (eds.) The Global Information Technology Report 2014—Rewards and Risks of Big Data. World Economic Forum, pp. 43–51 (2014)

Elmqvist, N., Irani, P.: Ubiquitous analytics: interacting with big data anywhere, anytime. Computer (Long. Beach. Calif.) **46**(4), 86–89 (2013)

EMC: Big data transforms. The life science commercial model. EMC (2013)

EY: Big data—changing the way businesses compete and operate. EYGM Limited. (2014)

Fan, W., Bifet, A.: Mining big data: current status, and forecast to the future. ACM SIGKDD Explor. News Lett. **14**(2), 1–5 (2012)

Fayyad, U., Uthurusamy, R. (eds.): Evolving data into mining solutions for insights. Commun. ACM **45**(8), 28–31 (2002)

Gobble, M.M.: Resources: big data: the next big thing in innovation. Res. Manag. **56**(1), 64–67 (2013)

Groves, P., Kayyali, B., Knott, D., Van Kuiken, S.: The "Big Data" Revolution in Healthcare-Accelerating Value and Innovation. McKinsey & Company, Chicago (2013)

Hampton, S.E., et al.: Big data and the future of ecology. Front. Ecol. Environ. **11**(3), 156–162 (2013)

Hartmann, P.M., Zaki, M., Feldmann, N., Neely, A.: Big Data for Big Business? A Taxonomy of Data-Driven Business Models Used by Start-up Firms. University of Cambridge, Cambridge Service Alliance (2014)
HM Revenue and Customs: Annual report and accounts 2012–13. HM Revenue and Customs (2013)
Huo, J. et al.: BESIU physical analysis on Hadoop platform. J. Phys. Conf. Ser. **513**(3), 032044 (2014)
Jacobs, A.: The pathologies of big data. Commun. ACM **52**(8), 36–44 (2009)
Jain, P.: New trends and future applications/directions of institutional repositories in academic institutions. Libr. Rev. **60**(2), 125–141 (2011)
Ji, C. et al.: Big data processing: big challenges and opportunities. J. Interconnect. Netw. **13**(3–4), 1250009 (2012)
Jinbao, Z., Wang, A.: Data modeling for big data. CA Technologies (2012)
Kaisler, S., et al.: Big data: issues and challenges moving forward. In: 2013 46th Hawaii International Conference on System Sciences, pp. 995–1004 (2013)
Kelly, J., Vellante, D., Floyer, D.: Big data market size and vendor revenues. http://wikibon.org/wiki/v/Big_Data_Market_Size_and_Vendor_Revenues (2014). Accessed 18 Nov 2014
Kwon, O., et al.: Data quality management, data usage experience and acquisition intention of big data analytics. Int. J. Inf. Manage. **34**(3), 387–394 (2014)
Lavalle, S., Lesser, E., Shock-ley, R., Hopkins, M.S., Kruschwitz, N.: Big data, analytics and the path from insights to value. MIT Sloan Manage. Rev. **52**(2) (2011)
Lohr, S.: The age of big data. http://www.nytimes.com/2012/02/12/sunday-review/big-datas-impact-in-the-world.html?pagewanted=all&_r=0 (2012). Accessed 18 Nov 2014
Louridas, P., Ebert, C.: Embedded analytics and statistics for big data. IEEE Softw. **30**(6), 33–39 (2013)
Madden, S.: From databases to big data. IEEE Internet Comput. **16**, 1–2 (2012)
Manyika, J., Chui, M., Bughin, J., Dobbs, R., Bisson, P., Marrs, A.: Disruptive technologies: advances that will transform life, business, and the global economy. McKinsey Global Institute (2013)
McAfee, A., Brynjolfsson, E.: Big data: the management revolution. Harv. Bus. Rev. **90**(10), 60–68 (2012)
Meeker, W.Q., Hong, Y.: Reliability meets big data: opportunities and challenges. Qual. Eng. **26**(1), 102–116 (2014)
Miluzzo, E.: I'm Cloud 2.0, and I'm not just a data center. IEEE Internet Comput. **18**(3), 73–77 (2014). doi:10.1109/MIC.2014.53
Mithas, S., Lee, M.R., Earley, S., Murugesan, S., Djavanshir, R.: Leveraging big data and business analytics. IEEE IT Prof. **15**(6), 18–20 (2013)
Morabito, V.: Trends and Challenges in Digital Business Innovation. Springer International Publishing, Cham (2014)
Mullich, J.: Adobe gets personal with customers. Adobe Systems (2014)
Obeng-Odoom, F.: The future of our cities. Cities **26**(1), 49–53 (2009)
Olson, B.M.: HADOOP: scalable, flexible data storage and analysis. IQT Q. **1**(3), 14–18 (2010)
Özcan, F. et al.: Are we experiencing a big data bubble? In: Proceedings of the 2014 ACM SIGMOD International Conference *on* Management of Data—SIGMOD'14, pp. 1407–1408 (2014)
Parmar, R., Cohn, D.L., Marshall, A.: Driving innovation through data. IBM Global Business Services (2014)
Parmar, R., Mackenzie, I., Cohn, D., Gann, D.: The new patterns of innovation. Harv. Bus. Rev. https://hbr.org/2014/01/the-new-patterns-of-innovation (2014). Accessed 18 Nov 2014
Pearson, B.T., Wegener, R.: Big data: the organizational challenge. Bain Co. (2013)
Piatetsky-Shapiro, G.: Comment on "A revolution that will transform how we live, work, and think: an interview with the authors of big data". Big Data **1**(4), 193–193 (2013)

References

Prophet, T.: Investing in transportation to improve supply chain efficiency at HP. http://www8.hp.com/hpnext/posts/investing-transportation-improve-supply-chain-efficiency-hp#.VGvO6IdJOjk (2013). Accessed 18 Nov 2014

Provost, F., Fawcett, T.: Data science and its relationship to big data and data-driven decision making. Big Data **1**(1), 51–59 (2013)

Qubole, A.T.: How big data is revolutionizing the food industry. WIRED innovation insights. http://www.wired.com/2014/02/big-data-revolutionizing-food-industry/ (2014). Accessed 19 Nov 2014

Russom, P.: Big data analytics. TDWI best practices report (2011)

Russom, P.: Managing big data. TDWI best practices report (2013)

Sagiroglu, S., Sinanc, D.: Big data: a review. In: 2013 International Conference on Collaboration Technologies and Systems, pp. 42–47 (2013)

Saleem, M.A.: Lightweight stack for big data analytics. Head of Department: Dr. Steve Linton, Supervisor: Dr. Adam Barker, Department of Computer Science, University of St Andrews, June 2014 Declaration (2014)

Schmarzo, B.: Big data business model maturity chart—EMC^2 InFocus. https://infocus.emc.com/william_schmarzo/big-data-business-model-maturity-chart/ (2012). Accessed 18 Nov 2014

Serenko, A., Bontis, N., Hull, E.: An application of the knowledge management maturity model: the case of credit unions. In: Proceedings of the Twentieth Americas Conference on Information Systems, Savannah (ICIS2014), pp. 1–10 (2014)

Stonebraker, M., Madden, S., Dubey, P.: Intel "big data" science and technology center vision and execution plan. SIGMOD Rec. **42**(1), 44–49 (2013)

Taylor, W.C., Labarre, P.: Mavericks at Work: Why the Most Original Minds in Business Win. HarperCollins e-books, New York (2006)

Wanderman-milne, S., Li, N.: Runtime code generation in Cloudera Impala. IEEE Data Eng. Bull. **37**(1), 31–37 (2014)

Wielki, J.: Implementation of the big data concept in organizations—possibilities, impediments and challenges. In: FEDCSIS, pp. 985–989 (2013)

Williams, K., Wu, J., Choudhury, S.R., Khabsa, M., Giles, C.L.: Scholarly big data information extraction and integration in the CiteSeer^X digital library. In: 2014 IEEE 30th International Conference on Data Engineering Work (ICDEW) (2014)

Yan, J.: Big data, bigger opportunities collaborate in the era of big data—Data.gov's roles: promote, lead, contribute, and collaborate in the era of big data. Data.gov, U.S. General Services Administration (2013)

Part III
Innovation Practices

Big Data and Analytics Innovation Practices

8

Abstract

This chapter focuses on examples of data intensive innovations in practice, providing fact-sheets of 10 interesting ideas in the field of big data and analytics worldwide in 2014. The genesis of the selected ideas lies mostly in innovative research projects that have developed successfully, becoming start-ups and spin-offs and reaching the market, where they are currently applied. For each innovation we provide an introduction to the main characteristics of the solution, information about its developer coupled with technology and market readiness indicators that can help in assessing the time-to-market, as well as some indicators of user value in terms of perception, such as the user experience aspect and the so called "Wow" effect.

8.1 Introduction

The combination of technological advances in data analytics, the increasing availability of large data sources, the attention the topic is getting and genuine innovative efforts have contributed to generating, in the last years, a number of start-ups focusing on the topic. The need for connecting physical actions, experiences, and characteristics with their digital counterpart is ever more urgent, as it allows to integrate the two worlds and act on them in a multi-dimensional level. Understanding the opportunities arising from this very dynamic area of innovation requires to observe directly the projects and topics research centers are working on. When the idea is valuable, the underlying research project often becomes a spin-off or a start-up, reaching to the market in short time and developing through experience and collaboration the execution capability to make it possible. The ideas selected and presented in this chapter originate mostly in effective research projects launched first by excellence centers all over the World, that have been developed and brought to the market, and are now being applied. The continuous scouting activity conducted to prepare this part of research gives us tools to evaluate and select interesting topics and ideas to keep in the innovation radar. This approach, together with the drivers of competitiveness relative to time-to-market and user value, has been developed and presented in Morabito (2014).

8.2 Sociometric Solution

The key concept at the core of Sociometric Solution is the "human cue": each person spreads around many cues that can be captured through voice and position in space, offering behavioral signals ready to be interpreted. The company that has turned into practice an MIT research stream, adopts the approach of a three-stepped process:

i. human metric identification,
ii. data sensing, by means of sensor-carrier badges,
iii. analysis and insights elaboration.

The Sociometric Badges are small sensor-rich tools that employees wear for a certain time, allowing the collection and tracking of a vast amount of data related to a set of human cues. Tracking includes tone of voice, time spent speaking versus listening, connections and exchanges among individuals, movement and routes around the offices. All data collected in this way is analyzed in order to understand the human dynamics in the organization, through quantitative and objective data representing, as much as possible, the reality. The kind of insights offered by Sociometric enable the testing of hypotheses on layout, organization and team structure that analytics intensive companies usually perform on their websites and digital platforms, allowing to modify organizations in order to increase effective communication and interaction between employees. As technology improves and the data accumulate, it becomes progressively easier to make those experiments.

8.2.1 Developer

Sociometric Solutions® was founded by Ben Waber, Daniel Olguin-Olguin, Taemie Kim, and Alex Pentland from the Human Dynamics Laboratory at MIT and Tuomas Jaanu from Aalto University in Finland (Sociometric Solutions 2014). The founders share research interests in the field of organizational dynamics, social sensing technologies, "human analytics" and "weak communication signals". While it is widely acknowledged that effective communication and knowledge transfer are crucial to an organization's success, these behaviors are very difficult to measure. According to Sociometric Solutions (2014) surveys and human observation provide often biased and limited views into communication behaviors. Thus, their results are actually of little practical usefulness for organizations or at least require for additional effort in terms of generalization. Consequently, developers were strongly committed to find a way to deploy in practice the "network intelligence" theory of

Table 8.1 Company competitiveness indicators for time-to-market

Solution	Sociometric Solutions
Founded	2009
No. of products	1
Clients	Enterprises
Partners	Different companies
Market dimension	Growing
Competitors	No
Enabling infrastructure	Not relevant

social signaling (Pentland 2008), describing how we can harness the intelligence of our social network to become better managers, workers, and communicators.

In Table 8.1 there is a synthetic representation of some of the drivers of competitiveness with a focus on a time-to-market relevant characteristics. The measures are intended to describe the readiness of the technology, of the company, of the market (both demand and offer side) and of the complementary infrastructure. In particular, year of foundation and number of products are included as a proxy of the stability of the company. Furthermore, the presence of clients substitutes a measure of the product readiness; while the presence of strong incumbent companies as partners in the development phase is another indicator of solidity.

The dimension of the market and its growth, combined with the presence of competitors, indicate a certain level of readiness of the demand, which signals a higher likeliness of a fast rate of diffusion of the product. Finally, the presence of the enabling infrastructure is a complement and, thus, dependent on the readiness of the technology itself, since whenever it is ready it can be effectively deployed only if the infrastructure is ready as well. As appears from the table, Sociometric Solutions is increasing its presence through different projects in a growing number of companies.

8.2.2 Applications

The value behind such kinds of innovation lies mainly in an increased understanding of companies' employees behavioral patterns. The company's research has supported the importance of face-to-face interactions and communication, and building larger networks among peers. One finding from the firm's research was that simple physical changes such as having larger tables in a cafeteria facilitated more interaction and collaboration among colleagues than smaller tables. Another finding emphasized the importance of group breaks and office spaces, which facilitate such breaks as having an important effect on employee morale and efficacy. While Sociometric Solutions collects full data through its sensors, it anonymizes the data in its customer reports, only plotting broader patterns and connections to productivity rather than individual tracking and performance (Sociometric Solution 2014).

Table 8.2 User value indicators

Fast learning	Yes
User interface	Good
User experience	Positive
Process impact	Medium
User feedback	Positive
"Wow" effect	Medium

Table 8.2 shows the set of drivers used to capture the concept of *User Value*. In this case the potential user is the employee in the company conducting the assessment, therefore a good user interface and user experience is crucial for increasing engagement and adoption.

The application is simple and does not require much learning. The impact is intended as a measure of how much the use of this innovation changes the established processes for the user, therefore impacting on their willingness to change it. The "Wow" effect is intended as the level of attraction and positive impact on the user, which in this case is "Medium" due also to the sensitive characteristics of the solution.

8.3 Invenio

Invenio is a process mining software that is able to design the organization processes by reading the structured and unstructured information of a given company (Invenio 2014). Invenio processes application log files, documents, email messages, and social signals to optimize an organization business processes. Its force resides in the quality and efficacy of the graphic representation of the processes, even the hidden ones, underlying companies operations. Through the interactive visualization it is possible to dive deep into specific processes, test changes and modify directly issuing new maps and workflows.

8.3.1 Developer

Invenio is a Malta based company, founded in 2012 with the goal of empowering companies to better understand and map operative processes. The founding team includes an Italian entrepreneur, who was fascinated by the prospect to understand in detail working flows. Thanks to his 20 years experience in IT consulting he could apply precious expertise to enhance working processes understanding.

In Table 8.3 the representation of the drivers of competitiveness on a time-to-market basis shows, in synthesis, an advanced development of the technology behind Invenio and a growing demand of the market.

Table 8.3 Company competitiveness indicators for time-to-market

Solution	Invenio
Founded	2012
No. of products	1
Clients	Enterprises
Partners	Distribution partner
Market dimension	Growing interest
Competitors	Few
Enabling infrastructure	Ready

Table 8.4 User value indicators

Fast learning	Yes
User interface	Positive
User experience	Positive
Process impact	Low
User feedback	Positive
"Wow" effect	Medium

8.3.2 Applications

The application matches and confronts event data (i.e. observed behavior) and process models (specific input or discovered automatically). This technology can be applied to any type of operational processes. Also, potential applications can be found where dynamic behaviors need to be related to process models, returning a decision tree, a collection of clusters, or frequent patterns.

In Table 8.4 the drivers show a very high level of *User Value*. The design of the application is simple and easy to grasp. The impact on established processes is low, as the analysis does not require specific data collection and happens automatically. Feedback from users has been very positive and is likely to foster a snowball effect in adoption.

8.4 Evolv

Evolv, named one of the world's top 10 most innovative companies in big data, is a workforce science platform that analyzes employee performance data and provides information for HR decision-making (Evolv 2014). Leveraging big data, it helps solve workforce performance issues for the C-suite by using a configurable cloud services platform. Evolv's patented technology platform unifies and supplements existing data from current systems, then using them to identify fact-based workforce insights that can drive measurable ROI (Evolv 2014). Thus, Evolv exploits data-driven methodology to help companies discover the core reasons behind workforce performance, enabling executives to make better operational business decisions.

Evolv was acquired in 2014 by Cornerstone OnDemand, a leader in cloud-based applications for talent management. The company's solutions help organizations recruit, train, manage and engage their employees, empowering their people and increasing workforce productivity. Thus, the acquisition of Evolv is expected to expand Cornerstone by providing a platform enabling organizations to use relevant internal and external data to factually evaluate the skills, work experience and personalities of their employees and job candidates. Furthermore, Cornerstone expects that same technology to serve as the engine to develop insights on the massive data set accumulated by the company over the past decade from its more than 1,800 global clients.

8.4.1 Developer

Max Symkoff co-founded Evolv in 2006 because he recognized the future development in aligning employer needs with employee talents, while today he supervises all aspects of Evolv strategy and operations as its CEO (Crunchbase 2014). Moreover, Jim Meyerle, Symkoff's co-founder, thought of Evolv as a mean to redefine how employers and job seekers go about finding each other. At first, the challenge was making sure they had the right team to build and develop the vision they had for using data to improve the match between employers and employees. Neither of them had a deep technological background, while the problem they wanted to solve required highly technical knowledge, so they hired other people who were technically competent to do it.

Because their biggest initial risk to growth was hiring a great technical team, they focused on making sure they had the right hiring model; thus, they established a competency model for success within their specific company environment, enlisting the help of industrial organizational psychologists to identify which technical and behavioral competencies would be critical for success in a company like theirs and they assigned each person on the hiring team to focus on evaluating candidates for each one of these competency areas (Fast Company 2014a).

In Table 8.5 the time-to-market drivers of competitiveness display an advanced development of the company and the market, with a ready technology and no issues

Table 8.5 Company competitiveness indicators for time-to-market

Solution	Evolv
Founded	2007
No. of products	1
Clients	Enterprises
Partners	Cornerstone performance cloud
Market dimension	Growing
Competitors	Few
Enabling infrastructure	Ready

Table 8.6 User value indicators

Fast learning	Medium
User interface	Very good
User experience	Very good
Process impact	High
User feedback	Positive
"Wow" effect	Medium

of integration with established processes and enabling infrastructures, also because it is provided as a cloud solution, while there is still a lack of competitors.

8.4.2 Applications

Evolv helps employers better understand employees and job candidates by comparing their skills, work experience, and personalities. However, Evolv takes it to a deeper level, crunching more than 500 million data points on gas prices, unemployment rates, and social media usage to help clients such as, e.g., like Xerox predict, for example, when an employee is most likely to leave his job (Fast Company 2014b). Some insights Evolv's data scientists have discovered are, for example, people with two social media accounts perform much higher than those with either more or less of two, and in many careers, such as call-center work, employees with criminal backgrounds perform better than those with clean records (Lawrence 2014).

Table 8.6 shows an extremely high level of *User Value*. The application design is simple and well-conceived, and the functionalities are straightforward and easy to use.

The impact on established processes is high as it requires a change of mindset and culture, although in the end the result is a simplification of an existing process. Feedback from users has been very positive, and the reception of Evolv has been enthusiastic at all the conventions and competitions it has taken part in, winning the company a widespread support and a number of awards.

8.5 Essentia Analytics

Essentia Analytics' decision support software uses latest behavioral finance research to provide professional investors with an enhanced understanding of where their skills lie when evaluating their own performance, so that "they can do more of what they're good at and less of what they're not" (Essentia Analytics 2014).

According to Essentia Analytics (2014) all professional investors share the problem that they are selling skill, but getting paid for performance. However, performance is a measure of outcome and not a measure of skill, which is a function of the decisions we make. Conscious decisions can be improved by implementing process in a disciplined way, while unconscious decisions are more challenging, requiring first self-awareness for optimizing their influence. Essentia's decision support software enables fund managers to capture richer data about their own behavior, while improving the productivity and referenceability of their investment processes (Essentia Analytics 2014). Indeed, on the one hand, a more accurate picture of the past enables better conscious decisions in the future. On the other hand, Essentia's coaching partners identify behavioral patterns and correlations, and reveal actionable insights, enabling awareness of the unconscious influences, helping fund managers convert that awareness into behavioral change, thus, increasing the probability of success.

8.5.1 Developer

Formerly a fund manager, Clare Flynn Levy is founder and CEO at Essentia Analytics. She is an entrepreneur specialized in hedge-fund and financial software, behavioral finance and financial analysis. Essentia Analytics is at the nexus of Behavioral Finance and Data Science, developed by leading neuroscientists, software engineers and ex-fund managers (Essentia Analytics 2014). The result is a simple, accurate, continuous feedback loop, the same sort that professional athletes use to achieve excellence. Essentia Analytics, which is headquartered in London, was founded in 2013. The software was launched in March 2014.

In Table 8.7 competitiveness appears to be high on time-to-market drivers. The company is growing and the technology is developing and integrating with more partner technologies. The hedge fund sector is interested, especially in design-intensive companies and for advanced decision making activity.

8.5.2 Applications

Appropriate for traditional active managers, hedge funds and multi-manager platforms, high and low turnover portfolios, the software has already been adopted by several of the world's leading investment managers, including GLG Partners

Table 8.7 Company competitiveness indicators for time-to-market

Solution	Essentia Analytics
Founded	2013
No. of products	1
Clients	Fund managers
Partners	Growing
Market dimension	Growing
Competitors	No
Enabling infrastructure	Not relevant

Table 8.8 User value indicators

Fast learning	Medium
User interface	Medium
User experience	Medium
Process impact	Medium
User feedback	Very positive
"Wow" effect	High

(Man Group), Talisman Global Asset Management, and Union Investment, despite being less than 2 years old.

Table 8.8 suggests a high level of perception for the *User Value*, but with the caveat of expectations on the application results.

8.6 Ayasdi Core

Ayasdi is a solution using a visual approach to take the guesswork out of big data (Ayasdi Core 2014). Indeed, users of Ayasdi, such as, e.g., companies like Merck and Citigroup, deposit related data into its platform to generate a 3D map that uncovers new trends (Fast Company 2014b). The mathematic technique it adopts is called topological data analysis, which analyzes the shape of complex data, identifying clusters and their statistical significance that, finally, deliver a more accurate "big picture" of the data, representing, for example, clusters of patients or customers. Thus, the Ayasdi's tools allow for automated discovery instead of the previous model of having people type in search-style queries, which works only if a person knows the right question to ask, as pointed out by Gurjeet Singh, co-founder and chief executive of Ayasdi (Lohr 2013).

8.6.1 Developer

The data analysis start-up has been founded with the expertise of Gunnar Carlsson, a professor of mathematics at Stanford University. Dr. Carlsson was the principal investigator on research projects that were financed, from 2000 to 2008, with $10 million from the National Science Foundation and the Defense Advanced Research Projects Agency (DARPA) (Lohr 2013). In 2008, when Dr. Carlsson and the other co-founders decided to attempt to commercialize the research they received $1.25 million as a Small Business Innovation Research grant, for "high-risk, high-payoff research" (Lohr 2013). The prototype technology has been developed 2 years later and in 2013 it has its commercial launch. Ayasdi is not the only big data start-up in Silicon Valley, but while most of the others are focused on producing software to more efficiently manage data and handle queries, Ayasdi focused and produced a new important technique of mathematical analysis.

Table 8.9 Company competitiveness indicators for time-to-market

Solution	Ayasdi Core
Founded	2008
No. of products	1
Clients	Enterprise
Partners	Growing
Market dimension	Growing
Competitors	No
Enabling infrastructure	Ready

In Table 8.9 time-to-market drivers show a ready and on the market company facing a growing demand. The company development is continuing. Competitors are few and exhibit a more traditional approach. The infrastructure is ready as there is no need for anything other than a PC and an Internet connection.

8.6.2 Applications

Ayasdi's work has revealed genetic traits of cancer survivors and tracked the source of an E. coli outbreak to name some of its applications (Fast Company 2014b). Then, it created a visualization to help the Institute for the Study of War, a Washington, D.C.-based think tank, to map terrorist behavior in and around Baghdad during a campaign to free some imprisoned Al Qaeda members (Fast Company 2014b). Ayasdi's technology has also been used to investigate cross-species databases to accelerate biomedical discovery and treatment and it has been reported to be extremely good at detecting patterns and presenting them (Lohr 2013). As said above, Ayasdi has about 20 customers including Merck, the Food and Drug Administration, the United States Department of Agriculture, and several unnamed large corporations. They are using the company's technology mostly for drug discovery, oil and gas exploration, and financial-market research.

Table 8.10 shows a good level of perceived *User Value*, based on a great user interface and user experience, a very high level of novelty and "Wow" effect. Feedback from users has been very positive.

Table 8.10 User value indicators

Fast learning	Medium
User interface	Very good
User experience	Very good
Process impact	Medium
User feedback	Positive
"Wow" effect	High

8.7 Cogito Dialog

Cogito's systems aim to constantly collect and interpret the social signals underlying telephone conversations, video chats, and smartphone behavior (Cogito Dialog 2014). The underlying algorithms have been developed based on clinical studies and post-traumatic stress disorder (PTSD) patients. The system automatically tracks and analyzes facial expressions, body posture, acoustic features, linguistic patterns and higher-level behavior descriptors (for example, attention and fidgeting), in real-time. Cogito Dialog helps people interact on the phone by giving the accounts a real-time visualization of how they and the customer sound as they are speaking. This feedback promotes active listening, leading to more caring and empathetic communications. Dialog can monitor large populations for specific behavior patterns such as pain or engagement and inform managers as those patterns are recognized (Cogito Dialog 2014).

8.7.1 Developer

Founded in 2006, Cogito is a Boston-based technology company developing new ways of analyzing and understanding human communication and perception (see also our discussion in Morabito (2014)). They combine a decade of MIT Human Dynamics Lab research, represented by the Co-founder Professor Alex Pentland in the Management Team, with advanced signal processing and computational engineering capabilities, in order to track and model social signals exchanged in conversation and monitored through Smartphone-enabled mobile sensing systems. Cogito has been supported by Venture Mentoring System of MIT, which matches entrepreneurs with skilled volunteer mentors selected for their experience in areas relevant to the needs of new entrepreneurs and for their enthusiasm for the program.

In Table 8.11 the time-to-market competitiveness appears to be high, with a solid company, facing some competition but with a large market to tap, showing no need for additional enabling infrastructure.

Table 8.11 Company competitiveness indicators for time-to-market

Solution	Cogito Dialog
Founded	2007
No. of products	3
Clients	Enterprises
Partners	Research institutes
Market dimension	Greenfield
Competitors	Few
Enabling infrastructure	Ready

Table 8.12 User value indicators

Fast learning	Medium
User interface	Very good
User experience	Very good
Process impact	Medium to high
User feedback	Positive
"Wow" effect	High

8.7.2 Applications

Besides its commercial application in supporting communication rich activities, Cogito has been partnering with Raytheon-BBN and the United States Government's Defense Advanced Research Projects Agency (DARPA) to develop and validate a privacy-assured, secure and scalable mobile sensing platform that gathers trustworthy data from mobile phones, analyzes that data for patterns of psychological distress, stores the data securely, and allows each individual to see and share feedback on their overall mental health status. The platform has been deployed as part of a major Boston-area clinical trial that looks at behavior from individuals experiencing PTSD and depression and generates automatic symptom assessment models.

Companies use Cogito to gain insight into buying behavior, satisfaction, follow-through, and intervention needs of their customers. This improves decision-making, workflows, consistency of service, and successful interactions. Feedback from clients reports benefits such as, e.g., increase in productivity, improved sales performance, better data collection, and higher customer retention.

In Table 8.12 the *User Value* is quite high, with positive feedback from users. The impact on existing processes is quite high, due to the fact that the solution requires to set specific actions and procedures to make use of it, unless it is integrated in an existing activity as an improvement of sentiment recognition.

8.8 Tracx

Tracx is a software indexing social media and delivering the most relevant, high impact audiences and conversations about a brand (Tracx 2014). The platform allows marketers to sort through streams of social media data and drill down to provide geographic, demographic, and psychographic insights and to monitor performance against competitors while planning, monitoring, engaging, and measuring influencers from a centralized dashboard. The technology analyzes masses of data across all social media and channels, providing insights into customer, competitor, and influencer behaviors. It delivers the most relevant, high impact audiences and conversations by capturing a 360° view of activity around a brand, product, or ecosystem (Tracx 2014).

8.8 Tracx

Table 8.13 Company competitiveness indicators for time-to-market

Solution	Tracx
Founded	2010
No. of products	3
Clients	Enterprises
Partners	Integrators
Market dimension	Growing
Competitors	Few
Enabling infrastructure	None

8.8.1 Developer

Established in 2008, the Tracx team is made of social enthusiasts and technology experts united in the desire to build the most compelling social media management system. Since going live, Tracx has conquered the trust of some of the biggest brands in the world including Microsoft, Johnnie Walker, BMW and Coca Cola.

In Table 8.13 the time-to-market competitiveness appears to be high, with a solid company, facing some competition but with a large market to tap, showing no need for additional enabling infrastructure as it is provided as a cloud solution.

8.8.2 Applications

The key to the startup's value proposition is its data engine. To give its customers a more accurate, real time view of audience segmentation across marketing, sales, and customer relations, Tracx goes beyond "listening and monitoring" platforms (Empson 2012). The platform satisfies different use cases, such as competitive benchmarking, audience analysis and segmentation, influencers' identification and management. Part of its value and growth are also due to its development, in part through local partnerships, of solutions also in languages other than English.

As shown in Table 8.14, the *User Value* is quite high, with positive feedback from users. The impact on existing processes is not too high as it blends easily with existing processes and systems. Bringing big data to social CRM can have a big effect on how deep marketers are able to go in planning the best ways to reach and engage their customers.

Table 8.14 User value indicators

Fast learning	Yes
User interface	Positive
User experience	High
Process impact	Medium
User feedback	High
"Wow" effect	Medium

8.9 Kahuna

Kahuna's engine provides real-time analytics, creating people profiles, which reflect individual's behavior and preferences across mobile and tablet (Kahuna 2014a). People are automatically divided into subgroups based on defined criteria and presented in clear visual images. Kahuna allows sending out personalized push notifications without requiring spreadsheets, data analysis or SQL. Marketers can use specific, highly targeted rules for engagement. Analytics solutions, typically, offer dashboards that show what is going on, but the user is still needed to figure out what to do about the analysis, which actually involves manually building marketing campaigns through other email/push/notification systems. When the number of campaigns increases this becomes a huge burden. Kahuna prompts marketing campaigns automatically, checking every day to see who has fallen into "dormant", or signed up as s "newbie", or has become active. Then, Kahuna automatically activates a campaign as needed as soon as a user changes state, whether that is a push notification, email, or any other means (Dunlap 2013).

8.9.1 Developer

Kahuna was founded in 2012, funded by Sequoia Capital, by Adam Marchick, its CEO (Kahuna 2014b), who started coding when he was 16, building GPS tracking systems in Matlab. The first start-up he joined had a $3B IPO (iBeam Broadcasting) (Kahuna 2014b). For the first 7 years of his career, Adam Marchick held Engineering and Product roles at Oracle (Siebel), Facebook and Jarna (Mobile Apps). He received his BS in Computer Science from Stanford University, then went back to get his MBA at the Stanford some years later. Jacob Taylor, the CTO, started his first funded programming project at age 14, prototyping his dream of a massively multiplayer online role playing game. He spent several years helping startups with their technology needs and building innovative technologies. He received his BS in Computer Science and Engineering and his MS in Artificial Intelligence from University of California, Los Angeles.

In Table 8.15 the time-to-market drivers show a very promising company, also given the relevance of its funding partner (Sequoia Capital). Enabling infrastructure takes a little to get ready, but once it gets running, it just gathers results and improves. Since most clients don't have a lot of extra bandwidth to maintain campaigns, Kahuna is found to be a great ROI of time invested to returns, and anyone from an entry level marketing manager to engineer can do it.

Table 8.15 Company competitiveness indicators for time-to-market

Solution	Kahuna
Founded	2011
No. of products	1
Clients	Digital enterprises
Partners	Enterprises
Market dimension	Growing
Competitors	Some
Enabling infrastructure	In progress

8.9.2 Applications

Successful mobile-focused companies engage with their users at every stage of the mobile lifecycle, where an important step is tailoring the communication to each user's current engagement state with the brand (Kahuna 2014c). There are different types of notification-push campaigns that can be carried out, e.g., to inform new users about the benefits of creating an account or signing in through an app or else encouraging them to make their first purchase by targeting new users who have shown purchase intent (such as, e.g., adding an item to their shopping cart) but have not yet completed their purchase. In this case it is worth to send personalized notifications based on previous user behavior and areas of interest to dormant users, that were active in the past, making sure segmentation so that dormant users do not receive a notification about a feature they have already tried (Marchick 2014).

These are just few examples of the possible applications, with the fundamental purpose of making sure the app delights its users. Customized push notifications that add real value to users' lives are one of the way in which to drive higher app adoption. Table 8.16 shows a good *User Value*, with very positive feedback from the first adopters. The impact on existing processes is positive in terms of time-saving and, even if there is no "Wow" effect, the value resides in simplification and reduction of unwanted expenses.

Table 8.16 User value indicators

Fast learning	Medium
User interface	High
User experience	High
Process impact	Low
User feedback	High
"Wow" effect	Medium

8.10 RetailNext

RetailNext is leader in Applied big data for brick-and-mortar retail, delivering real-time analytics that enable retailers and manufacturers to collect, analyze, and visualize in-store data (RetailNext 2014a). The solution uses video analytics, Wi-Fi detection, on-shelf sensors, data from point-of-sale systems and other sources to automatically inform retailers about how people engage with their stores (Retailnext 2014d). RetailNext platform is highly scalable and easily integrates with promotional calendars, staffing systems, and even weather services to analyze how internal and external factors impact customer shopping patterns, thus, allowing retailers to identify opportunities for growth, implement changes, and measure achievements (Retailnext 2014c).

8.10.1 Developer

RetailNext was founded by engineers during at Cisco Systems, recognizing that to stay competitive with e-commerce providers, retailers need business intelligence tools dedicated to in-store analytics (RetailNext 2014b). Having developed advanced solutions for a number of other industries at Cisco, the team applied their experience to build an analytics platform that would address the needs of retailers at global level.

In 2007, RetailNext established its headquarters in San Jose, California. It received the support of talented professionals from companies such as, e.g., Google, Oracle, Salesforce, Cisco, Motorola, IBM, Symantec, Intel, VeriSign, Palm Computing, and Accenture (RetailNext 2014b). In addition, RetailNext resulted in a combination of technology experts and professionals who have had years of experience at companies such as Saks Fifth Avenue, Tiffany & Co, Bloomingdales, Macys, Lancôme, Tommy Hilfiger, L'Oréal and Unilever (RetailNext 2014b).

In Table 8.17 the drivers for time-to-market describe a solid company facing a large and growing market, with a strong link to partners in the same technological ecosystem. Enabling infrastructure is quite ready and the demand is very large.

Table 8.17 Company competitiveness indicators for time-to-market

Solution	RetailNext
Founded	2007
No. of products	1
Clients	Retail enterprises
Partners	Integrators
Market dimension	Growing
Competitors	Few
Enabling infrastructure	Sensors and store data

8.10 RetailNext

Table 8.18 User value indicators

Fast learning	Yes
User interface	Good
User experience	High
Process impact	Medium
User feedback	High
"Wow" effect	Low to medium

8.10.2 Applications

RetailNext is tracking over 500 million shoppers per year, collecting data from nearly 100,000 in-store sensors across locations in 33 countries. Companies that use RetailNext include Bloomingdales, American Apparel, Brookstone, Montblanc, Ulta and Family Dollar. In 2013 RetailNext acquired Nearbuy, the in-store, opt-in data tracking service, which offers shoppers free Wi-Fi in return for letting retailers track where the customer is browsing physically and online as they traverse the store (Shieber 2014). As reported by Perez et al. (2013), actually the company focuses on crunching retailers' so-called "big data" from different sources such as, e.g., video surveillance, passive Wi-Fi tracking, point-of-sale systems, workforce management tools, credit card transactions, weather data.

In Table 8.18 the *User Value* is high, with very good feedback on user interface and experience, and a minimal process impact (it's actually an improvement and streamlining of existing procedures). The "Wow" effect is not very high, as in most innovations focused on cost reduction and simplification.

8.11 Evrythng

Evrythng (2014a) is among the British startups attempting to change the face of retail, considering the ambitious company's plan to give every single object in the world a unique web-addressable URL (Hern 2014). Furthermore, as pointed out by Hern (2014). Evrythng offers also a way to solve specific "smart" issues, such as the fact that smart fridges don't work without smart food, and smart food won't be sold without smart fridges. Indeed, if manufacturers start placing unique RFID chips in individual products to enable promotions as well as analytics, smart fridges could take advantage of that, for example, to advise owners when food is about to go off.

8.11.1 Developer

Evrythng was founded by Andy Hobsbawm, Dominique Guinard, Niall Murphy, and Vlad Trifa. It is based in London, United Kingdom. Niall Murphy, the CEO, has authored and presented numerous papers around the world, including at TED. He was a co-author of the WiFi International Roaming Access Protocols framework

Table 8.19 Company competitiveness indicators for time-to-market

Solution	Evrythng
Founded	2007
No. of products	1
Clients	Retail enterprises
Partners	Integrators
Market dimension	Growing
Competitors	Few
Enabling infrastructure	In progress

in 2005 (Evrythng 2014b). Andy Hobsbawm, Chief Marketing Officer, has been listed among the 100 top digital influencers by Wired UK and has been a weekly columnist about the new economy for the Financial Times, a member of GartnerG2's first advisory board on online advertising and spoken at numerous conferences, including TED (Evrythng 2014b).

Dom Guinard got his Ph.D. from ETH Zurich, where he worked on laying down the foundations of the Web of Things. He also worked 4 years for SAP on the software aspects of the next generation platform for integrating real-world services with business systems. Early in 2012, his Ph.D. research was granted the ETH Medal (Evrythng 2014b). Vlad Trifa is a recognized expert in the interconnection of networked embedded devices (sensor networks, robots, mobile phones, RFID, etc.) with higher-level applications using Web technologies. He also worked as a researcher in urban and mobile computing at the Senseable City Lab at MIT in USA and Singapore and in human-robot interaction and neurosciences the ATR International Research Center in Kyoto (Japan) (Evrythng 2014b).

In Table 8.19 the representation shows a longer time-to-market, if we consider the absence of a true ecosystem and the lack of enabling infrastructure. However growing, there is some doubt about the market dimensions, as the implementation of sensors is only useful from the perspective of a network.

8.11.2 Applications

The prototypes in Evrythng's offices in Clerkenwell, London, use QR codes and RFID chips to achieve the goal of tracking and communicating with items, and show applications that include, for example, bottles of whisky that can have promotions personalized to the location or time they were bought, or biscuits that can automatically redeem a free coffee on purchase from a machine (Evrythng 2014b).

In Table 8.20 the *User Value* is high in terms of learning and user interface, although the process impact is quite significant. Furthermore, the "Wow" effect is high, considering the potential impact on customer experience improvement and supply chain management.

Table 8.20 User value indicators

Fast learning	Medium
User interface	Good
User experience	Not available
Process impact	High
User feedback	Not available
"Wow" effect	High

8.12 Summary

This chapter has discussed examples of big data and analytics solutions in practice, providing fact sheets of 10 of the most interesting ones available worldwide in 2014. The evolution trends are going to concern a further focus on convergence of mobile services and social sensing, that is an increased exploitation of advanced analytics for behavioral analysis from intensive data streams as well as from big data.

Businesses and organizations from all sectors began to gain critical insights from the structured data collected through various enterprise systems and analyzed by commercial relational database management systems. However, over the past several years, web intelligence, web analytics, web 2.0, and the ability to mine unstructured user generated contents have ushered in a new data-driven era, leading to unprecedented intelligence on consumer opinion, customer needs, and recognizing new business opportunities. By highlighting several applications such as e-commerce, market intelligence, retail and sentiment analysis and by mapping important initiatives of the current big data and analytics landscape, we hope to contribute to future sources of value.

References

Ayasdi Core: http://www.ayasdi.com/product/ (2014). Accessed 11 Nov 2014
Cogito Dialog: http://www.cogitocorp.com/ (2014). Accessed 12 Nov 2014
Crunchbase: http://www.crunchbase.com/person/max-simkoff (2014). Accessed 18 Nov 2014
Dunlap, S.: What differentiates Kahuna mobile analytics from other mobile analytics companies? http://www.quora.com/What-differentiates-Kahuna-mobile-analytics-from-other-mobile-analytics-companies (2013). Accessed 18 Nov 2014
Empson, R.: Tracx secures $4.4 million to bring big data to social media management. http://echcrunch.com/2012/02/16/tracx-secures-4-4-million-to-bring-big-data-to-social-media-management/ (2012). Accessed 18 Nov 2014
Essentia Analytics: http://www.essentia-analytics.com (2014). Accessed 11 Nov 2014
Evolv: www.evolv.net (2014). Accessed 11 Nov 2014
Evrythng: http://www.evrythng.com (2014a). Accessed 11 Nov 2014
Evrythng: https://evrythng.com/about-us/our-team/ (2014b). Accessed 18 Nov 2014
Fast Company: http://www.fastcompany.com/3034748/worth-the-risk/how-evolv-is-arming-companies-with-predictive-data-on-employees (2014a). Accessed 18 Nov 2014

Fast Company: http://www.fastcompany.com/most-innovative-companies/2014/industry/big-data (2014b). Accessed 18 Nov 2014
cHern, A.: Cisco invests in UK internet of things startup Evrythng. http://www.theguardian.com/technology/2014/apr/30/cisco-internet-of-things-startup-evrythng (2014). Accessed 18 Nov 2014
Invenio: Cognitive technology. http://www.cognitive.com.mt/ (2014). Accessed 11 Nov 2014
Kahuna: http://www.usekahuna.com/ (2014a). Accessed 12 Nov 2014
Kahuna: https://www.kahuna.com/about/ (2014b). Accessed 18 Nov 2014
Kahuna: https://www.kahuna.com/blog/2014/07/ (2014c). Accessed 18 Nov 2014
Lawrence, J.: Big Data Renders College Diplomas Worthless; Billionaires Nonplussed, San Diego Free Press. http://sandiegofreepress.org/2014/04/big-data-renders-college-diplomas-worthless-billionaires-nonplussed/#.VGsbJ4dJOjl (2014). Accessed 18 Nov 2014
Lohr, S.: Ayasdi: a big data start-up with a long history. Bits. http://bits.blogs.nytimes.com/2013/01/16/ayasdi-a-big-data-start-up-with-a-long-history/?_r=0 (2013). Accessed 18 Nov 2014
Marchick, A.: 8 push notification campaigns your App should be running, right now. https://www.linkedin.com/today/post/article/20140728170145-2185326-8-push-notification-campaigns-your-app-should-be-running-right-now (2014). Accessed 18 Nov 2014
Morabito, V.: Trends and Challenges in Digital Business Innovation. Springer, Cham (2014)
Pentland, A.: Honest Signals—How They Shape Our World. The MIT Press, Cambridge (2008). ISBN: 9780262162562
Perez, S.: RetailNext acquires Eric Schmidt-Backed Wi-Fi analytics company, Nearbuy Systems. http://techcrunch.com/2013/12/03/retailnext-acquires-eric-schmidt-backed-wi-fi-analytics-company-nearbuy-systems/ (2013). Accessed 18 Nov 2014
Retailnext: http://retailnext.net/ (2014a). Accessed 11 Nov 2014
Retailnext: http://retailnext.net/about-us/ (2014b). Accessed 18 Nov 2014
Retailnext: http://retailnext.net/press-release/retailnext-picks-up-five-accolades-recognizing-growth-big-data-innovation-and-customer-results/ (2014c). Accessed 18 Nov 2014
Retailnext:https://www.linkedin.com/company/retailnext (2014d). Accessed 18 Nov 2014
Shieber, J.: RetailNext raises another $30 million to track in-store data. http://techcrunch.com/2014/07/08/retailnext-raises-another-30-million-to-track-in-store-data/ (2014). Accessed 18 Nov 2014
Sociometric Solutions: http://www.sociometricsolutions.com/ (2014). Accessed 16 Nov 2014
Tracx: http://www.tracx.com/ (2014). Accessed 12 Nov 2014

9. Conclusion

Abstract

The book has discussed and presented challenges, benefits, and experiences in big data and analytics to a composite audience of practitioners and scholars. In this chapter conclusive remarks are provided as well as key advices for strategic actions as a result of the issues discussed and analyzed in this volume.

9.1 Building the Big Data Intelligence Agenda

In this book we have discussed the key issues and impacts of big data and analytics to a composite audience of practitioners and scholars. In particular, we have focused the attention on their main strategic and organizational challenges and benefits. Thus, we have first framed big data and analytics to question how they can be utilized for achieving competitive advantage (Chap. 1). However, business is only one of the domains impacted by big data and analytics, other areas concern the public sector (Chap. 2) and education (Chap. 3), whose challenges have been consequently investigated. No matter the context and the sector, big data and analytics ask for a new understanding of the potential use of the actual information growth to design appropriate business models (discussed in Chap. 4). Furthermore, we have pointed out what needed at organizational level for improved big data governance (Chap. 5), business oriented evaluation (Chap. 6), and managing change for big data driven innovation (Chap. 7).

The different facets considered can be summarized in the key areas we have identified in 2014 (Morabito 2014a) as representative of a digital business innovative organization (see Fig. 9.1). In the case of big data we consider "business" in a more general sense as "an activity that someone is engaged in" or "work that has to be done or matters that have to be attended to" (Oxford Dictionaries 2014), thus, encompassing both private and public organizations. Consequently, to be innovative by exploiting big data and analytics in their digital business they need to take into account:

Fig. 9.1 Key areas for digital business innovative organization. Adapted from Morabito (2014a)

- *innovation* through appropriate business models (Chap. 4),
- *collaboration* through an effective governance (Chap. 5), and
- *control* through evaluation frameworks (Chap. 6), and accuracy in managing change (Chap. 7).

As a consequence, IT leaders have to be able to combine an appropriate knowledge of benefits and drawbacks related to big data and analytics utilization, in order to design effective digital strategies and implement them within they organization.

As for these issues, this book has tried to provide insights as well as inspiring "templates" for putting in practice digital business innovation through big data and analytics. A practice we inaugurated in a former volume (Morabito 2014a), and we actually find useful for managers know-how.

Accordingly, Chap. 8 tells what could be called "10 short stories" about those which have been selected as interesting "global" experiences of the 2014. As for this selection, it is worth mentioning that also in this case as in Morabito (2014a), the choice concerns innovations that are actually applied and "in use"; thus, a pragmatic approach have been adopted, balancing between the so called "Wow" effect (i.e. the perceived novelty and interest in the idea), feasibility, and actual user adoption. Consequently, not only digital innovations potentially inedited if not disruptive, but also "ready-to-use" ones, have been selected and analyzed.

The above arguments and cases lead us to the big data lifecycle management (shown in Fig. 9.2 and discussed in our 2014 contribution on big data, Morabito 2014b) and the main challenges and IT actions identified there for big data for business value:

- *Convergence information sources*: IT in the organization must enable the construction of a "data asset" from internal and external sources, unique, integrated and of quality.
- *Data architecture*: IT must support the storage and enable the extraction of valuable information from structured, semi-structured as well as unstructured data (images, recordings, etc.).
- *Information infrastructure*: IT must define models and adopt techniques for allowing modular and flexible access to information and analysis of data across

9.1 Building the Big Data Intelligence Agenda

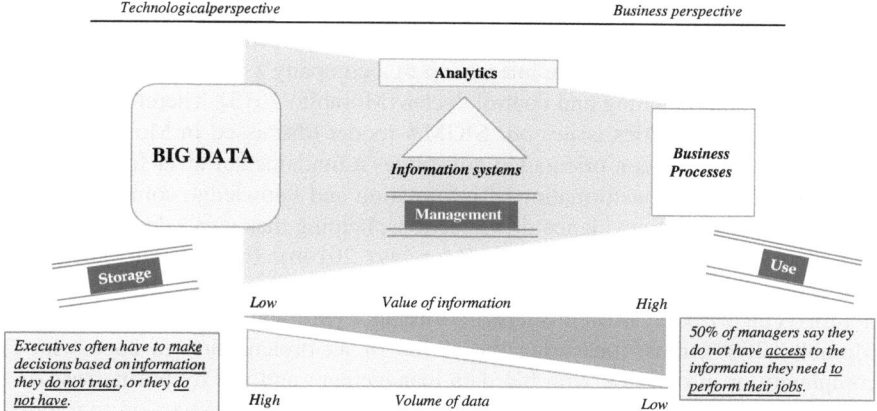

Fig. 9.2 Big Data management challenges. Adapted from Morabito (2014a), Pospiech and Felden (2012)

the enterprise. Furthermore, organizations must commit human resources in recruiting and empowering data scientist skills and capabilities across business lines and management.

- *Investments*: The IT and the business executives must share decisions on the budget for the management and innovation of information assets.

Taking these issues into account, as also discussed in Morabito (2014b), big data and analytics are key components of the digital asset of today's organizations (as shown in Fig. 9.3). Indeed, business decisions and actions rely on the digital asset of an organization, although requiring different types of orientation in managing the

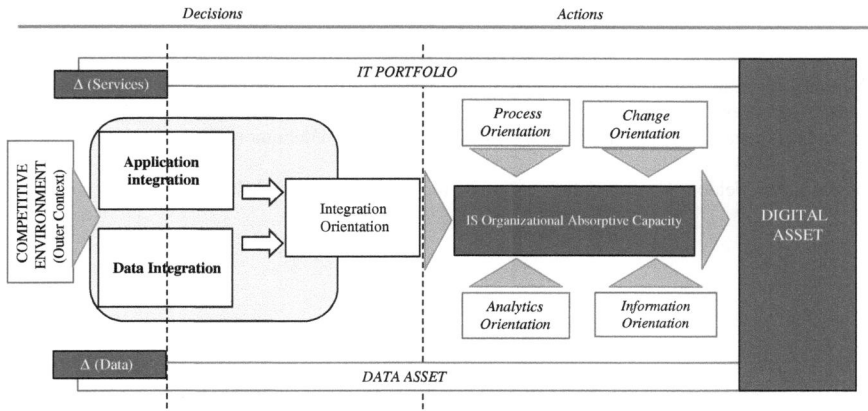

Fig. 9.3 A framework for managing digital asset. Adapted from Morabito (2014b)

information systems (IS). As for decisions, *integration orientation* seems to be required for satisfying the needs for optimization and effective data management of big data. Indeed, the greater the integration of a company's information system, the faster the overall planning and control cycles (Morabito 2013). Therefore, applying to big data and analytics issues our SIGMA model (discussed in Morabito 2013), we argue that integration orientation constitutes a fundamental lever for facilitating the absorption and transformation of information and knowledge coming from big data and analytics into evidence-driven actions, helping manager's decision-making and employees perform their work (Morabito 2014b). Furthermore, integration orientation is one of the determinants of organizational absorptive capacity, which, in turn, is theorized to affect business performance (Morabito 2013; Francalanci and Morabito 2008), thus, measuring the ability of an organization to cope with IT complexity or in our case with big data management and use by businesses. As a consequence, moving from decisions to action calls for an organization to improve *IS absorptive capacity* (Morabito 2013; Francalanci and Morabito 2008) in terms of the set of key orientations considered in the above mentioned SIGMA approach: analytics, information, process, and change orientation.

Considering these issues and what discussed in previous chapters, we point out that the framework in Fig. 9.2 is suitable to provide a systemic and integrated "working" representation of factors and drivers involved in managing digital assets, which aim to exploit the opportunities of big data and analytics for business performance and value. Finally, taking all the above issues into account, we hope the book has provided a toolbox for managerial actions in building what we call a *big data intelligence agenda* (Morabito 2014b).

References

Francalanci, C., Morabito, V.: IS integration and business performance: the mediation effect of organizational absorptive capacity in SMEs. J. Inf. Technol. **23**, 297–312 (2008)

Morabito, V.: Business Technology Organization—Managing Digital Information Technology for Value Creation—The SIGMA Approach. Springer, Berlin (2013)

Morabito, V.: Trends and Challenges in Digital Business Innovation. Springer, Berlin (2014a)

Morabito, V.: Big data. In: Trends and Challenges in Digital Business Innovation, pp. 3–21. Springer, New York (2014b)

Oxford Dictionaries: business. http://www.oxforddictionaries.com/definition/english/business. Accessed 16 Nov 2014

Pospiech, M., Felden, C.: Big data—a state-of-the-art. In: AMCIS 2012

Index

A
Academic analytics, 54
Adobe, 125, 147–150
Airbnb, 72
Amazon, 12, 15, 108, 109, 111, 115, 118, 120, 122
Amazon web service, 120
Apple, 8
Applied big data, 172
Artificial Intelligence (AI), 72
Asos.com, 8

B
22@ Barcelona, 36
Banorte, 71
Barcelona, 23, 36–38, 42
Behavior, 110, 111, 113
Behavioral finance, 164
Big data driven business models, 66, 79
Big data governance, 83
Big data management (BDM), 99
Bitcoin, 68, 72, 73
Business model, 65, 66, 68, 69, 73, 77–79
Business process integration, 89

C
California Report Card, 41
Capability Maturity Model (CMM), 95
Center of Excellence (CoE), 134
Chief Executive Officer (CEO), 130
Chief Information Officers (CIOs), 130
Chief Marketing Officer (CMO), 130
Citidirect BeMobile, 136
Citysourced.com, 24
Cloud computing, 31, 32, 120, 121
Cloudera, 138
CMOOCs, 52–54, 58, 62
Cognitive city, 27
Cognitive code, 69
Competitive advantage, 4
Coolest cooler, 74
Cornerstone, 162
Coursera, 50–52, 58
Course Resource Appraisal Model (CRAM), 56
Crowdflower, 38
Crowdfunded, 9
Crowdfunding, 10, 74, 75
Crowdreporting, 26, 27
Crowdsourced, 9
Crowdsourcing, 23, 24, 26, 29, 30, 38, 39, 42, 67, 70, 73, 75, 76
Customer Relationship Management (CRM), 71

D
3D printer, 10
3Sage, 87
Data analysts, 35
DataFlux, 94, 95
Data governance, 84, 87, 94, 95–97
Data mining, 107, 122
Data ownership, 23, 31, 33, 42
Data quality, 34, 39, 86, 89, 98
Data science, 164
Data scientists, 12
The Data Warehousing Institute (TDWI), 91
Deep thunder, 68
Demographics, 110, 111
Distance learning, 47, 48, 62

E
eBay, 108, 109, 111, 114, 115, 123
e-commerce, 4
e-government, 23, 32
Edification, 62

edX, 50–52, 60
Engine Health Management (EHM), 135
Enterprise information management (EIM), 95
Enterprise resource planning (ERP), 4

F
Facebook, 26, 30, 34, 76, 85, 106, 108, 116–119, 121, 122, 126, 140, 170
Financial markets, 127
FutureLearn, 50, 51

G
Gamification, 6, 57, 61, 63
Gartner maturity model, 95, 96
Google, 11, 12, 15, 73, 76, 105, 108, 111, 123, 126, 134, 140
Google ventures, 73
GPS, 83, 86
Greece, 25, 31
Grid computing, 32
Groupon, 5, 10, 14, 15, 19

H
Hadoop, 34, 71, 114, 118, 122, 123, 132, 137–139
Haiti, 23, 38, 42
HarvardX, 60
Health informatics, 33
Her Majesty's Revenue and Customs (HMRC), 131
Hewlett Packard, 125, 150
Human metric identification, 158

I
IBM, 11, 68, 95–97, 115, 136, 138, 149
Information governance, 85, 87
Information lifecycle management, 86, 89
Innocentive, 9
Instagram, 116
InStedd, 38
Intellectual property (IP), 9
Internet of Everything, 27, 28
Internet of things (IoTs), 8, 27, 66, 75, 76
iPhone, 8
IT service delivery, 32

K
Kaggle, 70
Kearney, A.T., 6

Key Performance Indicators (KPIs), 75
Kickstarter, 74
Kickstarter.com, 10

L
Learning analytics, 55–57
Learning Management System (LMS), 52
Lending, 127
Lifestyle, 110
LinkedIn, 6, 85
Livemocha, 61, 63

M
MapMyRun, 141, 142
Marine Institute of Ireland, 136
Master data integration, 89
McKinsey Global Institute, 27, 32
Megacities, 25
Metadata management, 89
Meteorological Assimilation Data Ingest System (MADIS), 27
Microsoft, 115
Money management, 127
MySpace, 116

N
Neighborhood planning, 30
Netflix, 108, 110, 116, 118–123
Network intelligence, 158
NoSQL, 132, 139, 151

O
One Laptop Per Child (OLPC), 48
Open Courseware, 49
Open government, 23, 24, 31, 36
Open innovation, 9
Open Universities, 47
Oracle, 115, 170, 172
Ownership of, 79

P
PartyX, 25
Peer 2 Peer University, 50
Pharmaceuticals, 5, 15–18
Predictive analytics, 30, 33
Privacy, 34
Privacy and security, 114, 122
Profiling, 34, 35, 41
Prosumers, 42

Index

Public–Private Partnerships, 31
Public service management, 31

R
Real-estate, 127
RedLaser, 109
RFID, 83, 86, 173, 174
Riff, 38
Ripple, 73
Rolls-Royce, 135

S
SeeClickFix.com, 26
Security and privacy, 89
Sequoia Capital, 170
Servitization, 75
Skype, 5, 14
Smart city, 26, 28, 29, 36–40
Smart City Personal Management
 Office, 36
Smart grid technology, 33
Social entrepreneurs, 9
Social sensing technologies, 158
Social signals, 160, 167
Software Engineering Institute (SEI), 95
SpigitEngage, 73
SQL, 170

T
Topological data analysis, 165
Twitter, 26, 85, 116, 123

U
Udacity, 50, 51, 58
Udemy, 50
Urban Habitat, 36
Ushahidi, 38
Utility from, 78

V
Virtonomics, 57
Virtualization, 32
Visualization, 108, 122

W
Waze, 136
Weather underground, 27

X
Xerox, 163
xMOOCs, 51–55, 57, 62

If you have any concerns about our products,
you can contact us on
ProductSafety@springernature.com

In case Publisher is established outside the EU,
the EU authorized representative is:
**Springer Nature Customer Service Center GmbH
Europaplatz 3, 69115 Heidelberg, Germany**

Printed by Libri Plureos GmbH
in Hamburg, Germany